COLD WAR

OTHER BOOKS BY ROY MACSKIMMING

The Perilous Trade: Publishing Canada's Writers

Gordie: A Hockey Legend

On Your Own Again (with Keith Anderson, M.D.)

Laurier in Love, a novel

Macdonald, a novel

Out of Love, a novel

Formentera, a novel

THE AMAZING CANADA-SOVIET HOCKEY SERIES OF 1972

COLD WAR

ROY MACSKIMMING

GREYSTONE BOOKS

Vancouver/Berkeley/London

Greystone Books Ltd.
greystonebooks.com

Cataloguing data available from Library and Archives Canada
ISBN 978-1-77840-026-1 (pbk)
ISBN 978-1-77100-059-8 (epub)

Editing by Barbara Pulling
Cover design by Peter Cocking
Text design by Val Speidel
Cover photograph of Phil Esposito and Alexander Ragulin by Frank Lennon

Printed and bound in Canada on FSC® certified paper at Friesens.
The FSC® label means that materials used
for the product have been responsibly sourced.

Greystone Books gratefully acknowledges the Musqueam, Squamish, and
Tsleil-Waututh peoples on whose land our Vancouver head office is located.

Greystone Books thanks the Canada Council for the Arts,
the British Columbia Arts Council, the Province of British Columbia
through the Book Publishing Tax Credit, and the Government
of Canada for supporting our publishing activities.

Canada

FSC
www.fsc.org

MIX
Paper from
responsible sources
FSC® C016245

BRITISH
COLUMBIA

BRITISH COLUMBIA
ARTS COUNCIL
An agency of the Province of British Columbia

Canada Council
for the Arts

Conseil des arts
du Canada

CONTENTS

●

Introduction   *1*

1   The Little Shrine in the West   *5*
2   Great Expectations: August 1972   *15*
3   The Puck   *31*
4   Game 1: Who Has Seen the Wind?   *41*
5   A Little Learning Is a Useful Thing   *56*
6   Game 2: Brother Night   *67*
7   Igor in Winnipeg   *78*
8   Game 3: The Win That Wasn't   *85*
9   The Soviet Way   *93*
10   Game 4: Into the Pit   *107*
11   The Lonely Mission of Ron Ellis   *119*
12   Team Ugly in No Man's Land   *128*
13   Game 5: Beyond Hope   *139*
14   The Canadiens Connection   *156*
15   Game 6: Staying Alive   *166*
16   Butch and Sundance   *179*
17   Game 7: Back from the Dead—Again   *189*
18   The Ineffable Grace of Paul Henderson   *202*
19   Game 8: Spirit to Draw On   *211*
20   Where Were You?   *232*
21   Where Hockey Has Gone   *242*

Summaries and Statistics of the 1972 Canada-Soviet Series   *253*
Sources and Acknowledgements   *265*
Index   *268*

CANADA'S ODYSSEY

"My country is not a country, it's the winter; it's hockey."

—DOUG BEARDSLEY, WITH ACKNOWLEDGEMENT
TO GILLES VIGNEAULT, *Country on Ice*

●

We learned to play the game about the same time we learned to skate. We first stumbled, then flew, along natural ice under an open sky—a frozen pond or river or slough fringed with trees, a school or community rink whose scarred and weathered boards were put up every fall and taken down every spring, sometimes a back-yard rink flooded late at night, sometimes an icy driveway, even a suburban street frozen hard enough to skate on, if the weather and passage of cars were just right.

For those of us who grew up before 1972, before the era of tightly scheduled, structured practices on artificial ice in enclosed arenas, and for the luckier of those who grew up later, the imagery is real. Having encountered hockey and nature together in our earliest, most impressionable years, we associate the game with the freshness and freedom and romance and private passion of childhood. And if this association lends a quality of pastoral idyll or paradisal myth to the sport, we can't help it. We come by it naturally. It's ours.

So hockey itself is—or at least was—imbued with innocence. We understood it not as big business, not as a rich man's sport or a route to wealth, but as everyone's joy, the common language of all classes and cultures across Canada. Whether at the level of the National Hockey League, peewee or bantam or junior or senior, A or B, or of a school or community house league, hockey was always a sport both to watch and to play, and thus to become enthusiastic, knowledgeable, even expert, about—the true pleasures of the *amateur*, in the French sense of the word.

Inevitably, hockey became for us more than a game: it became a symbol, an emblem of our uniqueness as individuals and as a society. Having been dominated politically, economically and culturally throughout our history by larger, richer, more powerful nations, Canadians needed the symbol of our "natural" hockey supremacy to affirm that uniqueness. And the symbolism was never more alive, more emotionally potent, than when our teams were pitted against other hockey-playing countries, and especially against the best of those others, the Union of Soviet Socialist Republics.

But until 1972, a confrontation between our best and their best had never been staged. History and politics had conspired to prevent hockey's leading professionals—the Canadian-born and -trained stars of the NHL—from competing against hockey's leading "amateurs"—the ten-time consecutive World's champions, the Soviet national team.

Their meeting in September of that year would be an unprecedented, primordial event. In the context of hockey, it would resemble the first contact between Europeans and the New World, a moment of profound revelation and impact. Throughout Canada, it created more sustained anticipation, excitement, anger, angst and ecstasy than any sporting event in the country's history—indeed than any event of any kind since the Second World War had ended twenty-seven years earlier.

It was billed as a set of eight exhibition games: four in Canada, four in the USSR. No trophy, no official championship was at stake. And yet everyone knew it meant far, far more than that. We called it a summit, a showdown, an epic trial by ice between hockey's two superpowers. Afterwards, Phil Esposito called it "war—our society against their society."

Most of us witnessed those eight astonishing games through the medium of television, and through the familiar quavering, nasal, high-pitched, slightly hysterical but bred-in-the-bone voice of veteran broadcaster Foster Hewitt, who came out of retirement to participate in the historic occasion. We witnessed the acting out of our national myth, put to the test at last. No wonder a mere hockey series shook us so much.

And it did more. By sharing in the enactment of the myth, Canadians—temperamentally so fractious and resentful a people, then as now, on grounds of language or region or ethnicity—joined together in a rare moment of unity. By surrendering to a process larger than ourselves, we transcended the pettiness of our usual concerns. By going so deeply into our national psyche, we were briefly able—ironically—to travel beyond our habitually narrow frame of national reference. The 1972 Canada-Soviet series swept us into a wider world, and in the end it changed us; we learned something vital about who we are, and where and what we've come from. It was an odyssey from innocence to experience.

Those are the same reasons, as the series' twenty-fifth anniversary approaches, for writing about it now. Of course the story has been told before. But with the benefit of a quarter-century of hindsight, reflection and subsequent hockey history, we can see more clearly how extraordinarily influential the series was, how ultimately it transformed our game in so many ways—many of them for the better. And we can appreciate even better one of the great mythic dramas in the history of sport.

ONE

THE LITTLE SHRINE
IN THE WEST

"A game is a game. But a symbol is not.
We had to win this series."
— KEN DRYDEN AND ROY MACGREGOR, *Home Game*

●

It began with a telephone call. And, in truth, an attempt to relieve boredom. Like many momentous events, there was little momentous about its origins.

During the long dark Moscow winter of 1971-72, they kept the electric lights burning all day long in the Canadian embassy on Starokonyushenny Street, at least when there wasn't a power failure. A Russian-speaking second secretary named Gary Smith, a handsome young man in the early stages of a distinguished diplomatic career, needed all the light he could get. One of Smith's less stimulating responsibilities was to read the daily papers: particularly the state newspaper *Izvestia,* which he combed front to back for potentially useful information about life in the USSR, and for clues about which way the Soviet political winds were blowing. Smith always read the sports section carefully, partly because he was also responsible for sports and cultural exchanges between Canada and the Soviet Union, partly for relief from the paper's numbing anti-Western propaganda.

One day Smith's eyes were running down a hockey article by sports editor Boris Fedosov, who wrote under the pseudonym "The Snowman," when something in the text jumped out at him. Fedosov was saying the Soviets had grown tired of defeating all other nations year after year at the annual *Izvestia* tournament and the World's hockey championships and the Winter Olympic Games: they needed a new challenge. To make another great leap forward, Soviet hockey required the stimulus of stronger competition.

Smith knew nothing appeared in the paper without a sanctioned political purpose. He telephoned Fedosov, whom he knew. He remarked on the column and asked, "Are you serious?"

Fedosov replied, "Come over for a drink and we'll talk about it."

Smith took with him first secretary Peter Hancock, now Canadian ambassador to Turkey. Over the obligatory vodkas, it quickly became clear to them that, after years of coyly refusing to match their world-beating national team against Canadian professionals from the National Hockey League, on the grounds that they feared losing their Olympic amateur status, the Soviets were finally ready to risk a "best vs. best" series involving NHL players. The three men did a little brainstorming. They amicably wound up agreeing in principle that such a series would be an excellent idea indeed—from the viewpoint of both countries.

They continued their informal discussion another evening at the newspaper's offices, when Fedosov brought in Soviet hockey boss Andrei Starovoitov. The main topic was how such a series would work in practical terms: a series of "friendly matches," they thought, some in Canadian cities and some in Soviet cities, Leningrad and Kiev as well as Moscow. The evening was a great success. It was accompanied by a showing of the embassy's print of the 1971 Stanley Cup highlights film, which would become an exceptionally popular item in the Soviet Union, borrowed by the military and eventually shown to audiences in the hundreds of thousands.

Circulating such films was one of the ongoing "hockey diplomacy" activities Smith was involved in. Another was the Moscow Maple Leafs, the hockey team he played on: wearing castoff Toronto Maple Leaf uniforms donated a few years earlier by Punch Imlach, the team consisted of Canadian embassy personnel bolstered by a few Americans, Swedes and Finns. They played against teams from the Soviet Ministry of Foreign Trade, Tass news agency, and suchlike.

But now, in their boldest foray yet into hockey diplomacy, the young diplomats had taken the initiative as far as they could. It was up to higher powers to make a Canada-Soviet series a reality. The Canadian ambassador, the moustachioed patrician Robert Ford, also known in literary circles as the poet R. A. D. Ford, prided himself on having carefully nurtured a thaw in Canada-Soviet relations over the years. He moved the matter smoothly up the diplomatic ladder to the level of state-to-state negotiations. It was out of the embassy's hands.

•

The idea of testing the true calibre of international hockey against the NHL had been around for years. Canada had never been represented abroad by its professionals. The last time Canada had won a World's title was 1961, when the Trail Smoke Eaters, an amateur senior team from British Columbia, defeated the Soviets 5-1. And it was even longer since Canada had won the Olympic gold medal in hockey: 1952, when it was sufficient for the country to send over an intermediate-level amateur team, the Edmonton Mercurys, to whip the Europeans.

Since then, European, and especially Soviet, hockey had advanced enormously. In 1963, believing Canada needed its own national amateur team that stayed together and trained under international conditions, Father David Bauer, a successful Junior A coach at St. Michael's College in Toronto, organized a group of top-level college players. Between 1964 and 1969, his Canadian national team competed creditably for World's and Olympic titles. Bauer's young Nats often finished in the medals, but never brought home the ultimate prize. An unforgiving nation, accepting in hockey only complete and final victory, disdained them.

Reacting to widespread public unhappiness with this situation, and to recommendations of its own Task Force on Sport, the federal government took steps. In 1969, it created a new body, Hockey Canada, to develop the sport at home and advance the country's interests in international competition.

Hockey Canada was an umbrella organization. Representatives of the NHL, the NHL Players Association (NHLPA), the Canadian Amateur Hockey Association (CAHA) and the government itself sat and often bickered on its board, moderated by the calming hand of big-business representatives such as its first chairman, newspaper tycoon and industrialist Max Bell. Hockey Canada took over the CAHA's mandate to negotiate with the governing bodies of international and Olympic hockey. One of the organization's avowed aims was to achieve what every hockey fan considered crucial to the national interest: getting Canada represented abroad by our very best players.

At first, Hockey Canada had a modicum of success. It negotiated a compromise agreement with the International Ice Hockey Federation (IIHF), permitting at least some professionals to play in the forthcoming World's championships to be held in Winnipeg. But when that deal collapsed in January 1970, scuppered in the Canadian view by the Soviets, Canada pulled out of international hockey altogether. We would no longer play under IIHF rules designed to defeat us. The consequences were the loss of both the national team program and the 1970 World's tournament.

Still, Hockey Canada didn't say die. The organization's president, Charles Hay, and CAHA executive director Gordon Juckes persisted in wearing down Soviet resistance to Canada's desire to play internationally using professionals. So two years later, when the signals came from the embassy in Moscow that the Soviets were ready to talk, Hockey Canada was ready and eager to respond.

One of Hockey Canada's board members was R. Alan Eagleson, then NHLPA executive director and agent for Bobby Orr and many other players. Eagleson, who had been doing some backroom lobbying of his own in Moscow, emerged as a key broker when he assured Hockey Canada of the association's commitment to deliver NHL players for the proposed series. But Eagleson was not part of the initial Canadian negotiating team that sat down with Soviet hockey authorities to hammer out the details.

Those meetings took place in April 1972 during the World's championships in Prague. The Canadian contingent of Hay, Juckes, CAHA president Joe Kryzcka and Hockey Canada board member Douglas Fisher, the newspaper columnist, laboriously nailed down the terms for an eight-game Canada-Soviet series to be played in September: four games in different Canadian cities, four games in Moscow.

It was a historic breakthrough. The series would pit our best against their best, without restriction. The artificial distinction between paid NHLers called "professionals" and paid Soviets called "amateurs" was waived at last. Eagleson joined the meetings near the end. Although not a member of the official delegation, he was able, according to Fisher, to grab some of the publicity surrounding the breakthrough by being first to phone the news to journalists back home.

In their eagerness to arrive at an agreement with the Soviets, the Canadians committed themselves to terms that seemed innocuous at the time but would prove to be handicaps for Team Canada.

The eight games were scheduled for the NHL pre-season. In those days, NHLers typically started the season out of shape and played their way into condition by Christmas; the Soviets, on the other hand, trained and practised year-round. The series would also be played under international rules, using the European officiating system. This involved just two referees, both of whom called penalties as well as everything else, as opposed to the North American system of one referee with jurisdiction over penalties and two linesmen to watch for offsides and icing. So Team Canada would play under an alien system, with very different conceptions of acceptable on-ice conduct, and very different officiating standards, from North American ones. Moreover, the Soviets insisted the four games in Canada be handled not by NHL officials but by amateur referees licensed by the IIHF; the four games in Moscow would be handled by Europeans.

The concessions by Canada were agreed to in some haste, and under bargaining pressure from the Soviets. But at the time, most people believed they weren't concessions at all—simply good sportsmanship. NHL players, after all, would have no difficulty winning under any set of conditions, at any time of the year. The CAHA's Kryzcka, however, who spoke some Russian, felt afterwards his delegation had been outfoxed. He would later tell veteran sportswriter Jim Coleman: "In retrospect, I'm convinced that even before we arrived in Prague, the Soviets decided privately that their hockey team was good enough to beat the NHL. They strung out those meetings to get every possible concession."

If the Soviets were eager for the series to prove a point, both athletic and political, so were the Canadians. In fact, we were desperate. A piece of our history shows it.

•

Seventeen years before the Canada-Soviet series, a hockey team emerged out of the far west to fulfill essentially the same mission that would fall to Team Canada in 1972. That team was the Penticton Vees. Based in a small city at the foot of Okanagan Lake in the fruit-growing interior of British Columbia, the Vees were a Senior A team, a widespread phenomenon in those days. They played in the Okanagan Senior Hockey League, one of two senior leagues in B.C. at that time. Senior teams of that ilk often boasted the occasional player on his way up to, or down from, the NHL. But mainly they consisted of talented but underpaid blue-collar workers with day jobs, for whom there was simply no room in the six-team NHL of that era. Today, many of those players would be making six-figure incomes in a twenty-six team NHL.

A prized trophy existed, the Allan Cup, for which the champions of the various senior leagues across the country competed. The Penticton Vees captured the cup in 1954, earning the right to call themselves the best in Canada by defeating the Sudbury Wolves in a best-of-seven series. With their victory, the Vees also inherited a heavy responsibility: to become Canada's representatives in the following year's World's championships, and thus to avenge a humiliating Canadian defeat in the 1954 World's at Stockholm.

That defeat had plunged an unsuspecting nation into mourning. A run-of-the-mill Toronto Senior B team, named (after a car dealership) the East York Lyndhursts, had lost the world supremacy that Canadians had regarded as our national birthright since winning the first Olympic hockey tournament in 1920. Not only had the hapless Lyndhursts lost; they'd been utterly crushed by an upstart team from the Soviet Union, which had never even competed before in international hockey—a team of certified nobodies who had come from nowhere (well, from Moscow) to skate like the wind under a mentor, the wily Anatoly Tarasov, who was a certified hockey genius. Tarasov had studiously, religiously, secretively developed a unique style of hockey based on coordinated team play and precision passing. Having waited to enter world competition until they felt reasonably confident of success (athletic supremacy being considered such a valuable propaganda tool by the Soviet regime), Tarasov and his men had ambushed the complacent Canadians. As any Canadian hockey fan who was alive and conscious at the time will attest, the defeat was traumatic. The sudden loss of illusions always is.

And so, in the 1955 World's tournament, the pressure on the Penticton Vees was enormous. The team's playing coach, Grant Warwick, willingly, even fanatically, assumed the burden. Late of the New York Rangers, Boston Bruins and Montreal Canadiens, Warwick was a gnarled nine-year NHL veteran who had won the Calder Trophy as rookie of the year back in 1942. Now reinstated as an amateur, he put all the hard-bitten savvy of his professional career into a hockey crusade, making it his personal and professional mission to salvage the honour of Canadian hockey. When the Vees travelled from Penticton to Krefeld, West Germany, Canadians were convinced that, this time, we were sending the best of our "amateurs" overseas—the toughest, meanest practitioners of the national black arts this side of the NHL.

Warwick's teammates included his brothers Dick and Bill; they'd grown up poor together on the Prairies during the Depression. Under the Warwicks' tutelage, the Vees adopted an unapologetically physical strategy against their gentle European opponents, taking no prisoners and losing no games. Their relentless bodychecking made them no friends among the spectators, except for the Canadian servicemen and servicewomen who flocked to the games from their West German NATO bases. The European crowd might whistle its disapproval of the Vees' roughhouse tactics, but the Canadians were simply playing the game as they always had. And when it came to the gold-medal game against the Soviets, played in front of a screaming, packed house and a Canadian media contingent including Foster Hewitt at the microphone, the "Battling Warwicks" and their merry men didn't falter. In particular, they targeted the Soviets' biggest star, Vsevolod Bobrov, whose scoring had decimated the Lyndhursts the year before. The Vees' heavy hitters stalked Bobrov all night long, ensuring he spent most of it on his backside and didn't get a single shot on goal. The most celebrated check of the tournament occurred when Hal Tarala sent Bobrov somersaulting through the air to land on the ice headfirst. It wasn't gentlemanly but it got the job done: Canada recaptured the World's title with a thumping 5-0 victory.

Seventeen years later, Bobrov would seek his own vengeance as the Soviets' head coach in the '72 series. But for the time being, Canadians savoured our bare-knuckle triumph, lionizing the boys from Penticton who seemed to have proved the good old Canadian way was still the best—the low road to hockey supremacy. As Jim Coleman remembered in his book *Hockey Is Our Game,* "The swashbuckling Vees were national heroes." At their hotel in Krefeld, they were flooded with congratulatory telegrams from home, starting with tributes from Governor General Vincent Massey and Prime Minister Louis St. Laurent. It all *mattered* so much: that gut-level vindication, that unreasoning pride, that deep gratification of our self-image as the world's best in a sport that other nations, far larger or more powerful ones, might attempt, might even play proficiently, but never master as we had.

Nor are the Vees forgotten. To this day, if you visit the old-fashioned Penticton Memorial Arena with its chill, garish, exciting electric glare and pungent damp smells of ice mist and soggy French fries, with whistle blasts ripping the moist air and echoing high in the rafters, you can walk along the promenade level circling the rink behind the top row of seats and come upon a shrine. Housed in a large glass-fronted display case overlooking the ice, it's about twenty feet long and eight feet high: the townspeople's lovingly preserved, adoring tribute to a team that was their own but also Canada's, a team that people across the country cheered one long-ago winter as we would not cheer another until 1972.

Like many shrines, it is a poignant work of naive folk art. Its centrepiece is a giant letter V, cut with a jigsaw out of plywood and painted forest-green and white, the Vees' team colours. Alongside, a typed card primly notes that the team was named after three local varieties of peaches: Valiant, Vedette and Veteran. Up and down both arms of the V, black-and-white head shots of every member of the 1955 team are democratically arrayed, each within a cardboard star, none bigger than the others—not even Grant Warwick's. They're all here: the three Warwicks, Bernie Bathgate, Don Moog (father of Andy, the future NHL goaltender), Hal Tarala, Mike Shabaga, George McAvoy, Kevin Conway, Ivan McClelland, Jack McIntyre . . .

The central features of the shrine are a pair of two-dimensional hockey players, also cut out of plywood and hand-painted. Emblematically they stand eternally awaiting the next faceoff. One of the figures sports a green and white Vees jersey, the other the red, white and blue jersey the team wore in West Germany, "CANADA" daubed across the chest above a red maple leaf. Suspended within the arms of the V, as if held there by powerful electromagnetic forces, hangs a globe. It's the kind you'd have found in a fifties classroom, with all the British Commonwealth countries highlighted in pink.

The spirit of the times comes shouting through the headlines of another relic preserved within the shrine, the yellowing front page of the *Penticton Herald* of March 7, 1955:

5-0 WIN RESTORES CANADA'S PRESTIGE
VEES CRACK RUSSIAN HOCKEY MACHINE
CITY GOES WILD AT GREAT NEWS
OTTAWA CHEERS VEES' VICTORY

Already our media were characterizing the Soviet national team as a "machine," foreshadowing our 1972 portrayal of them as "robots," not quite human. One other headline from the *Herald* contains an unmistakable note of gloating: "RUSSIANS HUDDLE IN STADIUM CORNER AS VEES HUGGED AND KISSED BY FANS."

The crowing self-congratulation, the bloodlust and ecstasy, so thoroughly unCanadian, proclaim that craving to be once again the world's hockey superpower. It's a reminder that the Soviets weren't the only ones to regard athletic triumph in political terms. To rub the point in, the shrine's anonymous creators have listed the scores of all eight tournament victories, starting with the 12-1 skinning of the United States, and ending with the skunking of the USSR. And in the base supporting the giant V, preserved under a sheet of yellowed plastic like trophies of war, are embedded the national pennants of the defeated enemy armies—among them the Swedes, the Swiss, the Czechs and, of course, the feared and loathed Soviets.

In its humble yet fiercely self-assertive way, the shrine is redolent of the emotions of 1972. Then too, Team Canada simply *had* to win. Then too, it was imperative to restore Canadian supremacy after humiliating defeat. And then too, we set out to teach the Soviets a lesson they'd never forget.

When the '72 series ended, many Canadians felt we'd done just that. But who, in fact, taught lessons to whom?

GREAT EXPECTATIONS: AUGUST 1972

"We're representing our country and finally getting the chance to prove we are what we believe, the best hockey players in the world."

— BOBBY CLARKE, on the eve of Game 1

●

Arriving home after a summer holiday in Europe, Ken and Lynda Dryden are puzzled by the billboard they pass on the drive into Montreal from Dorval Airport. The message is clever but cryptic: "TO RUSSIA WITH HULL." It's evidently a reference to the forthcoming hockey series against the Soviets, mixed with some James Bond–ish jocularity. But what does it mean, exactly? Who paid to put it there? Something strange has been happening while they've been away, Dryden realizes; he has some catching up to do.

A few weeks earlier, while relaxing in the cafés of Vienna, the longish-haired, twenty-four-year-old Montreal Canadiens goaltender accepted an invitation from Team Canada coach Harry Sinden to attend training camp in Toronto. Camp won't begin until August 13, still three weeks away. But the expectations of Canadian fans are already building to a fever pitch, and a furor has already erupted over the make-up of the team. The people have been expecting, reasonably enough, that the best team possible will be assembled to represent them in the showdown with the USSR; now they're afraid it won't be.

What Dryden learns when he phones around to family and friends is that Bobby Hull, owner of the most lethal slapshot in hockey, breaker (in 1966) of Maurice Richard's once-indestructible record of fifty goals in a season, and newly minted millionaire, is being kept off Team Canada's line-up. Not in the least to Dryden's surprise, this has precipitated a national emergency.

Although now edging past his prime, the thirty-three-year-old Hull is the highest-scoring left winger in NHL history and still considered, along with the younger Bobby Orr, to be hockey's reigning superstar. Because of the severe knee trouble that will eventually force him out of hockey prematurely, Orr appears an unlikely starter in the series. Hull's presence is therefore all the more crucial. No less an authority than Anatoly Tarasov, architect of the Soviet national team but recently deposed as its coach, has said of the Canadians: "Their best players are Bobby Hull and Bobby Orr. . . . Hull against us would be worth one or two goals a game."

At issue is Hull's highly publicized, highly lucrative jump from the Chicago Black Hawks to the nascent World Hockey Association. By signing with the embryonic Winnipeg Jets for $2.75 million, Hull has conferred instant credibility on the upstart league— and instant trauma on NHL owners, who are still getting used to paying the higher salaries forced by their own league's expansion from six teams, only five years earlier, to twelve and now sixteen.

Hull's sensational news breaks just as Sinden and assistant coach John Ferguson are assembling Team Canada. When Sinden phones Hull to ask if he'll play in the series, Hull agrees—on condition that his share of the money goes to the WHA players' pension fund. Aware of the delicacy of the situation, yet still assuming he has access to all Canadian-born players, Sinden asks Hull to keep the matter under his hat until it can be smoothed out with the NHL.

But two days later, unable to contain himself, Hull goes public. NHL President Clarence Campbell then declares that if a single WHA player joins Team Canada, the NHL will bar all its players from competing in the series. Some NHL owners are contemplating legal action against the WHA, and the last thing they want is to appear to be accepting the opposition as equals, thus providing the rival league with an international showcase for its players.

The NHL doesn't actually have jurisdiction over Team Canada. Participation in the series is in the hands of Hockey Canada, which is supposed to function as an independent body. But in practical terms, the cooperation of the NHL, and in particular its U.S. owners, who control all but three of the sixteen franchises, is essential. American owners such as Bill Jennings of the New York Rangers have been grumpy and grudging towards Team Canada from the start, reluctant to let their chattels risk injury by playing the Soviets.

Canadians are outraged. They furiously phone call-in shows, pen letters to the editor, sign petitions and contribute money to billboard campaigns, demanding that Hull be permitted to play for his country. The controversy penetrates Parliament. Prime Minister Pierre Elliott Trudeau is suddenly possessed by a passion for hockey previously hidden from the voters. He sends telegrams to the NHL, the NHLPA and Hockey Canada: "You are aware of the intense concern," Trudeau writes, "which I share with millions of Canadians in all parts of our country, that Canada should be represented by its best hockey players, including Bobby Hull and all those named by Team Canada, in the forthcoming series with the Soviet Union.

"On behalf of these Canadians, I urge Hockey Canada, the NHL and the NHL Players Association to take whatever steps may be necessary to make this possible. . . . I would ask you to keep the best interests of Canada in mind and to make sure that they are fully respected and served."

The day before, Trudeau has summoned Hockey Canada representatives to his office. He's doing everything he can to bring political pressure to bear on resolving the Hull impasse. The cynical would think the prime minister has an opportunistic eye on the general election he will soon call, and the cynical would be absolutely right; but it's also true the government of Canada has invested several years of diplomatic effort in making this series happen.

As early as 1966, government officials have been anxious to improve Canada's performance in international hockey. They've been motivated by our lack of success on the ice, but also by concern for our image abroad, which has been tarnished in Europe by charges of "hooliganism" against our players. Hence Hockey Canada's double mandate: to develop the quality of minor hockey within the country, and to promote Canada's international participation.

This thrust has been quietly promoted by the Department of External Affairs as part of Trudeau's policy of seeking closer relations with the USSR. According to sports historians Donald Macintosh and Donna Greenhorn in their article "Hockey Diplomacy and Canadian Foreign Policy," Trudeau's exchange of visits with Soviet Premier Alexei Kosygin in 1971 included discussions about renewed hockey competition between the two countries. Now Trudeau doesn't want to see his initiative sunk by a few dog-in-the-manger NHL owners. He's encouraged by bombastic Harold Ballard, owner of the Toronto Maple Leafs, who declares, "I don't give a damn if Hull signed with a team in China. He's a Canadian and should be on the Canadian team."

Millions agree. They don't give a damn about closer relations with the Soviet Union, either: they just want to give those upstart Russians a licking.

Canadian fans have been dying to see this showdown for years. In a 1969 cover story, *Weekend Magazine* published a poll of its readers in which nearly 40,000 responses, or 99.1 per cent, were in favour of a confrontation between the NHL and the Soviets. The magazine, a Saturday supplement to major newspapers across the country, reported that the majority wanted to see a five- or seven-game series in which the previous year's Stanley Cup champions, not an all-star team, played the Soviet nationals. Now the people's wish is coming true—at least most of it—and on election eve, Trudeau doesn't want to see them disappointed.

But in the end, the NHL owners hold more cards than the Canadian government. Their business interests prevail over what Canadians fondly like to call "the good of hockey." Without the league's blessing, the great majority of the stars selected for Team Canada would have to play with the threat of legal action hanging over their heads, and few if any of them are willing to alienate the teams that pay their salaries. As Alan Eagleson will put it later, describing his own role on behalf of the Players' Association, "My choice was either blow the tournament or blow Bobby Hull."

So Team Canada will have to go to Russia and win, not only without Hull but without three other stars selected by Sinden but now signed by the WHA: Boston Bruins goalie Gerry Cheevers and playboy centre Derek Sanderson, and Montreal defenseman J. C. Tremblay. Add to the scratch list a disabled Orr, and Team Canada is starting out with a considerable handicap.

Still and all, once Canadian fans adjust to this reality, few of them really believe the missing stars will make the difference between victory and defeat. Reinforced by media "experts," our nearly unanimous view is that the NHL is simply too rich with talent for the Soviets to have any chance of winning. It's an article of faith.

•

With the Hull affair settled, Team Canada opens training camp in Maple Leaf Gardens on August 13. The country is over the top with excitement. Like the early weeks of the First World War, it's a time of sweet innocence: everyone looks forward blithely, heedlessly, to the honeyed taste of victory, blind to the terrible struggles yet to come. For Sinden and Ferguson, the main problem appears to be an embarrassment of riches. It will be a delicate task to select nineteen starters from the hand-picked thirty-five NHLers in camp—all of them invited because they're outstanding at their positions, big stars on their teams.

The coaches started by compiling separate lists of thirty-five, then comparing and combining them to arrive at a master list. They have assembled, in effect, two Team Canadas. They need all those bodies in order to hold intensive scrimmages and full-dress intrasquad games to bring the players up to a competitive level. Given that some members of the team haven't played hockey since the previous April, they need to be whipped into physical condition quickly and also to regain their sharpness in game situations. It's only three weeks less a day before they face off against the Soviets.

Regardless of his large complement of players, Sinden has promised they'll each have an opportunity to play in at least one of the eight games. With so much firepower at Team Canada's disposal, there's no reason why every player shouldn't get his taste of glory. It's the least Sinden can offer them for giving up a month of their summer holidays, or sacrificing the money they'd otherwise be earning at summer hockey schools or other jobs (in fact, some are partially reimbursed for lost income).

Several players have turned down the invitation to participate. The New York Rangers' Ed Giacomin (whose goaltending style has been studied by the Soviets) has a serious knee injury. Others simply feel they have higher priorities than to represent their country. The Bruins' Dallas Smith has to harvest the crop on his Manitoba farm; the wife of Montreal's Jacques Laperriere is about to have a baby; the Rangers' Walt Tkaczuk won't leave his hockey school obligations.

As camp begins, the all-stars arrive for their medicals in various states of flabbiness. Chicago Black Hawks defenseman Pat Stapleton, although not in top condition, has at least been physically active on his farm during the off-season. Toronto Maple Leafs left winger Paul Henderson hopes having stayed in shape will give him an edge in competing for a starting spot. Others are anything but svelte: the Bruins' big Phil Esposito is even bigger than normal, weighing in at a good fifteen pounds over his playing weight. "The only one fatter was Peter Mahovlich," Esposito recalls. "Both of us couldn't fit through the door at the same time." The two go off together to do extra exercises designed to bring their weight down.

Sinden and Ferguson start putting their charges through two workouts a day, ninety minutes in the mornings and sixty in the afternoons. It's your basic NHL training program: Sinden wants to keep the preparations on a purely physical level, since it's far too early to begin psyching the team up for the Soviets, and there's plenty of sheer sweat-hog work to be done.

In tape-recorded impressions that will later become a book, Ken Dryden notes that most of the players throw themselves into the camp with spirit and energy: "We are training with an obvious air of enthusiasm that is not often found at most training camps." Esposito will remember it the same way: "I never trained that hard in my life!" But then, training has never been the NHL's strong point.

Nonetheless, with stars of that calibre putting out—Esposito has scored a league-leading 66 goals and 133 points the previous season, and a record-setting 76 goals the season before that—lesser lights can't afford to be seen taking it easy. Everyone wants to make the starting line-up for opening night, the historic first game of the series, to be played September 2 in Montreal.

Some are sure-fire bets to start: Esposito, forwards Frank Mahovlich and Yvan Cournoyer of the Canadiens, defenseman Brad Park of New York. There's also the Rangers' GAG (Goal-a-Game) Line of Jean Ratelle, Vic Hadfield and Rod Gilbert, who placed third, fourth and fifth in league scoring the previous year with 139 goals and 312 points among them—an NHL record for a forward line.

Other Game 1 starters are less obvious. Three relatively unsung forwards Sinden puts together on the first day impress him more and more as camp goes on, because they skate hard, check assiduously and work smoothly together: the Philadelphia Flyers' rising young centre Bobby Clarke and two Toronto linemates usually centred by the aging Norm Ullman—Henderson and right wing Ron Ellis. At first, Henderson isn't too sure he wants "that diabetic kid from Philadelphia" as their centreman; he'd prefer an established star like Stan Mikita. But he quickly appreciates Clarke's work ethic and dedication to making the team. By their performances, these three are the most conspicuously determined to prove they belong with the big names.

The rest of the camp are a mixture of solid veterans and promising newcomers who will be valuable when young legs are needed. Among the most experienced are defensemen Stapleton and Bill White of Chicago, Don Awrey of Boston, Gary Bergman of Detroit and Rod Seiling of New York, who in 1964 played for the Canadian national team; Red Wings forwards Red Berenson, who played for the Belleville McFarlands in their successful defence of Canada's World's championship in 1959, and Mickey Redmond; Wayne Cashman of the Bruins, Black Hawks Mikita and Dennis Hull, and the Canadiens' Peter Mahovlich. The gifted youngsters include forwards Richard Martin and Gilbert Perreault of Buffalo and Marcel Dionne of Detroit, and defensemen Jocelyn Guevremont and Dale Tallon of Vancouver. Also at camp are Montreal defenseman Guy Lapointe, forwards J.-P. Parise and Bill Goldsworthy of Minnesota, and defenseman Brian Glennie of Toronto.

The goaltenders are Dryden and the Black Hawks' Tony

Esposito—generally considered the two best in the NHL—with backup from Eddie Johnston of Boston, replacing Cheevers. Canadiens defenseman Serge Savard is an uncertain starter because of a leg injury. But the biggest question mark remains Orr: the media are constantly running contradictory "Will He or Won't He?" stories, and nobody knows for sure.

Meanwhile Orr's money is playing, even if he isn't. Eagleson—who says he's always willing to put his mouth where Orr's money is—engineers a partnership between Bobby Orr Enterprises and Harold Ballard to pay Hockey Canada $750,000 for the lucrative broadcasting rights to the series. The partnership outbids MacLaren Advertising, rights-holders to *Hockey Night in Canada* on CBC Television, which has offered $500,000. Although Eagleson sits on the board of Hockey Canada, that body apparently evinces little concern over a possible conflict of interest.

The series promises to be profitable all around. The public has snapped up the tickets to the games in Montreal, Toronto, Winnipeg and Vancouver, many of them raffled off in lotteries by retailers and radio stations. Travel agencies have sold out the 3,000 packages available to Canadian fans to attend the Moscow half of the series, with airfare, hotel, sightseeing and game tickets included.

The players themselves will make only $3,000 and expenses, with a trip to Moscow thrown in for their wives or girlfriends. They'll receive $500 for each of six exhibition games—three intrasquad games, two matches in Sweden in the middle of the series, and one in Czechoslovakia afterwards—and nothing but the glory for the eight games against the Soviets. But that's okay, they reason, because their pension fund will benefit. Profits from the series will be divided evenly between Hockey Canada and the NHL on behalf of the pension fund, with a smaller amount going to the CAHA.

While the national ego is being gratified, hockey will be the winner financially. Or so the story goes. It all depends on your definition of "hockey."

•

With money being made left and right, and the public's excitement swirling around them, the players struggle to get a grip on exactly what they're preparing for. It's all so unfamiliar and out of character for them. Most have little conception of what it's like to compete internationally, except that there's no money in it. At this time of year, they'd normally be out on the golf course, not sweating it at camp.

Phil Esposito recalls his brother Tony asking him, "Why are we going? Why are we doing this? Who are we playing?" And Phil remembers replying, "I don't know, we're playing the Russians. How good can they be? They've won World's championships and they've won Olympics, but they've never played against the pros. So how good can they be?"

Paul Henderson's memory is of his own arrogance about Canada's prospects: "It didn't really matter how good they were, we were better."

Apart from simply wanting to win, some players do sense the historic importance of the occasion. Bill White remembers feeling honoured to be asked to play on Team Canada, but also feeling he has a duty to do it, "like going and being on jury duty. You can't turn it down." For Henderson, part of the motivation lies in the expectations of the country: "We were representing Canada and we were expected to win. I had a sense of responsibility."

After the Red-White intrasquad games, Harry Sinden's *real* problem, aside from selecting his nineteen starters and telling the other sixteen they won't be dressing for Game 1, is to make the entire team feel as Henderson does—proud, even exhilarated, about playing for their country. "These guys are used to playing for money," Sinden muses. "The pot of gold that goes with the Stanley Cup has always been their inspiration. Will they give their best now because Canadians want them to beat hell out of the Russians? I don't know."

Sinden has his own memories of how it feels to win for his country. When he captained the Whitby Dunlops to the World's championship in 1958, defeating the Soviets 4-2 in Oslo, Norway, he experienced "beautiful moments when I stood on top of the world." He and his teammates fulfilled the urgings of a telegram sent to them by Prime Minister John Diefenbaker and signed by thousands of Canadians, telling them to win it for Canada.

Again, there was a revenge motive: after the Penticton Vees' 1955 triumph, Canada lost to the USSR in the 1956 Olympics. Of the Dunlops' win, Sinden says, "We regained our pride." Fourteen years later, he's anxious for his players "to pick up the sense of pride and patriotism our team had that day." So, figuring a picture is worth a thousand words, Sinden sits them down in the media room at Maple Leaf Gardens to view a jerky, out-of-focus, black-and-white film of the 1958 championship game. It's the first stage in his psychological strategy "to get the guys sky-high for Saturday night."

The tactic backfires. The small, dark, crewcut figures flickering across the screen on a snow-rimmed Norwegian rink date from another era; the Soviet players of that day hardly resemble intimidating opponents. And when Sinden himself, then twenty-five years old but looking much younger, appears in close-up for the trophy presentation and hugs the cup to his chest, his players actually burst out laughing: "Who's that little kid with the hat?" Phil Esposito asks the darkened room. "Coach, you look like Charlie Chaplin!" another player exclaims.

Sinden cuts the meeting short. And yet his memories of Oslo remain as alive as burning coals—especially the intoxication he felt standing on the victory podium, the Soviet and Swedish captains below him on either side, as "O Canada" was played and the flag rose majestically, "the goose bumps popping out all over me."

"I hope," Sinden prays, "before this 1972 series is over, these kids can experience that feeling. Money can't buy it. Not even Stanley Cup money."

•

On August 30 at 8:30 p.m., an Ilyushin passenger jet from Moscow known as Aeroflot flight 301 touches down in the darkness at Dorval Airport. The USSR national hockey team has finally arrived on Canadian territory.

The next morning at nine, the Soviets are out on the ice in suburban St. Laurent for a "light" ninety-minute drill that would would put most Canadian workouts to shame—as if jet lag from the seven-hour time difference between Moscow and Montreal doesn't even exist for them. It doesn't, as it turns out. One of their interpreters explains they've been living and practising on Montreal time for the past two weeks. This team has prepared.

For Team Canada, the reality of the series is just beginning to sink in. But for the odd man out, the thoughtful, intellectual law student Dryden, the reality process accelerated five days earlier, the day of an intrasquad game in Toronto. In the afternoon, Dryden watched the televised opening ceremonies of the Summer Olympic Games from Munich. Struck by the grand pageantry of it all, he felt the parallels with international hockey and the upcoming series, and started to feel nervous: "I shivered for a few seconds. My heart seemed to be beating faster. Pressure had hit me."

But then Dryden has played internationally before. He has played the Soviets before. *He* knows how good they can be, having been heavily bombed while in goal for Father Bauer's national team in 1969, just three years earlier. His teammates, nearly all innocent of such knowledge, only begin to feel that pressure once they fly to Montreal wearing their spiffy new Team Canada blazers on September 1, the day before the series starts. They travel in two different aircraft, arriving just in time to take in the Soviets' practice at the Forum. Unfortunately, what they see doesn't impress them.

There is no dazzling display of passing pyrotechnics, no power shooting, no flashy goaltending: quite the opposite, in fact. The Soviets practise at a deliberately slow, low-key, even clumsy pace. Watching from the stands, the Canadian players grin and smirk as they see only soft shooters and stumbling defensemen. They salivate at the sight of the fresh-cheeked, twenty-year-old goaltender, Vladislav Tretiak, backing too deep into his net, flubbing easy shots—apparent confirmation of the one and only Team Canada scouting report brought back from Moscow, which alleges Tretiak's weak glove hand will make him a sitting duck for NHL sharpshooters.

Team Canada's scouts, Toronto Maple Leafs coach John McLellan and his chief scout Bob Davidson, spent only four days in the Soviet Union and saw only two games. One was an exhibition between the national team and Central Army, in which Tretiak, playing for Army against the best Soviet marksmen, including some of his own teammates, gave up eight goals. As John Ferguson remembers it, McClellan and Davidson estimated that weak Soviet goaltending would give Team Canada a five- or six-goal advantage every game. What the Canadian scouts weren't told—surprise!—was that Tretiak was getting married the next morning and suffering from a severe hangover after pre-nuptial celebrations with his Army buddies. Later, Phil Esposito will say, "Geez, no wonder the Maple Leafs end up in last place all the time!"

Even Bobby Orr, who will now definitely be prevented from playing the Canadian half of the series, asserts confidently that the young goalie will be easy pickings. Sinden, Orr's former coach with Boston, knows the canny Soviets don't show everything they have in practice—their habit when he played them back in 1958, and again at the 1960 Olympics in Squaw Valley. He frets about his team's overconfidence. And yet, when they take to the ice for their own practice, with the Soviets now looking on, he can't help feeling gleefully proud of his boys "unloading all kinds of bombs"—just like, he thinks, little kids showing off for their parents.

The Soviet book on Team Canada is infinitely more thorough and accurate. *Their* two scouts—national team assistant coach Boris Kulagin and former assistant coach Arkady Chernyshev, who worked closely with Tarasov in building the Soviet machine—have spent two weeks attending every Team Canada practice and intrasquad game, sitting in Maple Leaf Gardens scribbling endless notes and drawing copious diagrams. Soviet coach Vsevolod Bobrov and his brain trust have watched films of the 1971 and 1972 Stanley Cup playoffs to see the NHL stars at their best. When Sinden and Ferguson down a few friendly pre-series vodkas with their Soviet counterparts, they discover the other side knows "everything about our players."

For the Soviets, espionage isn't confined to nuclear secrets. They've already appropriated a couple of Team Canada drills, Sinden notices at the Forum. It seems like a flattering homage to Canadian hockey, as does the polite request from an official for multiple copies of Bobby Orr's autograph, sought by the Soviet players. But is it homage or psychological warfare?

"When you look back on it, we'd been had," Pat Stapleton says years later. And not only by the Soviets' wily machinations.

For weeks, even months, the North American media have been reinforcing the myth of NHL invincibility. Team Canada players have been reading the same papers and watching the same sportscasts as everyone else. Predictions of the series' outcome are everywhere in the media, and virtually all are variations on the following, published in the Montreal *Gazette* on the eve of Game 1—and note that U.S. pundits, their judgement unclouded by Canadian nationalism, concur:

Red Storey, former NHL referee: "Canada in eight straight— but the toughest win will be the opener."

Jim Coleman, Southam News Services: "Canada will win seven, with one game tied on Russian ice."

Johnny Esaw, CTV network: "The Russians will win one here, one in Russia. Six-two."

Jacques Plante, All-Star NHL goaltender: "Eight straight for Canada."

Gerald Eskenazi, *New York Times*: "The NHL team will slaughter them in eight straight."

Milt Dunnell, *Toronto Star*: "Canada will win handily. Say seven-one."

Claude Larochelle, *Le Soleil*, Quebec City: "We may lose one in Russia. Seven-one for Canada."

Mark Mulvoy, *Sports Illustrated*: "Canada, seven-one."

Fran Rosa, Boston *Globe*: "Eight-nothing Canada—and that's also the score of the first game."

Dissenters from this view are considered eccentric, unpatriotic or soft on Communism. One is Billy Harris, the former Toronto Maple Leaf who played on three Stanley Cup winners in the 1960s. Harris publicly warns that the Soviets will be considerably better than anyone expects, and even predicts they'll win the series, largely on the strength of Tretiak's goaltending. Harris is dismissed as a bit of a crank. His only qualification is that, earlier in the year, he has coached the Swedish national team to a 3-3 tie against the Soviets at the Olympics.

The other crank, and the only prominent eastern Canadian journalist to depart from the cozy consensus of the media, is John Robertson of the *Montreal Star*. In his columns and on television,

Robertson crawls out on a prickly limb to predict six *Soviet* wins—two in Canada and all four in Moscow. Assailed as insincere, a mere attention-seeker, and invited to go write for *Pravda*, Robertson is in fact palpably angry and indignant for the most patriotic of reasons: "We have taken one hundred years of hockey heritage and shoved it into the centre of the table and staked it on the outcome of an eight-game series in which we sat back and allowed the deck to be stacked against us."

Robertson marshalls some strong arguments to support his case. The skills gap between the NHLers and the Soviets, he writes, is actually narrow and can be bridged by the team with superior conditioning—and at this time of year, we know who that is. The Soviets also have an edge in skating ability. And they are tough enough that they won't be intimidated by our traditional bully tactics. To clinch his arguments, Robertson quotes several good Canadians. Aggie Kukulowicz, a former pro hockey player and now an Air Canada official who speaks Russian and acts as a liaison with the Soviets, cautions, "The Russians are too physically strong, too well-conditioned to be upset by bodychecks." Team Canada's Red Berenson admits, "We're certainly not in mid-season form, not in condition or timing." And Harry Sinden himself acknowledges to Robertson, "I'm nervous as hell. My main worry is the pace they play at."

Yet even Sinden's prophetic words are drowned in the torrent of calls for a Team Canada sweep. Reflecting on the impact of the media's mood on the players themselves, Stapleton remembers: "Harry kept telling us, 'They'll be ready. They're not coming over here without being ready.' But Harry's message kept being lost among everybody else's messages. You read all about how they don't have goaltending, they don't have this, they don't have that, and you just get to be part of the information flow from the newspapers and TV. All the experts are predicting eight straight, and Harry's just one man saying something different."

Sinden was even saying something different from his close colleague Alan Eagleson. By this time, five men—Eagleson, Sinden, Ferguson, and two people who worked for Eagleson, Bobby Haggert and Mike Cannon—have taken control over the day-today operations and management of the team, shutting out Hockey Canada officials from any direct involvement. They call themselves "Team Five" and will remain a tight, united crew to the very end. But on the eve of the series, there's Eagleson in the newspapers blaring, "We gotta win in eight games. Anything less than an unblemished sweep of the Russians would bring shame down on the heads of the players and the national pride."

Eagleson is only reflecting what folks are saying in the coffee shops and bars and offices and factories and living rooms of the nation. But that attitude makes it virtually impossible for Team Canada to win any real credit: if they sweep the series, they will simply be doing what everyone expected. As Dryden records in his notes, he and his teammates have been set up by their own countrymen's expectations: "We Canadians find ourselves on a one-way street. We must score an overwhelming 8-0 victory. Anything less will be a shattering defeat."

Such a universally mindless attitude is only possible amid the blinkered, black-and-white, Us-against-Them paranoia of the time. Indeed, the Cold War almost intervenes to end the series before it begins. A young Czech immigrant in Montreal has a grievance against the Soviet Union: not only did it invade his country four years earlier, trampling all over the heady new political and cultural freedoms ushered in by the 1968 "Prague Spring," but a Warsaw Pact tank demolished his car. After seeking financial compensation for three years, the man succeeds in winning a Quebec court order to seize the Soviet team's hockey equipment for non-payment of his claim for damages: a total of $1,889. The equipment is seized and locked up.

Whatever the justice of the man's claim, the visiting Soviets are also justified in their anger over the unwarranted intrusion of politics into what's supposed to be a hockey series. Just as Team Canada will feel harassed in Moscow later in the month, the Soviets feel themselves the target of Canadian harassment: they refuse to play unless they get their equipment back.

Both the Canadian government and Hockey Canada are flummoxed by the diplomatic embarrassment. Squeezed between setting an international legal precedent and caving in to Soviet pressure, they feel damned if they do and damned if they don't, so they do nothing. But not R. Alan Eagleson. Always a man to get the thing done as expediently as possible, Eagleson shocks his Hockey Canada colleagues by writing a personal cheque to the plaintiff, handing it to the man's lawyer in Montreal's Queen Elizabeth Hotel on the morning of Game 1 and stating, "There, he's paid. Now hand over the bloody equipment." The series is on again.

The day before, Prime Minister Trudeau exuberantly announces his first bid for reelection. Trudeau is unaware his Liberal Party electoral machine is as unready for battle as Team Canada, and seemingly uncaring that his high-handed policies and personal behaviour have turned many Canadians against him. He's confident the national euphoria over the hockey series will favour his campaign and speed his way to another majority government. Trudeau's campaign slogan is "The Land Is Strong." His arrogance, too, will turn out to be misplaced.

THREE

THE PUCK

"An athlete is a lot like an artist—you have to let him go,
you can't structure him too much."
— PAT STAPLETON, 1995

●

The most celebrated hockey puck in history must surely be the one Paul Henderson slipped behind Vladislav Tretiak one September evening in Moscow in 1972.

That singular puck, you imagine, must radiate light from its rubbery heart. Its radiance has nothing whatsoever to do with the electronic glow of the FoxTrax Puck, a cyberpuck used for the first time in the 1996 NHL All-Star game. Devised by the Fox Network to permit puck-blind viewers to follow the game on the small screen, that puck of doubtful lineage has no heart. It is a virtual puck, a hollowed-out impostor. Implanted with twenty infrared emitters, it sends electronic signals to a computer that visually tracks the puck by enveloping it in a blundering blue blob. The blob, transforming hilariously into a red comet-tail when the puck is shot at high speeds, actually hides the puck instead of revealing it, obliterating hockey's poetry-in-motion and turning it into a cartoonish video game. Nothing is left to the viewer's imagination or intuition.

No, Henderson's fateful puck must be altogether different. But where can we behold it? Where can we go to worship this Canadian Holy Grail?

For twenty years, nobody knew.

Then a clue appeared on September 26, 1992, almost twenty years to the day after The Goal was scored. Sports columnist Jim

Kernaghan of the *London Free Press* was researching some background for a twentieth-anniversary story and found himself talking to the last player to touch the puck when the final horn sounded in Moscow, thirty-four seconds of playing time after Henderson's triumphal shot: Pat Stapleton.

According to Kernaghan, Stapleton acknowledged he'd casually slipped the puck into his glove as the other members of Team Canada, 3,000 visiting Canadian fans and some twelve million Canadians back home watching on television or listening to the radio went out of their minds. Before letting loose a little himself, Stapleton, a practical soul and a farmer by vocation, had the lucid presence of mind to scoop the game puck. Nobody in that repressed land stopped him.

•

Now it's nearly a quarter-century later, a full generation. The Soviet Union no longer exists, and you're driving a rented green Neon through the expansive farmlands of southwestern Ontario, deep into the heart of hockey country, thinking how this massive flat landscape could easily be the Prairies, and wondering if, somewhere miles ahead, Pat Stapleton still has possession of his little souvenir from Moscow.

It will be extraordinary to witness it. You picture it enshrined, somehow—perhaps mounted in a place of honour on the barn wall, above a pair of crossed hockey sticks, guarded by cattle and horses. There's something wonderful about that idea, a national treasure being stored in such an unpretentious, unlikely, out-of-the-way place. As if the Americans had hung the Liberty Bell in a pool hall.

Now, chances are Pat Stapleton isn't the first name you think of when you think of the '72 series. Apart from Paul Henderson and Phil Esposito, you sooner recall Bobby Clarke or Yvan Cournoyer or Ken Dryden or the other goaltender, Esposito's brother Tony. Or Brad Park, Serge Savard, the Mahovlich brothers. Hell, you even remember *Soviet* names—Tretiak, Kharlamov, Yakushev—before Stapleton's.

Although he'd made the All-Star team three times, Stapleton was never a big star in the NHL. Just extremely good at what he did. By '72, he'd already played twelve seasons as a pro, and that experience, that reliability and steadiness, were what appealed to Sinden and Ferguson when they selected him to play against the Soviets. Team Canada was so overstocked with NHL stars, however, that Stapleton sat out the opening game of the series along with his Black Hawks defense partner, Bill White. After the shock of defeat in that first meeting, the coaches urgently needed to strengthen their blueline. Injected into the line-up for Game 2, Stapleton and White were such an effective combination that they played the rest of the series.

Stapleton's big contribution was his consistency: an asset both on the ice, where he stood up to the ever-dangerous Soviet attack and ended the series with an excellent plus-minus total of plus-six, second-highest on the team (the highest was White's plus-seven), and off. Stapleton's comradely nature and puckish humour also helped stabilize Team Canada's volatile mix of bona-fide stars, would-be stars and gold-plated prima donnas. It was a team that badly needed stabilizing. At one point, after four players had defected in Moscow and gone home because, they said, they weren't being played enough (and more likely because they feared being associated with a lost cause), Stapleton went up to Sinden and said: "Harry, I'm leaving. Here I come to Moscow for a nice holiday and I've had to play every damn game!"

You exit the main highway onto the township road leading to Stapleton's farm. As you turn up the long drive, an image comes to mind from the broadcast film of Game 8 in Moscow, which you've just viewed. Soviet defenseman Alexander Gusev shoots the puck in a last desperate attempt to steal Team Canada's victory, but he's wide of the mark. Dryden steers the puck carefully behind the net to Stapleton, who carries it up ice, taking his time before moving it out of harm's way. As the horn sounds, Stapleton suddenly accelerates in apparent pursuit of the puck—but we never actually see him nab it, because the camera moves off him to capture the ecstatic embraces of his teammates.

●

Emerging from the rear door of his farmhouse, Pat Stapleton is still as recognizable as any player you watched repeatedly on television during the years before helmets. Never exactly slim, he's become even more rotund; he must be at least twenty pounds over his playing weight of 185 pounds. Despite the belly and jowly neck, however, the face hasn't changed much: still open and boyish, the eyebrows and lashes pale against a pink complexion, the hair that gave him the nickname "Whitey" still blond and thick.

In the big high-ceilinged kitchen that once fed the six Stapleton children, now grown up, a pot of chili burbles away on the stove below a sign on the wall: "Soup Kitchen: Praise the Lord and Stay in Line." Stapleton and his wife, Jackie, bought the farm over thirty years ago, when they were still in their twenties. They moved there permanently after he retired from hockey in 1979. Back in the mid-1960s, buying a farm of his own seemed an excellent idea to a young father who'd already played professional hockey in four cities and two countries—Sault Ste. Marie and Kingston, Ontario; Portland, Oregon, and Boston—after his Junior A years with the St. Catharines Teepees. "In the hockey business," he explains, "it's not always real stable for the family. This way, the kids always could say they had a home. They always knew they were going home in the summertime. It had a stabilizing effect."

He and Jackie, as Stapleton puts it, "like a little more space than people who live in town." Over the years, they've had their three hundred acres mostly in corn, wheat, oats and barley, and at one time they fed a herd of eighty to ninety cows. Stapleton has always loved being out in the elements, whatever the weather. "There's days when you're up to your knees in mud, and there's days when you can't penetrate the ground with a spike. That variety is kinda the neat thing about farming."

In 1980, not long after he'd retired to the farm, Stapleton accepted an invitation to assist with the minor hockey program in New Brunswick. He visited seventeen communities across the province and taught a series of drills of his own devising to local coaches and their players. Invited to return the following year, he found his coaching methods had caught on so well that he agreed to his hosts' request to commit them to paper so others could use them. In the process, he realized he'd created much more than a set of hockey drills: it amounted to a developmental program for young people, for which hockey was simply the context. Today he calls it "a personal-growth program to help kids believe in themselves."

Stapleton's motivation had been his unhappiness with the way hockey was being taught to young people—not only in terms of technique but of human values. He saw kids being pushed and pressured through hockey, and being taught to push and pressure themselves and each other, with negative results for the individual. "I asked myself, 'What are we trying to do in this sport? Are we trying to help kids or hurt them? Are we trying to demoralize them? Are we trying to punish them?' "

These are questions that any adult involved in minor hockey, whether as coach or parent, needs to ask. But for Stapleton, they led to a new, holistic approach to the game: "I believe hockey can be a vehicle to make things happen for you. The skills you learn are transferable to whatever other aspect of life you want."

He called the program "Fundamentals in Action." The name is a significant, if unintended, echo of "Athletes in Action," the Christian pro sports ministry in which Paul Henderson became involved around the same time. That echo hints at the inescapably spiritual nature of Team Canada's odyssey, which has imbued some of the players with a messianic zeal.

Obtaining financial backing from Pepsi-Cola, Canadian Tire and other corporate sponsors, Stapleton took his program into—by his count—some 1,300 communities across Canada over the next decade or so, from the west to Newfoundland, a province that became for a time like his second home. For this ambitious undertaking, he recruited thirty-one former professional hockey players to deliver the program.

The program is no longer as active as it was, but Stapleton still burns with the conviction that got him started. He points out there were always players who were bigger, stronger or more talented than he was, who skated faster or shot harder, but who fell by the wayside en route to the NHL. What they lacked was self-worth: a quality he believes our minor hockey system—and society at large—fails to nurture in young people. Instead, we impose disabling limits on kids before their true potential can possibly be known or realized: "Every child who puts on skates is given a reason to fail: 'You're not big enough, you're not strong enough, you didn't make the right team, or play in the right league.' And consequently, a lot of them go by the boards. You really need that belief in yourself to overcome the obstacles people put in your way, and a support system to keep you going."

The support system he's created is meant to stay with young people long after they've completed a Fundamentals in Action program, even after they no longer have much need of the stick-handling or passing or shooting skills they've developed. "I offer them choices: if you say you can, you can; if you say you can't, you can't. Your choices create your habits, your habits make you or break you. It's that simple."

Rhyming off his precepts and the thinking behind them, Stapleton the hockey philosopher will suddenly veer off into some aphorism. Such as: "You can lean like a willow, but you can't break like an oak—yet you need the strength of an oak."

Or he'll ask if you know how a Chinese bamboo tree grows. You don't, as it happens: "The Chinese plant a seed. They watch it and cultivate it every day for a month and nothing happens. Two months, nothing happens. Five months. They make sure it gets lots of sunshine, they water it, cultivate it, and this goes on for a year—nothing happens. Two years—nothing happens. Three, four. It goes into its fifth year before it actually comes up through the ground. And when it does, it grows ninety feet in six months. Now I ask you, did it grow ninety feet in six months, or in five years and six months? So children are like that. You have to keep fertilizing them, watering them, encouraging them." He tries to get this point across not only to minor hockey coaches but to parents.

Within his amalgam of parable, positive thinking and plain common sense, Stapleton keeps circling back, as a man with his experience must, to the '72 series. To illustrate his precept about creativity, he tells you Team Canada was able to win because of its creative responses to the Soviet team's regimentation and predictability. Superskilled as they were, the Soviets had been trained to play in certain set patterns. The Canadians learned to anticipate those patterns, break them up in the later games, and exploit the advantages that resulted: "Our creativity within the individual athlete came out, and we found ways to beat them. Each act of individual creativity is important. An athlete is a lot like an artist—you have to let him go, you can't structure him too much."

In Stapleton's view, there is excessive emphasis today on structuring the way hockey is coached and played. Although this is considered a Russian and European influence, he also sees in it an American import from coaching football: "Let X hit O, let X move here, etc., etc. But hockey doesn't happen that way. I can study you and analyze your movements ten times over, but the eleventh time you're going to go the other way. The quickness, the agility, the creativity, the ability to surprise—that's what makes a hockey player. I still believe hockey players are the greatest athletes in the world. To skate while carrying the puck, keeping your head up and watching out for your own teammates and six other guys who want to interfere with you and keep you from the goal, that takes an awful lot of skill."

Stapleton argues adamantly that the '72 Soviet national team was overrated, whereas Team Canada was underrated. He acknowledges that the Soviets were excellent athletes: "Your game picked up very quickly against them because you had to play at a higher level." He also mentions individual players who stand out in his memory. But unlike some of his teammates, he refuses to be drawn into recognizing *any* of them as the greatest he ever played against.

Was the legendary Valery Kharlamov the toughest Soviet forward to defend against? "Not necessarily."

What about Alexander Yakushev? "He came down my side a lot. They'd criss-cross."

Which others does he remember best? "[Vladimir] Petrov was a pretty good one. [Boris] Mikhailov was a rugged competitor, he liked to get physical in the corners. And number ten, who was that? Oh yeah, [Alexander] Maltsev. He was a smooth athlete, very smooth stride, he moved the puck well."

Faint praise for one of the greatest hockey teams of all time: a team that lost to the NHL's best by only a single goal in the final minute of 480 minutes of play. But as evidence for his argument, Stapleton points to the wide disparity in penalties during the series, which provided the Soviets with many more power plays than Canada enjoyed: "If they were *that* good, they should've wiped the floor with us, considering how many opportunities they had. So maybe they weren't as good as everybody thought. Or we were better than we were given credit for!"

It's true that North Americans were awed and overwhelmed by the Soviets' power in the first four games in Canada, all the more so because their skills had been unheralded, their success unexpected. But, Stapleton argues, "Motivation's a funny thing. Like you need a bath every day, you need a little motivation every day. So did they take it easy on home ice? Was their game plan not as solid as when they came to Canada? Was their motivation not as high? They were well-prepared for us, but it's like in any sport—you can prepare all you want, but the other guy never lets you play like you want to. That's why you've gotta be creative in this game. If you start getting predictable, that predictability brings you down. The human element comes in."

Hockey and the human element: it isn't surprising that these are Stapleton's preoccupations because, by rights, Team Canada should never have won that series, given the deep dark pit they'd dug themselves into in the first five games. We should have lost it, and with it an enormous chunk of national pride and self-worth, given the almost incomprehensible importance Canadians place on hockey. But miraculously, Team Canada didn't lose. And so it isn't surprising, either, to hear Pat Stapleton say his convictions about hockey and life aren't derived from religion, yet do have something in common with religious faith:

"You can look at any religion, and you'll find the same idea: believe, believe, believe. Take action—you have potential for something, so believe in it and take action on it. As long as it isn't against the laws of God or man, you can have it.

"In fact, with those two qualifications, there isn't anything you can't have, provided you ask and answer three questions: What is it I really want? What will I sacrifice to get it? And am I willing to do the necessary work? You can have it! There are no boundaries!"

If anyone had written down a credo for Team Canada '72 to follow, that would have been it. *Something* helped them pull themselves out of that pit and climb over the top, where they received an ecstatic glimpse of something else—God, or Grail, or possibly just their own throbbing human potential—that has been driving some of them ever since.

•

Over lunch, Stapleton introduces another of his precepts, wearing a faint grin: "I also tell kids, 'Do something for someone else every day with no expectations of return.' That's why I've taken the time to talk with you, buddy. I've gotta practise what I preach, right?"

The time has definitely come to broach the subject that's been dangling invisibly in the air, an unpopped question. In fifteen minutes Stapleton has to leave to drive Jackie to the airport; she's catching a flight to Toronto and then to Phoenix, to visit their daughter and her family. So casually you inquire if there's time to take a little stroll outside, maybe see The Puck, which for some reason you still visualize as being in the barn.

Stapleton swallows the last of his sandwich. He leans back in his chair, grinning some more, sunlight glancing through the window and glinting off his blue eyes: "Here I thought you were interested in interviewing me," he says, only half-kidding, "and you're only interested in seeing the *puck!*"

You keep things light—what else, you ask, returning his smile, have you been doing for the past couple of hours but interviewing him?

"Yeah, well, I'd have to go dig it out. All our stuff is stored away somewhere."

Reasonably enough, it turns out he's worried about thieves, souvenir hunters. "But oh, I'll think of something to do with it," he adds quickly, "something that'll be neat for the whole country. We'll raffle it off for charity, or put it on display somewhere. Ronnie Ellis wanted it for the Hall of Fame. I remember the guys there saying, 'Come on, it's just a puck.' But it isn't, really—it's a part of history."

He ponders some more. "There's no way of telling who really has it. I guess I'm the only one who knows, because I picked it up, right? We had pretty good control of the puck for the last thirty seconds or so, and it came around to me and I actually was going to shoot it down the ice. And at the last second, as everything broke loose, I just kind of let up. It went ahead of me eight or ten feet and I just skated and picked it up. I don't know why. I never thought at the time it was such a significant puck. In the film, the camera sees me with the puck and then pans away somewhere else."

That's right, you tell him, you've seen the film too. But does he know for sure it's the same puck Henderson fired past Tretiak?

"Well, I can't remember them ever changing the puck. And it was only thirty-some seconds of play after the goal."

In that case, like so many others, you'd love to see it. Just a brief glimpse, to be able to say you've witnessed it—even touched it. It would be a bigger thrill than seeing the Stanley Cup, and we know how much it means to people to see *that*.

"What's the significance of you actually *looking* at it?" he asks pleasantly, still playing the Trickster. "I could go out to the shed and get any old puck and say this is it, you know? And how would you know the difference?"

Hard to argue that one. So you mutter something about a national talisman, a Holy Grail, and he laughs appreciatively, "That's good, that's good!"

He issues a challenge: "What can we do with this puck so *all* Canadians can see it? In a way that would benefit everybody? Because if there's no benefit, why show it?"

You take him up on it: "Okay, what about displaying it on Parliament Hill? It could be on view in the rotunda, in a Plexiglas case. Just inside the main entrance. Then everybody could see it when they visit the capital."

He seems to like the idea. "Yeah! Not bad! I'd take it to Ottawa, but first you and I'd take it out onto the Rideau Canal and bang it around a bit."

By now you're outside in the warm afternoon, and Stapleton is piling Jackie's luggage into the trunk of their big North American car. As you prepare to make the long drive back down the highway, you know you won't be discovering the Grail—not this trip, anyway.

You shake hands, you drive off. You try to be philosophical. You like the man very much. Yet somehow, as the miles of farmland melt away in reverse order and vanish behind you, the Grail seems to have vanished, too. It seems to have become just a bit doubtful in its authenticity—not unlike, you suddenly think, Team Canada's victory in 1972.

FOUR

GAME 1: WHO HAS SEEN THE WIND?

"You learn only when you lose. I hope we learned a lot."
— KEN DRYDEN, *Face-Off at the Summit*

●

On the Saturday the series opens, it's Labour Day weekend and the country is in a party mood, all set to celebrate the last blast of summer. The weather in Montreal fits the mood perfectly: sunny and hot, with temperatures in the high eighties (the Celsius scale hasn't arrived in Canada yet), better suited to barbecuing than hockey—but then, hockey isn't entirely what this series is about.

The McGuinness distillery of Ontario runs a full-page ad in Toronto newspapers for "the capitalist vodka." Across the top half, the ad reads: "If they can play hockey, we can make vodka"—a lighthearted variation on the series' dark political subtext.

The subtext isn't lost on the players themselves. They know well how much victory means to the people, and equally what defeat will mean.

Phil Esposito: "The country's at stake here. I mean, that's my thought. It's our society at stake against theirs."

Serge Savard: "It really became a battleground between two systems. It was not only a game. They were expecting to shock the world."

The Canadian players also fully expect to deliver what their country expects of them. Just a few hours later, not only these players, not only the sport of hockey, but the country itself will have entered a profound state of shock. Sixty minutes of hockey will have the shattering force of revelation: and ultimately, of revolution. In one evening, a large piece of the cherished bedrock of Canadians' understanding of ourselves is exploded. In the space hollowed out by that explosion, new understanding, and gradual but massive transformation, will grow. A more influential hockey game has never been played.

•

Harry Sinden is nervous. Entering the Team Canada dressing room at 7:00 p.m., one hour before game time, he notices he's already sweating. Even coaching in the Stanley Cup playoffs, he's never begun to sweat until the puck is dropped.

As his players pull their equipment on, Sinden detects an air of high anxiety among them, too. They can't wait to get out on the ice and show their stuff to the world. Still, Sinden worries: that's what coaches do. He worries that his team has had only seventeen days to prepare. He worries that they come from different clubs and haven't played much together. He worries that the Soviets are in better condition. Then he worries the most unthinkable worry of all: "Maybe we're not quite as good as I thought we were."

And yet he knows his game plan is sound. Essentially, it's to pit the Canadians' greatest perceived strength—offensive power— against the Soviets' greatest perceived weakness—poor goaltending. Sinden has instructed his men to shoot early and often and from every possible angle, even bad angles; the Soviet goalie might blow some easy ones, and a quick Team Canada lead could panic the visitors into making mistakes. And Sinden has ordered his men to play the style of game they're used to; he doesn't want to make adjustments "that might start our players thinking too much." This means being aggressive, NHL-style—although not fighting, since under international rules, fighting will get them ejected.

Defensively, Sinden has told his men they have to forecheck ceaselessly—"That's the game of Stanley Cup champions"—and bodycheck cleanly, taking away the Soviets' trademark short-passing game, their tactic of manoeuvring gradually in for the kill: "Take out the man making the pass so he can't get it back." But, since he's emphasizing offense, he utilizes his seventeen skaters (less the two goalies) by dressing four lines to carry the play to the Soviets, and just five defensemen.

The defense pairings are Don Awrey and Rod Seiling ("the best pair in training") and Brad Park and Gary Bergman, with Guy Lapointe as backup and point man on the power play. Dryden will be in goal. Like Lapointe, he'll be playing in front of his hometown fans, and although Dryden hasn't outshone Tony Esposito in camp, Sinden figures he'll play his best at home.

Meanwhile, in the Forum dressing room assigned to the Soviets, an unexpected visitor has arrived. Vladislav Tretiak is astonished to look up from lacing his skates to see one of his goaltending idols, Jacques Plante, standing before him. "It was about an hour before the first game," Tretiak has recalled, "and out of nowhere appears Jacques Plante. Our coaches brought him to me."

The two have met before. Three years earlier, when Tretiak was seventeen and visiting Canada with his national junior team, Plante worked with him on his technique. Now Plante, age forty-three, greying and playing with Toronto, his fourth NHL team, will be the colour commentator that night on the CBC's French television network. He's already made his public prediction that Team Canada will win eight straight; he's worried how young Tretiak will manage.

"He showed me on a [chalk] board how the Canadian players shot the puck," Tretiak remembers. "He talked about Cournoyer, Mahovlich, Esposito. I think he felt a little sorry for me. He didn't think I'd do well." Tretiak has since acknowledged that Plante's advice helped him in Game 1. But for now, even the former Canadiens' hero is underestimating his protégé's chances against the NHL sharpshooters, just as the rest of the country is underestimating Tretiak's teammates.

Soviet head coach Vsevolod Bobrov has hinted at this in a pre-game interview with the *Toronto Star*'s Milt Dunnell: "I know Canadians have said in the past that we try to mold everybody into the group," Bobrov tells Dunnell with a grin. "In my opinion, Kharlamov will stand out, even against your best Canadians. By North American standards, he is small but he has an excellent shot. I think he will be effective."

Bobrov quickly follows up this charming bit of understatement with the obligatory flattery of his opponents: "I expect there will be some surprises for us when we meet your Canadian stars. Some things will not surprise us. For example, I know your goaling is superior."

To which Arkady Chernyshev, one of Bobrov's scouts during the Canadian training camp, adds slyly: "There is so much talent [on Team Canada]. I hear it asked whether Bobby Hull will play. I hear it asked whether Bobby Orr will play. When you have so many excellent players, I wonder whether it matters?"

•

Whereas the Soviets have compiled acute observations and astute assessments of Team Canada's strengths and weaknesses, for most Canadians—fans and hockey professionals alike—the Soviet team may as well be creatures from another planet. Our curiosity about these mysterious alien visitors begins to be satisfied shortly after eight o'clock. A domestic audience estimated at 12 million (out of a national population of 21 million, and a worldwide viewership of 100 million), the largest Canadian audience ever for any television program, watches as the camera catches the Soviet players emerging from their dressing room. Wearing small, tight-fitting red helmets oddly reminiscent of a cosmonaut's headgear, and old-fashioned white sweaters with "CCCP," the Cyrillic abbreviation for USSR, in tiny red letters on their chests, they file quietly into the corridor. They seem unperturbed by the restless rumble of the capacity crowd awaiting them.

Their absence of facial expression—actually a form of Soviet correctness—contributes to the disparaging "robot" image we'll soon hang on them. The helmets, which we're not yet accustomed to, also create that impression. Only three members of Team Canada, Berenson, Henderson and Mikita, will not play bareheaded.

But in fact, the Soviet players are feeling the tension as much as any mortal. Tretiak's knees are shaking inside his heavy pads. Later, he'll admit frankly that he and his team were afraid of the Canadians, awed by their reputation for sheer physical power. The Soviets held a team meeting the evening before, at which they vowed to show Soviet hockey at its best even if they had to lose. To Alexander Yakushev, his teammates seem more anxious than usual, even veterans of international competition like defenseman Alexander Ragulin and forward Evgeny Mishakov, or men who are glamorous superstars back in Europe such as Valery Kharlamov and Alexander Maltsev.

To Canadians, these aren't superstars, merely unpronounceable names on a roster. We don't appreciate either that the Soviets have their own equivalent of a missing Hull and Orr. Thirty-one-year-old Anatoly Firsov, long the preeminent Soviet forward and coveted even by NHL scouts, was ready to come out of retirement to play against Canada. But like Orr, he's sidelined with a knee injury; and like Hull, he's had his conflicts with the hockey establishment. In addition, outstanding thirty-three-year-old defenseman Vitaly Davidov has stayed at home: he's either injured or out of favour with coach Bobrov.

Bobrov has tried to calm his men in the dressing room. He's reminded them of their superiority in skating and passing. His game plan is to outskate the larger, slower Canadians, using the swift pass-and-go to get by them. Knowing how tight his team is, Bobrov has cautioned them not to panic if Canada scores a quick goal or two: it will be a long game, they must stick to their plan. In contrast to Sinden, he'll use seven defensemen, hoping to spike Canada's big guns, and just three complete forward lines.

The teams line up at their bluelines to be introduced—not only to the fans but in a sense to each other. The 18,818 overheated spectators, many in shirtsleeves, give the unsmiling visitors a respectful round of applause as each unfamiliar name is announced. And when it's the home team's turn, the crowd lets loose all those years of pent-up anticipation.

Visually a knockout in their newly designed red sweaters, a massive, stylized white maple leaf exploding jaggedly across their chests, the Canadian players receive warm roars of appreciation.

The warmest are reserved for the boys from les Habs—in order, Cournoyer, Peter Mahovlich, Lapointe and then (the noisest and most prolonged ovations) Frank Mahovlich and Dryden. Standing at his blueline and witnessing the deafening adulation of "the professionals," as the Soviets always term them, Boris Mikhailov—a top scorer and a veteran himself at twenty-eight—realizes he feels "terrified."

Pierre Trudeau, his hair and sideburns fashionably long, treads the red carpet to centre ice at the head of the official party. Fresh from kicking off the election campaign, the PM wears an ascot tucked into his striped shirt, and a red rose in the lapel of his sporty summer jacket—throwbacks to the free-spirit image that got him elected four years earlier. Trudeau is almost as resplendent as John Ferguson: the retired Canadiens' battler resembles a barroom bouncer in his white summer suit with bell-bottom pants and receives a louder cheer than either boss Sinden or the prime minister.

Trudeau presides over an exchange of pennants and pins among the captains, three to a side—Ragulin, Victor Kuzkin and Vladimir Vikulov; Jean Ratelle, Phil Esposito and Frank Mahovlich—then drops the puck for the ceremonial faceoff. Esposito, who couldn't get to sleep that afternoon for his customary nap, "wins" the faceoff with a fired-up effort. He awards the puck to Trudeau. With a pleased toothy smile, the PM bears the souvenir back to his box seat where his young wife, Margaret, awaits him, radiating a fatal glamour in her dark glasses. Near the Trudeaus are seated former Prime Minister Lester Pearson, Conservative leader Robert Stanfield, CTV mogul John Bassett, NHL president Clarence Campbell, and, a few rows up, a young lawyer and aspiring Tory named Brian Mulroney.

During the playing of the national anthems on the Forum's organ, the hammer-and-sickle and maple-leaf flags flutter in an artificial breeze. A stirring of gleeful impatience, of incipient mass celebration, emanates from the crowd.

At last the formalities are over, and the game begins. Cournoyer is so pumped he streaks offside before the puck drops. Esposito loses the *real* faceoff to Vladimir Petrov. But moments later, the NHL scoring champ barrels into the Soviet zone with linemates

Cournoyer and Frank Mahovlich after a breakout pass by Bergman. They swarm the net: Mahovlich, standing untouched by the left corner, flicks a quick backhander that Tretiak kicks out, and Esposito, parked in his customary spot right in front, swings his stick at the rebound and bats it out of the air and into the net. Not pretty, but easy: it's taken a mere thirty seconds.

As the Forum erupts with delight, millions of viewers at home shake their heads in pleasant wonderment. Such immediate confirmation of Team Canada's mastery! A small seed of compassion for the outmatched Soviets begins to sprout in some Canadian hearts.

The next six minutes of play are extremely instructive, however. Remembering Bobrov's warning, the Soviets do not panic or fall apart, nor drop back into a respectful defensive posture in fear of Team Canada's awesome might. Instead, they take over. Their forwards darting and weaving cross-ice as they form their attack, they play *their* game, carrying the play decisively to the Canadians. For the next several minutes, they own the puck.

Granted, Canada has to play a man short for two minutes after Henderson—of all people—takes the first penalty of the series at 1:03, needlessly kicking a Soviet attacker's legs out from under him. The Canadian defenders manage to kill the penalty. But the Soviets continue attacking in wave after wave, constantly in motion, hitting each other cleanly with short passes, long passes, drop passes, moving the puck with calm certainty about where their teammates will be on the ice. Startlingly, they exhibit all the signs of a well-moulded team in late-season form. They put veteran North American viewers in mind of nothing less than the old Montreal Canadiens and their style, once thought unique, of "firewagon hockey."

Yakushev and Mikhailov both get excellent scoring chances. Dryden foils them, deflecting Mikhailov's hard shot off his arm; he must be wondering where his defensemen are hiding. Just in time, he slides across the crease on his pads to rob Evgeny Zimin on the first of the Soviets' tic-tac-toe passing plays, where they work the puck close-in to the open man standing by the corner of the net.

Team Canada's puck handling, by contrast, is tentative and clumsy. Like nearsighted old-timers who haven't been on skates for a while, they have to look for each other before passing. Whereas the

Soviets' rushes are swift and purposeful and authoritative, the Canadians' are ponderous and vague. It's becoming obvious Team Canada won't be able to compensate by manhandling its opponents, either. The Soviets can clearly look after themselves physically; they knock big Vic Hadfield off the puck with nonchalant ease. In fact, the Rangers' line of Hadfield, Ratelle and Gilbert, considered Canada's most Sovietlike for its passing prowess, is being completely neutralized, dominated by the Maltsev-Kharlamov-Vikulov line.

Surprisingly, the next goal is Team Canada's, and it's a little gem of teamwork. Right off the faceoff in the Soviet end, Clarke deftly passes to Ellis on his right, Ellis slaps it immediately back to Henderson at the top of the faceoff circle, and Henderson one-times it low and hard past Tretiak's outstretched pad into the right-hand corner of the net. Talk about tic-tac-toe: the Soviets never even touch the puck. Now, for perhaps the last time until the late stages of the series, they begin to doubt themselves. Boris Mikhailov will say later that his thought after the second Canadian goal was simply, "It's over. We're beaten. We're dead."

Tretiak experiences similar fears—"Maybe this game shouldn't have happened"—compounded by a weird sense of disorientation. He's having trouble getting used to the boisterous, unceasing crowd noise, so different from the orderly, well-behaved crowds at home. And the blasted organ: "I remember the organ man. He started playing funeral music. . . . For the first five minutes it was as if I was in darkness, I couldn't get out in the light." On the other hand, he'll recall, "when the two goals were scored, we decided we had nothing to lose and we became a bit more relaxed."

In fact, an objective observer would have to say all the momentum has been with the Soviets, even if they don't realize it themselves. On Team Canada's bench, they realize this better than anybody. A sickening sense of dread is creeping over some of the players. Henderson can't get over how he's gasping for air while his Soviet check, who's kept up with him stride for stride, is scarcely breathing. He remembers telling Clarke and Ellis after their very first shift, "This is going to be a long, long series." Henderson can't shake the feeling that he and his teammates have somehow "been sucked in."

After Henderson's goal, the fans are treated to several minutes of exciting all-out attack hockey seldom seen on this continent before the Stanley Cup playoffs. In end-to-end action, the teams seem equally matched. Frank Mahovlich sets up the onrushing Esposito beautifully in front of the net, and although Esposito faults his own rusty timing for not scoring, it's Tretiak (coming into the light now) who robs him with a fine save to prevent Team Canada from going up 3-0.

Instead, the margin is suddenly cut to 2-1. The Soviets' first goal comes quickly, unexpectedly, like a magician's sleight of hand plucking a gold coin out of the air. But in fact it results from their hard-working offensive pressure, with their defensemen Yuri Liapkin and Evgeny Paladiev shooting accurately from the point, and their forwards—in this case, the Yakushev-Vladimir Shadrin-Zimin line—recovering the rebounds, controlling the puck and keeping it in motion. They pass it back and forth like basketball players, so that the mesmerized Canadians—Ratelle, Hadfield and Gilbert, Seiling and Lapointe—lose their bearings and chase pointlessly hither and yon. From the right point, Paladiev passes up to Yakushev alone in the corner, who centres it perfectly past Shadrin's screen to Zimin, alone by the left side of the net, who fires it up high. Dryden, left unprotected from the attackers on his doorstep, doesn't have a hope. A surprised Jacques Plante observes on French-language television that Team Canada looks *"complètement désorganisé"* on defense.

When Mikhailov goes off for tripping Mickey Redmond, the Canadians get it together on the power play. They generate several scoring chances; Frank Mahovlich blows one of them at point-blank range, but for the rest, Plante's young protégé gives the lie to his bad scouting report, absolutely robbing Henderson from close range.

No sooner do the Soviets kill the penalty than Ragulin too is called for tripping. This time, Sinden sends out an all-Rangers power play: Ratelle, Hadfield and Gilbert, with Park and Seiling on defense. Far from impressed, the Soviets erupt brilliantly to tie the game with a short-handed goal.

Petrov wins the faceoff in his own end and passes up to

Mikhailov, busting out past Park. Lunging at Mikhailov, Park falls and almost breaks up the attack with a sweep of his stick, but unhappily the puck bounces over to Petrov, who sends it right back to Mikhailov with a lead pass at the Canadian blueline. Mikhailov powers past Seiling and fires a high hard wrist shot from fifteen feet—who the hell said these guys can't shoot?—and although Dryden gets his glove hand on the puck, he can't hold it. Petrov, trailing on the play, beats Dryden's good sliding second effort by backhanding the rebound into the corner.

Maybe the GAG Line, which was also on the ice for the first Soviet goal, should be renamed the Choke Line. Sinden pulls them from the power play in favour of the Esposito-Mahovlich-Cournoyer line, who come close several times but can't solve Tretiak. As the siren wails to end the first period with the score 2-2, an eerie mist is rising off the ice into the Forum's sultry, suffocating atmosphere. The faces on the Canadian bench look haggard, drawn and drenched—as if they've just played three tough periods, not one.

•

In the dressing room, Bruins' tough guy Wayne Cashman, one of the Team Canada players not dressed tonight, pays a visit to his regular linemate Esposito. "We got serious problems," Phil tells Cashman. "These guys can really motor. Whoever scouted them should be shot. . . . No fooling around, Cash, this is like the Stanley Cup finals."

Cashman nods thoughtfully. "Let's spear a few of them," he suggests. "We'll see how tough they are. Let's get them in the corners."

Sinden rallies his sluggish troops with different advice. "We're in a hockey game," he tells them, sweating as much as anyone, his tie askew. "You didn't expect anything else, did you?" Greeted by numb silence, he tries to settle them down by reminding them of the basics, as he would a team of bantams: sticking to their positions, not running around after the puck.

The thing that strikes Sinden so far, apart from the Soviets' great technical ability, is their penchant for long passes out of their own zone to break a man up the middle. He warns his men to watch for that manoeuvre, and also relays a tip from Bobby Orr, who has rushed excitedly into the dressing room: the defensemen have to stop dropping in front of the puck to block shots. "The Russians don't even *shoot* from out there," Orr insists.

But these adjustments are of little avail against Valery Kharlamov. The second period is all his. The little left winger—five feet, six inches, 154 pounds, according to the Soviets' press kit—takes a pass from centre Alexander Maltsev and streaks out of his own zone up the right side. As he hits the Canadian blueline, he feints Don Awrey "out of his intimate apparel," as sportswriter Dick Beddoes will say. Making as if to split Awrey and Seiling with a dip of his left shoulder, Kharlamov swoops to the outside instead, blowing right around Awrey, then, protecting the puck smoothly with one hand on his stick, cuts inside and brings it back to his forehand. Awrey, now behind Kharlamov, hurls himself desperately at the puck. He nearly gets his stick-blade on it, but the Soviet star puts another fake on Dryden and flicks a shot straight between his pads.

It's a stunning display. Distinguished by speed, agility, guile and perfect timing, Kharlamov's manoeuvre is worthy of Gordie Howe. Esposito and Frank Mahovlich recognize this; watching side by side from the bench, they turn to each other in amazement and shrug. Sinden is also impressed, since he considers Awrey "one of the toughest men in the game to beat to the outside." Suddenly a stereotype has been turned inside out: the quaint notion that the Soviets are regimented robots, mere cogs in a well-oiled machine, without individual inspiration or creativity.

Driving the point home, Kharlamov scores a second superb goal less than eight minutes later. He collects a loose puck off the faceoff in his own end and explodes out of the zone. His flight path takes him on a diagonal trajectory from right to left across centre. At the Canadian blueline, Seiling and Awrey are ready for him, but this time Kharlamov doesn't even bother faking them out. Veering to the left of Seiling, going away from the net instead of towards it, he fires a precision slapshot—usually a contradiction in terms—from the top of the faceoff circle. The puck catches the far corner of the net almost before Dryden can move on it, his long arms and legs flailing like broken masts in a gale.

As with Kharlamov's previous goal, this one is a completely solo effort, yet utterly different in execution from the earlier one—even scored from the opposite side of the ice. Both plays are accomplished with the dead-calm assurance of a player whose finely tuned instincts are matched with exquisite physical skills. Plante compares the second goal to a move by his old teammate Bernie Geoffrion.

The other second-period standout is that kid with the lousy glove hand. Frank Mahovlich, brother Peter and Rod Gilbert successively test Tretiak at close range: he faces each of them down with steady stand-up goaltending, catching the puck with his glove or trapping it in his pads, not allowing a rebound. The Canadians' frustration begins to show: Clarke, irritated by Maltsev's grabbing his stick, upends the Soviet player, recovers his stick and cracks Maltsev hard across the top of the helmet. He gets two minutes for slashing.

By the end of the period, the Soviets are well in control. Dryden has kept Canada within reach with some good saves, but the Soviets have now scored four unanswered goals. The Canadian heavy artillery has failed to blast even one past Tretiak in over thirty-three minutes.

Nobody expected this—almost nobody. In homes and bars, people are asking each other if it's just some kind of fluke. And if it isn't? What then?

•

In the dressing room, Sinden looks at his exhausted defensemen and sees it was a mistake to go with only five. There's nothing he can do about it now, but since Awrey is having a bad night, Sinden replaces him with Lapointe. He also decides to play the Ratelle line more sparingly, since it has been conspicuously ineffective. He needs an inspired comeback from his men, but in that heat, their reserves are close to spent.

Still, they start the third period drawing on all they have left. As the mist billows more thickly off the ice, both teams have good scoring opportunities—particularly Esposito and Kharlamov, who continues to be dangerous—but the goaltenders prevail. Cournoyer sets up Frank Mahovlich right in the crease, but tonight Mahovlich lacks his touch around the net; Tretiak stymies him, then makes a dramatic glove save on a blast from the point by Seiling.

The Clarke line gets the next shift. Henderson controls the puck along the right boards in the Soviet zone. He backhands a pass to Ellis in the high slot, Ellis one-times it on the net, keeping the puck flat on the ice, and Clarke, standing unmolested by the right corner, deflects it behind Tretiak. Another piece of fine timing, the line's second goal of the game is Team Canada's first in forty-two minutes. But now they're back in it.

Under international rules, the last period is broken into two halves with a change of ends, a legacy from the days when European hockey was played on variable outdoor ice. It's 4-3 at the break, and the crowd gets excited again, clapping rhythmically, energized: Canada finally seems to have seized the momentum, with a full ten minutes to turn things around.

Briefly the Canadians dominate, pressing for a goal. Cournoyer moves in and rings a wicked low shot off the post. But on a Soviet rush to centre ice, Yuri Blinov passes to Mikhailov on the left wing going over the Canadian blueline. Unchallenged by Seiling and Lapointe, Mikhailov drifts laterally to his right into good scoring range, waiting patiently until he sees a wide enough gap between the two defenders, then releases a quick backhand shot going away. He catches Dryden moving with the flow; the puck lodges in the left corner.

A heady play, and the point of no return for Team Canada: the Soviets have restored their two-goal lead with a little over six minutes left. The Forum falls deathly quiet.

Moments later, the pall of gloom deepens. Zimin zooms in on a loose puck in the high slot above Dryden. Cannily, he fakes a shot to throw Bergman out of position, then fans on a shot as Park pokes the puck off his stick. Unwittingly, however, Park has assisted Zimin; Dryden is now down and out of position, having committed himself on the shot he thought was coming, so when Zimin tenaciously recovers the puck off his skate blade, he's able to beat Dryden cleanly. Another gutsy solo effort, unassisted, making the score 6-3.

There's an intelligence at work producing these Soviet goals. Intelligence is also evident in their final scoring play, although the pathetic state of their opponents makes them look even smarter.

With an agile bit of stickhandling, Vladimir Shadrin manoeuvres his way between Seiling and Lapointe to feed Yakushev, who gets in behind the Canadian defensemen. All alone in front of the net, Yakushev takes his sweet time, floating teasingly past Dryden with the puck on his forehand, waiting until the goaltender has flopped prematurely to the ice before sweeping the puck to his backhand and throwing it high over Dryden's prostrate form into the far upper corner. Seiling futilely waves an arm at the shot, like somebody waving good-bye to his sweetheart.

Meanwhile Lapointe, having helped allow the goal, gets "even" with Shadrin by driving an elbow into his face. On CBC Television, colour man Brian Conacher comments, "Foster, the tolerance level of a Soviet hockey player has to be higher than anybody."

In the final minute and a half, the visitors continue the attack, looking to run the score up, and Team Canada continues responding stupidly to the frustration of defeat. After being called for cross-checking in front of his net, Lapointe swings his stick at Boris Mikhailov in the corner, and Esposito takes a run at Vladimir Petrov after the whistle. The Forum crowd, always the most discerning and demanding in the NHL, boos the bush-league behaviour. They even mock Dryden, their hometown favourite, by cheering when he blocks a long easy shot—an unfair jibe, given that he's had inadequate protection all night and little chance on most of the goals.

The Soviets, Sinden notices, finally show some feeling—a gloating defiance at the childish behaviour of "the professionals": "At the end, they were actually laughing at us. . . . Phil Esposito punched one of them in the face with his glove. The Russian just grinned at Phil as much as to say, 'Look at the scoreboard, you jerk.'"

The Russian in question is Petrov, who remembers: "That night in Montreal was so *beautiful* for us. It showed everyone we were able to compete with the Canadians."

The sense of vindication is even sweeter for the Soviets, according to Alexander Yakushev, because of the contempt they felt coming from the Canadians before the game. Yakushev recalls: "They judged us very superficially, without much thought. . . . We could see from their gestures, the way they acted and the remarks they made during our practice, that they didn't consider us worthy opponents. We could hear their laughter. We could all *feel* it—that arrogance."

When the siren wails to end the game 7-3, the Canadians compound these impressions. They fail to stay on the ice and line up for the ritual handshake, the tradition in international matches. Sinden has already headed for the dressing room five seconds before the siren; his players clomp glumly after him. As the Soviets cluster expectantly, only Dryden and Berenson—who have both played internationally—and Peter Mahovlich remain on the ice. Finally, even they give up on the possibility that their teammates will return. Before he steps through the gate, Dryden communicates with his adversaries with a nod of his head and a wave of his stick in acknowledgement of their fine play. It's a touchingly human moment.

Alone on the ice, the Soviet players look up in surprise as they hear loud applause: the aficionados in the crowd refuse to let patriotism interfere with their appreciation of great hockey. The Soviets return the salute by raising their sticks in the air, then file off in happy bemusement.

Meanwhile, someone has reminded Alan Eagleson of the handshake protocol. He races to the Canadian dressing room and yells at Sinden to get his players back out on the ice, but they're already stripping off their gear. When they reluctantly pull their sweaters on and return, the Soviets have vanished. Eagleson makes an apology over the public address system, explaining that Team Canada was unaware of the ceremony. Eventually, Hockey Canada officials will contradict him.

"No one had ever told me or the players that we were supposed to meet with the Russians on the ice after the game," Sinden insists later. If true, it's the least of what they weren't told.

But Canadians' disillusionment with our NHL heroes is only beginning. Being Canadians, and this being hockey, we take the whole thing very personally.

A LITTLE LEARNING IS A USEFUL THING

"The public was totally devastated. People were in a state of shock.
Deep down inside they were scared to death, and so was I."
— JOHNNY ESAW, CTV broadcaster

●

Johnny Esaw's recollection of the aftermath of Game 1 may seem, in the cold light of today, exaggerated, alarmist, excessively emotional—more suited to a mass murder than a hockey game. That's why it reflects so perfectly how Canadians felt the morning after. We did not react to "our" defeat in a measured, temperate, reasonable spirit, consistent with the national stereotype. We freaked. We wept. We raged. We despaired. We agonized. Ultimately, we mourned. Harry Sinden himself said it best: "A little piece of all of us died today."

Like any mourning process, it began with disbelief. Our difficulty in coming to grips with what had happened was first expressed in the voice that had signified hockey for us as long as we could remember. When Game 1 ended, Foster Hewitt told us the score over and over, as if even he couldn't quite believe what he had just witnessed and reported, play by play: "And the game is *over!* And the USSR have defeated Canada in the first game of an eight-game series by a score of *7 to 3!* The Soviets 7, Canada 3. The final score, the Soviets 7 and Canada 3. . . . This is Game 1 from Montreal!"

If Foster said so, it had to be. And yet somehow, coming from him, keeper of the faith on countless *Hockey Nights in Canada* on countless dark and snowy Saturday evenings, first on radio, later television, the truth was even harder to accept. In the end, what we accepted no longer were the assurances that every hockey "expert" west of the Black Sea had been feeding us for years about the supremacy of brand-name NHL hockey. Our faith was shattered. Even the players' faith in themselves was seriously shaken. Ken Dryden, as usual a step ahead of his colleagues in frankness as well as imagination, noted: "I too have lost the feeling that the Canadian professional hockey player, by definition, is superior to all other hockey players in the world."

And so the next stage of our mourning was anger. Stripped of our most cherished and comforting certainty about ourselves, we felt raw, exposed, vulnerable. Even worse was the realization that we'd blindly colluded in our own deception.

The media quickly voiced the sour public mood. In Montreal, sports columnist Ted Blackman of the *Gazette* wrote of our "arrogance" and "humiliation." *Dimanche-Matin* headlined, "Le Canada humilié 7-3." The *Sunday Express* simply ran tall funereal capitals: "WE LOST."

In Toronto, the *Globe and Mail* called it "a shocking, incredible result" on page one, and inside, the late Dick Beddoes asked: "Has the National Hockey League been perpetrating a fraud all these years?" The *Star* editorialized in "Hockey Humiliation" that "our team represented us too accurately," observing: "In their world hockey debut, our pampered professional darlings played as if they had scarcely been introduced to one another. . . . Is it too much to expect that $50,000- to $100,000-a-year hockey players should be in shape in September, like the Russians?" The McGuinness "If they can play hockey, we can make vodka" ad still ran in the papers, but with the "If" crossed out.

Of course, the Jeremiahs of the media were the same ones who, until very recently, had been predicting a crushing Team Canada victory. At least Beddoes had the grace to eat his words—literally. Having vowed three days before the series that if the Soviets won a single game he'd "eat this column shredded at high noon in a bowl of borscht on the front steps of the Russian embassy," he did just that, more or less—in front of the Soviet consulate in Toronto, with a *Pravda* correspondent, several Soviet hockey players and a *Globe* photographer as witnesses.

The other bit of comic relief came in the ample form of Harold Ballard, who declared he'd pay $1 million for Valery Kharlamov if the Soviet star could be released from the motherland—a promise Ballard knew he'd never have to keep. "He's the best young forward in the world," declaimed the Emperor of Maple Leaf Gardens.

The only journalist who resembled an expert any more was the *Montreal Star*'s John Robertson. His disillusioned column on the day of the game had turned out to be remarkably prophetic. Robertson had not only warned that Team Canada was too poorly prepared and out of condition to win—a situation he termed "unforgivable"—but pilloried the NHL for its indifference to Canada's hockey pride and to the fans themselves: "This, the most important hockey event of our time, has been tacked onto the front of the NHL season as something only tolerated by the owners, and endorsed by the players as a means of enriching their pension plan. But from the moment the puck is dropped it will dwarf in stature the Stanley Cup, and any other hockey championship you can name. What is the NHL but a house league combining 13 U.S. branch offices and three Canadian branch offices, which succeeded by default as the only game in town until someone else set up shop across the street?"

By "someone else," Robertson meant the new and as yet untested World Hockey Association. "But," he argued, "the long-suffering hockey fan suddenly has something real, something meaningful to get excited about—international hockey, where he can root for a country instead of a corporation of grasping little men."

The major-domo of international hockey, J. F. (Bunny) Ahearne himself, was tickled pink by the result of Game 1. Described by Jim Kernaghan, then of the *Toronto Star*, as "the little Irishman Canadians love to hate," Ahearne had been president of the International Ice Hockey Federation practically forever. On not one but two never-forgiven occasions, Ahearne's backroom finagling had been responsible for doing Canada out of Olympic hockey medals: a gold at the 1936 Winter Games at Garmisch-Partenkirchen, Germany, and a bronze in 1964 at Innsbruck, Austria.

Informed by Kernaghan that the Soviets had won the first game of the series, Ahearne responded in character: "Good God, I'm delighted."

"Ho, ho, ho," Ahearne chortled, "I didn't visualize anything like this. Out of eight games, the Russians will more than hold their own. I always said the Russians were better skaters, shooters and passers, but all I've ever heard from Canada is, 'Wait until they meet our professionals.'"

The Soviet state news agency Tass gloated less than Ahearne but pontificated more. Tass said pointedly that Team Canada had not been "fastidious" about the tactics it employed on the ice, especially in the last period. "The myth of the invincibility of the best Canadian professionals is no more," Tass pronounced with high moral seriousness. The galling thing about it was, they were absolutely right.

●

As the wave of hurt and shame rolled across the land, it unleashed a growing public backlash against unsuspecting Team Canada. Those unfortunate few would soon discover how fragile and hockey-centric is the national ego. Suddenly the entire burden of it rode on their slumping shoulders.

The war now began in earnest. It would be a singular test of our national character: unreasoning primal emotions had been activated. The country had been riding an airy crest of feel-good self-regard and self-congratulation for five years, ever since Expo 67 and Centennial fever and Trudeaumania; now we had to contend with possible defeat in the international spotlight, possible inferiority, and already a strong dose of humiliation on our chosen field of battle. Game 1 had been lost, after all, in our own first temple of hockey.

Any war triggers a primitive human archetype, genetically imprinted from time immemorial: Us vs. Them. The emotional equations are elemental—when threatened, when attacked, you go for the throat or you run. Fight or flight. How would we respond? With what measure of courage or cowardice, cruelty or dignity?

The first signs from Team Canada itself were encouraging. The man charged with the team's success and authorized to speak for it was gracious in defeat, calm enough to realize the series was far from over. In spite of the unfortunate faux pas of the post-game handshake incident, which had reportedly upset even the prime minister himself, a man with his own notorious reputation for rudeness, Harry Sinden was generous to his opponents and realistic in assessing his team's revised prospects. Looking drawn and reserved at the post-game news conference, and feeling worse inside than he'd ever felt about losing a hockey game, Sinden said, "The explanation is simple. They outplayed us in almost every aspect of the game, from goaltending to shooting to skating to passing. We got beat by one fine hockey team. We knew the Russians were good, but we had no idea they were that good. I was stunned how well they played at times. You play just about as well as the other team permits you, and they didn't allow us to play very well."

Sinden's praise for the Soviet performance was even higher in the book he wrote after the series: "They took apart the best in the world like no one ever had before."

Looking ahead at the news conference, the coach bravely insisted his team would still win the series. But he qualified his statement immediately: "Unless we play absolutely flawless hockey, we'll be life-and-death to win against this team." They would not, of course, play flawless hockey.

Phil Esposito's prediction, meanwhile, was more modest but blunter: "We'll get better," Espo promised the press ruefully. "We can't get any worse."

•

Ken Dryden has observed that you learn only when you lose. Game 1 was undoubtedly a learning experience, but did it have to be such a traumatic one? Rather than being stunned by the Soviet team's excellence, why wasn't the nation better prepared for the test of a hockey lifetime? Why were Canadians, and more particularly Team Canada, so pitifully ignorant of the might of Soviet hockey?

There was, after all, a valuable repository of knowledge about the Soviets right here at home. It would have been a simple matter for Team Canada to consult the collective memory of the former Canadian national team, the band of college amateurs recruited by Father David Bauer. Most of those players were still around, some of them in the NHL, and Father Bauer was on the Hockey Canada board. But the men running Team Canada had turned their backs on Hockey Canada, illustrating how implicitly NHLers believed they had nothing to learn from anyone outside the NHL.

Equally, this attitude illustrates the value system operating in our society: value is measured by money. Professional hockey is profitable and therefore esteemed, whereas amateur hockey is nice but unprofitable—and therefore second-rate. That condescension had been the perpetual fate of the players who'd formed Canada's national team during its competitive years, 1964 to 1969. The Nats were termed "the world's best third-place club" after winning the bronze medal at the 1966 World's championships at Ljubljana in what was then Yugoslavia.

Trouble was, Canadians didn't realize how good you had to be to finish third; we just expected our boys to bring home gold because they were Canadians. It was all or nothing, so theirs was a thankless task, even when they played their best. As the Nats' coach Jackie McLeod once put it, "What makes me so downhearted is that people back home don't care. All they know is that we lost, and they don't care how."

On top of that, NHL clubs resented Father Bauer and his team for tempting away talented young players. Instead of making the usual jump directly from junior hockey to pro ranks, which precluded a college education, some promising juniors were attracted by the package Bauer offered: the chance to attend university—first the University of British Columbia, later the University of Manitoba—while playing hockey at a high level and representing your country. One of these bright recruits was an agile nineteen-year-old left winger from Weyburn, Saskatchewan, named Morris Mott.

Today Mott teaches Canadian history at Brandon University in Manitoba and gives a course on the history of sport. After joining the national team in 1965 out of the Saskatchewan Junior League, he played in three World's championships and one Olympics, remaining with the team until it was disbanded in 1970. Eventually, like many of his teammates (Wayne Stephenson, Marshall Johnston and Fran Huck, to name three), Mott played in the NHL—in his case, with the California Seals. Then he got his Ph.D.

Over lunch at the Royal Oak Inn in Brandon, against a backdrop of children's squeals and splashes from the swimming pool, Mott recalls how much he enjoyed his five years with the Nats. He also acknowledges readily that "the concept was more successful than the team." Mott believes that if the team had taken gold even once, the public's perception of them would have been very different. They always lacked scoring punch, yet weren't so inferior to the Soviets that they couldn't stay in the game with them: "We were always competitive with the Russians, although we didn't beat them very often. And I always felt they played against us as well as they could. We had a good skating team, a good checking team, but we didn't have any real bombers, guys who could really zing that puck in there, an Yvan Cournoyer or a Bobby Hull."

Having acquired a healthy respect for the Soviets, Mott knew there would be no eight-game sweep for Team Canada in '72. The Nats had played exhibition games against NHL teams and were in a good position to compare and contrast the two adversaries. Mott thought the Soviets would win at least a couple of games, maybe more, but expected them to play better in the Moscow half of the series. And, like practically everyone else, he didn't expect Tretiak to deliver such an outstanding performance.

Mott chuckles at the near-universal assumption that Team Canada would clobber the Soviets even without Hull and Orr. "The NHL always felt they knew it all, but on the national team we saw it the other way around. We tended to think the Russians were doing a lot of things right and the NHL a lot of things wrong."

The first thing he'd have told Team Canada about was the Soviets' conditioning: "Anybody who'd played against the Russians knew, before the NHL caught onto it, that they were in a different kind of physical condition from North American players. You always felt more tired after playing the Russians than you did playing *anyone* else."

Along with their conditioning went exceptional physical strength, pound for pound, which emerged in their skating, stick-handling and puck control. Mott and his teammates were always impressed by how strong and stable the Soviets were on the puck. When they'd point this out to Canadians, they'd be reminded that Europeans didn't know how to bodycheck; a little NHL muscle would soon put them on their behinds. But in Game 1, it became obvious that a player like Kharlamov, as small he might be, was very hard to knock over. When Soviet and Canadian players collided, it was more often the Canadian who fell down.

"They never gave up on the puck," Mott remembers. "You'd think you had it frozen on the boards, but they were always moving their feet and they'd dig it out somehow. They always managed to keep their feet underneath them. I guess it was their soccer training. No other team I played against, whether Swedes or Czechs or NHL pros, was as well balanced."

The Soviets showed the same strengths against Team Canada as they'd shown in international competition—forechecking, for instance. Mott recalls a game in the 1969 World's championships, the first tournament that Petrov, Kharlamov and Mikhailov played together, in which the line's forechecking penned veteran Canadian defenseman Terry O'Malley in his own end for the better part of a shift: "The puck never left O'Malley's corner. He'd try to carry it out and a Soviet would knock it off his stick into the corner, so he'd go back again for it—meanwhile, the rest of us were circling around waiting to get a pass, and it seemed like Terry was the only one working the whole shift. Finally we came off the ice, and Terry's huffing and puffing and says, 'Jesus Christ, don't those guys know you're only supposed to send two guys in to forecheck?' "

For a stretch in Game 3 of the '72 series, which Mott attended in Winnipeg, something similar happened: "When the Russians' Kid Line came out for the first time, they were forechecking and backchecking and going so fast, any Canadian who had the puck didn't have time to do anything constructive with it."

There were other things Team Canada could have benefited from hearing about, such as the Soviets' creative puck handling— "Some of the better Soviet players were doing some amazing things with the puck at that time"—or how the game changes when you play on the bigger ice surface in Europe. Your checking has to be much more disciplined in your own end, Mott explains. If you get drawn down off your point and the puck goes back to the point man, he can walk in twenty feet before anybody challenges him.

Team Canada did, in fact, include three players who had briefly been members of the national team—Rod Seiling, Toronto Maple Leaf defenseman Brian Glennie (who didn't see game action in the '72 series) and Ken Dryden. But even though Dryden told his teammates a thing or two about the Soviets, Mott doubts they even listened: "You have to get into the mentality of the pro hockey player at that time. Some of those guys would have the attitude, 'If Dryden says it, it's probably not true.' Dryden was different from them: they saw him as the egghead."

They also might have heard that the national team on which Dryden had played won only four out of its ten games in the 1969 World's championships, or that the Soviets scored nine goals against him in an exhibition game later that year in Vancouver. That would have made Dryden even less credible to his teammates—and yet it should have taught them greater respect for their opponents' abilities.

•

When you visit Herb Pinder Jr. at his penthouse office in Saskatoon, the sign on the door reads "The Goal Group." The office, with its spectacular view of the wide South Saskatchewan River and the campus of the University of Saskatchewan, which Pinder attended while playing junior hockey in the sixties, houses his player agency and other business interests. His clients have included Ryan Walter, Andy Moog, Joe Nieuwendyk, Mike Richter and Trevor Kidd.

On entering, you sit and wait. Pinder, a casually dressed man with curly hair, mobile features, a sharp, driving voice and an MBA from Harvard, is busy on the phone with one of his draft-age clients, outlining a contract offer from an NHL club. It's early July, one day before the NHL draft in Edmonton.

"They're offering four years firm," Pinder tells his client, leaning back in a designer swivel chair. He speaks into a tiny microphone attached to a headset, leaving his hands free to scribble notes and gesticulate as he runs down the annual salary levels his client will earn if he makes the team: $300,000, $350,000, $375,000, $400,000. "There's a signing bonus of three-fifty and minor-league totals of four hundred over four years. So the most attractive part of the offer is the guarantee you'll reach seven-fifty on a worst-case scenario."

On the office wall, in a simple wooden frame, an Olympic bronze medal hangs suspended from its multicoloured ribbon. Pinder won the medal in 1968 in Grenoble, France, playing with Canada's national team for nothing.

Getting off the phone, he says, "I'll tell you a funny story about that medal. You're about my age, so you'll remember the climate was, 'Those Europeans are bums.' There was a Canadian smugness about hockey, fostered by the NHL. But it was widely held: 'Hockey is our game, and we're so clearly superior at it.'

"But those of us on the national team *knew* the Europeans were good. We'd played against NHL teams and we'd played against the Europeans—and they could skate and shoot and they were strong and they could move the puck better than most Canadians. We went to Grenoble in '68 and played all the best European national teams and we earned the bronze. But we didn't win the gold, so in the eyes of Canadians, we'd let the country down. The perception was, 'Aw, the bums've let us down again, let's get some *real* players in there.'

"So I put my bronze medal in a drawer. I didn't buy the attitude that we were bums. I knew I wasn't an NHL-calibre player at that time, but I also knew the Europeans were a lot better than our public realized.

"Flash forward sixteen years to the 1984 Olympics in Sarajevo. James Patrick is on the Canadian team, and I'm representing him as he gets ready to make the jump to the New York Rangers. They get to the medal round. The bronze medal game is against Sweden, and Canada loses 2-0. James comes back to Canada and stays at my place while we do his contract. He says, 'I'd give anything to have won an Olympic medal, even a bronze.' And I say, 'Well, do you want to see one?' and pull mine out of the drawer.

"James can't believe it. 'What's *that* doing *there*?' he says. 'You should be proud of it. Put it up on the wall!'

"So that helped to change my attitude. But 1972 helped too."

Pinder almost fell out with his best friend over the series. When he described for his buddy some of the Soviets' strengths before the series began, his hard-won knowledge was taken for a lack of patriotism. "So the night of Game 1, boom, Team Canada scores twice. My buddy gets on the phone: 'Hey, Herb! How do you like this?' Now, I'm not cheering against Canada, but it's been four years since we took that bronze, and it's been no fun being maligned for it. So when the period ends and it's 2-2, I phone my buddy back. And he won't even come on the line!"

The next person Pinder phoned was Morris Mott in Winnipeg. Only a former national teammate could really understand what he was feeling. After the game that night, "All the guys who'd been on our team, our phone lines were just buzzing. We were ecstatic. That game reestablished our self-respect and gave some measure to our accomplishment as a team."

But inevitably, Pinder, Mott and their teammates became swept up in the great national anxiety to see Canada, suddenly and astonishingly the underdog, take the series. "There was nobody cheering louder for Team Canada than us. We'd been there, so we respected the enormity of their accomplishment."

In the meantime, Team Canada still had a lot of learning to do. To their credit, they would realize that and go to school for a while. "There was a whole different [international] hockey culture to understand: the style of play, the style of refereeing. There's a whole knowledge base that we really understand well now—our junior teams are unbelievably well-prepared, and at every level we know how to compete intelligently in international play. But in '72, we were ignorant—arrogant, smug and blind."

All the more reason why the shock of losing Game 1, as Herb Pinder says today, was the best thing that could have happened to us.

SIX

GAME 2:
BROTHER NIGHT

"The game isn't fun unless you win."
— HARRY SINDEN, *Hockey Showdown*

●

The hockey authorities of the USSR keep calling the series games "friendly matches." They insist they've brought their team to Canada to learn, not to win. After dominating international hockey for a decade, they face no more challenges in Europe; their game is in danger of stagnating, even declining. So the exhibition games of '72 give them an opportunity to acquire a new understanding of the sport, to develop new skills and new approaches, by playing against and emulating the best in the world. But it's become painfully obvious the learning process is going the other way now. And the remaining friendly matches aren't going to get any friendlier.

As Harry Sinden acknowledges, it's the Canadians who will have to change, not the Soviets.

During Game 1, that reality was written in the knitted brows of spectator Bobby Orr: his puzzled, then frustrated, finally disgusted facial expressions. Sitting nearby, Pat Stapleton found himself feeling a twinge of fear. Stapleton saw teammates—some of the NHL's best, chosen ahead of him to start the series—struggling terribly: "It wasn't lack of desire or lack of trying—the cohesiveness of the team just wasn't there. That was the most unnerving thing." Now Stapleton will be thrown into the battle to see if he can do better.

Another player who will now get his chance is Tony Esposito, replacing Dryden in goal. On the Sunday between Games 1 and 2, the team is back in Toronto, and the Esposito brothers are sharing a room at the Sutton Place Hotel, not far from Maple Leaf Gardens. Phil Esposito remembers his younger brother trying to prepare by bombarding him with questions about being on the ice with the Soviets:

"Tony says, 'Are they really as quick as they look?' I say, 'Yeah, they're as quick as they look.' And I say, 'But the thing that surprised me is they're tough. You run into them, it's like running into a wall.' "

The brothers decide to phone their father, a building contractor in Sault Ste. Marie, before he comes down to Toronto to watch Game 2. "He only gave us this advice," Phil recalls later: " 'You S.O.B.s better dig down as deep as you can or you guys got a big problem.' We said, 'Dad, I realize that. Believe me, I realize that.' "

Phil's consolation is that whenever his dad comes to watch him play, his team wins. Avowedly superstitious, Phil takes this as a good omen. But his father's attitude is typical: suddenly Team Canada is finding friends and admirers are scarcer than teeth in a hockey player's mouth.

Further helpful comments come Team Canada's way from NHL President Clarence Campbell. In the media, Campbell criticizes Sinden for his choice of players in Game 1, particularly Dryden and Lapointe. Perpetuating the anti-Canadiens bias he showed with his playoff suspension of Maurice Richard back in 1955, Campbell implies the two players somehow didn't belong on the ice with the Soviets and alleges Sinden played them merely to appease the Montreal fans.

Sinden is furious. He has problems enough rebuilding his team's shattered morale in twenty-four hours without being second-guessed by the NHL president—especially after Campbell has barred him from recruiting WHA players.

Sinden is already worried the big loss has undermined his players' self-confidence. On the late-night flight from Montreal, he has taken pains to confront that danger. With the curtain drawn to separate the team from the rest of the passengers, he has told his exhausted, disconsolate men that none of them should blame himself for the loss: "All of us lost this game tonight," he declared.

"Every coach and every player had a hand in it, even the ones who weren't dressed. We accept that because we're a team. . . . When we win it will be as a team, and when we lose it's as a team." Before long, he'll give Campbell a piece of his mind, too.

So will Dryden, who's already feeling guilty about the loss—"empty . . . like I have done something wrong." He's depressed about being benched for Game 2, even though he understands the reasons perfectly: "I had failed, and now I was discarded. I am not used to the feeling. Here is the goaltender thought to be the best possible man for the first game, and now he is out in the cold. Very humbling. Very humbling indeed."

Dryden is far from alone. On Sunday before the team practice, Sinden and Ferguson sit down to analyze Game 1 and watch the film, then make eight personnel changes for Game 2—a 40 per cent different line-up.

At least there is advantage in having played one game against their opponents: now the Canadian coaches know far more about the Soviets' strengths and can strategize to play them differently. Canada has to slow the Soviets down, Sinden decides, not try to match their speed. Clearly a more rugged defense is a priority. And Canada needs to defend more vigilantly against the Soviets' swift transition game, their ability to break a man up the middle. We need to find ways to disrupt their quick game around the net. The defensemen also need to stay fresh enough to last the game: the coaches switch to three pairs and just three complete forward lines.

Sinden and Ferguson decide the Park-Bergman pairing is working well enough to play again. But Awrey and Seiling, beaten too frequently in Game 1, will sit this one out. Serge Savard didn't impress enough in camp to start the first game—an indication the coaches weren't really worried about appeasing Montrealers—but now Savard is inserted alongside Lapointe, his sometime partner with the Habs. The other pairing will be Chicago's Stapleton and Bill White, also well experienced as a unit. Both Savard and White are tall and have long arms; reach will make a difference in checking the shifty Soviet forwards, who often move too fast, or pass too elusively, to bodycheck.

Changes to the forward lines are dictated by a new strategy

Sinden and Ferguson adopt for Game 2. They conclude the text-book style of NHL defense just doesn't work against the Soviets' explosive attack. The Soviets would have scored even more goals in Game 1 if they'd shot more often instead of passing the puck in search of the perfect set-up. Their forwards were constantly outmanoeuvring the Canadians in our end of the rink; watching the game film, Sinden counts six occasions when the Soviets beat his men cleanly in one-on-one situations.

So he needs forwards who can backcheck. The Canadian wingers have to come back deep to help out their defensemen. The Soviets don't shoot well from the point anyway, Sinden reasons, so he'll have his centres stay high in the middle to cover the points, and have four defenders concentrate on preventing the Soviets from working the puck in deep.

Offensively, Sinden tells his forwards just to dump the puck into their opponents' end, NHL-style, and outfight the Soviets for it in the corners. He trusts his shooters to get sharper around the net as the series proceeds, but they'll need diggers and grinders to control the corners and get the puck out to them in the slot. Into the line-up go Wayne Cashman and the Minnesota North Stars' Jean-Paul Parise as new wingmates for Esposito; Cashman has set up many of Esposito's 66 goals during the preceding season in Boston.

Bill Goldsworthy of the North Stars, another hard-nosed fore-checker, will be an alternate forward, along with Peter Mahovlich. Sinden figures he'll need Goldsworthy to play right wing in case Cashman gets into a fight and is ejected, even though he and Ferguson have been working on Cashman for days, psyching him to control his violent tendencies. Stan Mikita, the Black Hawks' great play-making centre, now on the downward slope of his career, takes Esposito's place between Frank Mahovlich and Cournoyer.

The only line remaining intact from Game 1—and the only one that will remain so throughout the series—is Clarke-Henderson-Ellis. The reasons are clear to everyone: they can check as well as score, having netted two of Canada's three goals on Saturday night. The only problem is that Ron Ellis injured his neck in a fall against a Soviet player's leg, and the neck has stiffened up so painfully he can't look down to shoot. Although Ellis is afraid the disability may keep him out of the series, Sinden gives him a special defensive assignment: to act as Valery Kharlamov's shadow.

For equally clear reasons, the Ratelle-Hadfield-Gilbert line is gone, never to reappear as a unit for Team Canada. Against the Soviets, they couldn't check their hat or control the puck along the boards. When Vic Hadfield hears his line won't be dressing, he comments gracefully, "Sure I'm surprised, but this is not the time to gripe. This is the time to pull together." His forbearance and team spirit will soon wear thin.

•

If Game 1 was preceded by an enormous buildup of national attention, the excitement before Game 2 is just as intense—but with quite a different cause and quite a different texture. Now the predominant public mood is high anxiety, bordering on panic. It is suddenly conceivable Canada could lose the series. If the team goes down to defeat a second straight time at home, the outlook will be black indeed. Everyone is desperate to know if Game 1 was an aberration—or are the Soviets superior to the NHL after all?

Looking back years later, Alexander Yakushev has observed of the Canadians, "They completely underestimated us at the beginning. For them, the series was a novelty, not a serious competition. . . . For us, it was perfect. We were ready."

One game late, the Canadians are ready too. They underestimate their opponents, and overestimate themselves, no longer. Game day, September 4, is Labour Day. The players are tense but try to keep the positive focus that Sinden has given them. Arriving at the Gardens early, Yvan Cournoyer is observed standing motionless and staring at the ice for over half an hour as if in a trance, his hands resting on the boards, then ritually spitting, twice.

Frank Mahovlich puffs morosely on a cigar, his face ashen, nerves seething, fists clenching and unclenching: "I hate to lose. I can't take that sort of thing," he tells the *Montreal Star*'s Red Fisher. Mahovlich is incensed when he sees Progressive Conservative leader Robert Stanfield posing for a campaign photograph in a Team Canada sweater. "Damn it," he says, "we're not playing for the bloody politicians, we're playing the bloody Red Army!"

Indeed, as the crowd take their seats, all three national party leaders are there, although some more visibly than others. Pierre and Margaret Trudeau occupy a box directly behind the Soviet bench. Stanfield sits behind the Canadian bench with Ontario Tory Premier William Davis. And New Democratic Party leader David Lewis, supplied with tickets by the prime minister's office, is lodged with his son Michael high in the upper greens. Lewis comments that the view is fine but notes he's been "carefully shielded from any great exposure."

People are now wondering how the outcome of the series will affect the election campaign. A backroom party organizer muses on the front page of the *Toronto Star* about the mood of the voting public if Canada loses the series: "Will the Canadian inferiority complex increase and thus affect the electorate's thinking on such issues as Canadian-U.S. relations? Will voters, 90 per cent of them hockey fans, blame the government? They blame the government for everything else, so who knows?"

Just before the game, Pat Stapleton feels the tension not only in his stomach but throughout the 16,485 unnaturally silent people jamming the Gardens. The crowd tension is even greater than before the first game, Stapleton remembers: "Could we recover? The crowd was so quiet. It was tight as a banjo string in there."

From the beginning, it's clear this is a very different hockey game from the last one—and a very different Team Canada. No quick goals, no instant jubilation or equally instant letdown. Just poised positional play. Just solid stand-up defense. Just old-style, elbows-up, gum-baring, inelegant physical intimidation.

From the start, Sinden aggressively outstrategizes Bobrov, using his home-team prerogative to make the last line change before a faceoff and to match, in particular, the Ellis line against the Kharlamov line. Ellis, sore neck and all, goes up and down and around with the Soviet superstar and holds him to three shots all night. Meanwhile, Cashman and Parise charge into the corners and hack and flail away along the boards, two pit bulls unleashed from their kennels. The Soviet players are soon hesitating before setting up their passing plays, which previously clicked so automatically. They're not used to worrying about getting their heads knocked off. Now they're looking nervously over their shoulders in case they have to duck a flying stick or elbow.

But for nearly a period and a half, the hard-line approach doesn't generate any Canadian goals, either. So all the more important that Tony Esposito comes up big when he has to, giving his teammates some needed confidence with an early save on Evgeny Zimin from short range. Right away the Canadian goalie is steady on his feet, unfazed by the Soviets' fancy footwork. Their two power plays in the first period (on penalties to Park and Henderson) fail to produce a goal. Early in the second, with his team short-handed, Kharlamov pounces on a loose puck to create a solo breakaway, but Esposito robs him too. Although full of exciting offensive chances, the game is a stalemate, 0-0, until nearly the halfway point.

The Soviet players notice something else has changed besides the Canadians' hyperactively rough play. Boris Mikhailov, no softie himself, recollects a complete change in their attitude, which he attributes to a newfound respect for the Soviets' abilities: "In the second game, they were much more collected and concentrated. A hockey player can tell things from his opponents' appearance. I remember looking into their eyes in Toronto and seeing more fire and intensity."

That intensity finally explodes where it has to—in front of the Soviet net. In the eighth minute of the second period, Cashman's relentless digging pays off. Phil Esposito is dumped just to the right of the Soviet net by *his* shadow, Vladimir Petrov. With the referee's arm up to signal a penalty, brother Tony lumbers to the bench to make way for a sixth attacker, while Phil unhurriedly rises from his knees as if he has all day. Meanwhile Cashman is controlling the puck and, eyeing Phil heading for the goal mouth, flicks a pass to him through some Soviet skates. Suddenly animated, Esposito in one swift gesture pulls the puck across the top of the crease, right past Tretiak's hungry eyes and lunging stick, and fires it up high into the left corner—undeterred by defenseman Victor Kuzkin slamming his stick across his back.

First blood to Canada, again. First blood to Esposito, again.

Novelist Jack Ludwig in his book *Hockey Night in Moscow* will call it "a garbage goal"; it's nothing of the kind. True, it's a patented Cashman-to-Espo-in-the-slot number, but executed with its own panache and grace under pressure, before you can say "Rocket Richard"—another instinctual genius around the net who was accused of getting his share of "garbage goals."

The teams continue their sustained end-to-end action, working the fans into a frenzy, reminding them how comparatively uninspired and uninspiring the watered-down competition in the expansion NHL has become. Still the score remains 1-0. These are two closely matched teams. Things don't break open until 1:19 of the third period.

With Canada on a power play during Gennady Tsygankov's penalty, and Kharlamov unable to play his penalty-killing role after receiving a ten-minute misconduct for shoving a referee, Brad Park takes off from behind his own net. Streaking to centre, he has Cournoyer keeping pace ahead of him on his right. Just as Cournoyer hits the blueline, Park lays a perfect pass on his tape so that the Canadiens' right winger doesn't break stride as he bursts between Alexander Ragulin and the boards. Making Ragulin and his mate Vladimir Lutchenko resemble men standing on a platform as the train pulls out, Cournoyer blows around them, cuts inside and fires a hard fast one between Tretiak's pads. He has done to the Soviet defensemen what Kharlamov did to Awrey and Seiling in Game 1. Foster Hewitt exults, "This game and the last one are different as night and day!"

Four minutes later, the fans, remembering the Soviets' scoring bursts in Montreal, feel Canada's bubble bursting. Clarke is in the penalty box. In a startling give-and-go, Evgeny Zimin hands off to his defenseman Evgeny Paladiev at the side of his own net, then circles behind the goal and sprints straight up the middle. In an instant, Paladiev threads a long lead pass back to Zimin just inside the centre line and Zimin's gone, accelerating between Park and White and going in alone on Tony Esposito. Aiming for the upper left-hand corner, Zimin shoots wide—but defenseman Yuri Liapkin, trailing on the play, collects the puck off the boards and centres it to Alexander Yakushev in the slot, who makes no mistake, powering it past Esposito's stick side.

With Team Canada's lead cut in half, they receive another blow twenty-one seconds later—a penalty to Stapleton for hooking. Disaster! The Soviet power play presses relentlessly once again, methodically moving the puck around for a close-in scoring chance. Lapointe, White, Phil Esposito and Peter Mahovlich stay tight in their box, matching wits with the attackers. Lapointe almost clears it but not out. Then Esposito throws a blind backhander up the boards and over the blueline, and Peter Mahovlich strides up to take it, leaving all but one of the Soviets, Paladiev, behind.

The next moment is among the most thrilling in hockey. With gawky grace, Mahovlich drives ahead in a low crouch over the red line, his six-foot-five frame covering immense stretches of ice. Moving diagonally into the middle, bearing down hard on Paladiev just across the Soviet blueline, Peter draws his stick back for the slapshot that one would expect of him—but something tells him to hold his fire. The fake slapshot freezes Paladiev to the spot for a split-second. It's just long enough for Mahovlich to step nimbly to the right and around the defenseman, a blur of pumping knees and elbows, and bull in all alone on Tretiak. Recovering the puck off his own skate like a soccer-trained Soviet, Mahovlich moves left as if for a forehand shot, feints Tretiak to the ice, then pulls the puck to his backhand and drives it over the goaltender's skates as he slides into him and arrives victorious, a triumphant gladiator, above Tretiak's fallen body.

The goal never fails to amaze on repeated viewings. Tretiak himself says he remembers every detail, every movement to this day, and still can't figure out how Mahovlich managed to score: "Technically, I played it perfectly." Watching it on video years later, Mahovlich can only grin in helpless wonderment at his own spontaneous masterpiece: "Who *is* that guy?"

Whoever he is, he's put the game out of reach. With a little over thirteen minutes to play, there's only one more goal to be scored, and that by another Mahovlich. Big brother Frank, nine years older, has rushed onto the ice after the goal and with a giant joyous leap joined the mob of teammates congratulating Peter. Two minutes later, Frank gets his own moment. Stan Mikita, forechecking industriously, steals possession and carries the puck behind the Soviet goal. Emerging on the left side, Mikita sees Frank moving into the slot and passes to him across the top of the faceoff circle. As Cournoyer ties up Kuzkin right in front of Tretiak, partially screening him, Mahovlich beams the puck into the upper left-hand corner, making the score 4-1.

And that's how Game 2 ends—with the widest margin Team Canada will enjoy in the series.

•

Gracious in defeat two nights earlier, Harry Sinden is judicious in victory. "Now look," he tells the boisterous celebrants in his dressing room, "enjoy the victory, but don't gloat over it. We've got six games to play. Enjoy it tonight, savour it, but we've got a lotta games to play!"

As the coach leaves to attend the post-game news conference, Phil Esposito and Peter Mahovlich are standing side-by-side in terry-cloth robes, a Coke in one hand and a microphone in the other, waiting to be interviewed on national television. Phil and brother Tony have been selected game stars. Peter and brother Frank scored big goals. It's Brother Night in Canada, and all's well with the world once more.

In the Gardens press room, Sinden attributes his team's win to those old-fashioned tried-and-true virtues, close checking and positional play, the kind of unspectacular tactics that used to win Stanley Cups for Hap Day's Maple Leafs in the 1940s. (Later, in his book, Sinden will be more frankly—and justifiably—self-congratulatory: "I was proud of myself and John Ferguson. I think we had as much to do with winning this game as coaches can have. All the changes we made worked.")

Then he alludes briefly to another matter on his mind. "I don't want to get into recriminations," he says civilly, "but I hope you gentlemen understand that we found out a lot of things by losing Saturday." He doesn't mean just tactically. He means who your friends are and aren't, Mr. Campbell.

Sinden has the media spotlight to himself. Oddly enough, the Soviet coaches are no-shows—odder still after assistant Boris Kulagin chided Sinden on Saturday night for not staying in the news conference longer, commenting then: "It is an old Russian custom that the two opposing coaches get together with the press after a sporting event and exchange views of the game."

Now the old Russian custom is left in the lurch as the Soviet hockey authorities indulge in another old custom, thoroughly familiar to North Americans: blaming the referees for their defeat.

Head coach Bobrov complains that the two U.S. referees, Frank Larsen and Steve Dowling, allowed the Canadians to get away with bad behaviour, if not outright murder. He says that if Wayne Cashman had been playing in Europe, he'd have spent the entire game in the penalty box. To which Cashman replies in the press, with blunt and simple honesty: "I played like we do it on the Bruins." A clearer illustration of the difference between European and North American hockey does not exist.

All the violence wasn't committed by Team Canada, however. Cashman himself alleges, backed up by linemate Esposito, that the Soviets "bring their sticks around pretty good after they're hit. . . . They're also very skilled at hooking you around the stomach and on some occasions up higher."

A more neutral and objective observation comes from Murray Williamson, coach of the U.S. national team, which took the silver medal at the Olympics earlier in the year: "I've seen teams intimidate other teams before. But Canada laid on the lumber so viciously I think they even intimidated the referees. . . . Everyone knows you can't intimidate the Russians by running at them and using your body. But no one gave them a dose of their own medicine and used sticks in this manner before."

Even Dryden finds some of the Team Canada stickwork embarrassing: "A lot of high sticks were rubbed under the noses of the Russians to suggest what might happen later. There were also a few cheap shots. . . . If I had been one of the Russian players, I'd have thought: 'These Canadians must be awfully brutal to be going around and doing these things all the time.' "

Lest any of us regard the Soviets as gentle lambs led to the slaughter, it is well to note that the head of the USSR Hockey Federation, Andrei Starovoitov, actually charged the door of the American officials' dressing room after the game and kicked chairs over.

"The American referees," he screamed, "let the Canadian players perform like a bunch of barbarians!"

Cold War, indeed. Given what Team Canada will endure from the referees in Moscow, the Soviets' discomfiture merely seems—with hindsight—poetic justice.

SEVEN

IGOR IN WINNIPEG

"For Canadians, hockey is more than just entertainment."
— BRUCE KIDD AND JOHN MACFARLANE,
The Death of Hockey

●

The day after Team Canada won Game 2, the Montreal *Gazette*'s banner headline ran, "Hey! We're not so red-faced now!" In the *Toronto Sun*, the blackline was, "WE DID IT! 4-1." The visual treatment featured great symbolic shots of Peter Mahovlich bent like a giant pretzel over Tretiak's fallen body.

Suddenly we were okay again. Team Canada was okay again. The sense that they not only represented us, they *were* us, would only grow as the series wore on. Canadians identified so closely with the team that this was the hugest case of fan loyalty the country had ever known. The loyalty wasn't as total as in, say, Langenburg, Saskatchewan, or Foxwarren, Manitoba, where they erect highway signs honouring the NHL players the town has produced, but it was powerful and ubiquitous all the same.

One city where the loyalty was initially a bit doubtful was the site of Game 3. Although Winnipeggers were no less appreciative and knowledgeable hockey fans, and no less dedicated Canadians, than citizens elsewhere, they held a grudge of their very own against Team Canada. The grudge grew bigger with the NHL's mistreatment of their adopted favourite son, Bobby Hull, the most Golden of the newborn Winnipeg Jets of the World Hockey Association, who hadn't yet played a single league game in the city. But Winnipeggers' sense of grievance originated in even deeper matters: the NHL's inflexible refusal to accept a franchise there, on the grounds that the city and its then 10,000-seat Winnipeg Arena were too small; Hockey Canada's decision to pull out of international competition in 1970, and thereby pull both the national team and the World's championship tournament from Winnipeg; and deepest of all, the East's historic lording it over the West.

Local media personalities often articulate and reinforce local grievances, and *Winnipeg Tribune* sports editor Jack Matheson was typical. One of his columns during the series—elevated onto page one—was headlined: "THE BIG, FAT NHL HAS LOST ITS PATENT ON THE GAME OF HOCKEY." Grooming his readers for a switch of loyalties to the WHA, Matheson wrote: "We have sundry things to be proud about in this country, and the NHL isn't one of them."

It's startling to realize how much anti-NHL feeling was floating around the country by 1972. Much of it resulted from the league's turning its back on Canada (with the exception of Vancouver) in its eagerness to expand into the rich urban markets of the U.S. In Winnipeg especially, but elsewhere too, Team Canada got dubbed "Team U.S. NHL."

Earlier in the year, a Canadian book entitled *The Death of Hockey* had become a best-seller. Written by ex-Olympic runner Bruce Kidd and journalist John Macfarlane, the book was an eloquent indictment of the NHL's commercialization and debasement of hockey. The authors argued that the NHL had ripped hockey away from its roots and diluted its quality in pursuit of profit.

A quarter-century later, you might well ask, "So what's changed?" Winnipeggers finally got their NHL team in 1979, when the WHA folded and the Jets' franchise became one of four absorbed into the older league—the others being the Quebec Nordiques, the Edmonton Oilers with nineteen-year-old Wayne Gretzky, and the Hartford Whalers with fifty-one-year-old Gordie Howe. But by fall 1995, the Jets were a lame-duck franchise. Playing out their final season in a city that loved them despite their lousy playoff record, they were preparing to fly south to Phoenix, Arizona, and metamorphose into

Coyotes. Once again, NHL demographics—market size, tax base, arena revenue-generating capacity, ratio of corporate executives and luxury boxes per capita—had found Winnipeg, in fact all of Manitoba, wanting. Once again, American money had talked.

This is not the place to go into the bitter trauma of the sometimes heroic, sometimes venal, and ultimately tragic efforts to keep major-league hockey in Winnipeg. Suffice to recall that between spring and fall 1995, Manitobans endured a mercilessly dragged-out off-season of fragile hopes and low despairs.

There was the day in May when they held a public funeral for the Jets in the Winnipeg Arena, and the team's longest-serving player, Thomas Steen, sobbed into a microphone as his sweater was retired, "If there is anyone out there who can save this team, please do it!" There were the hopes aroused when a group of local businessmen made a bid to buy the team before it could be sold to U.S. investors who wanted to move it to Minneapolis, itself a hockey-deprived city. There was the high-stakes political cooperation among three levels of government, all of them grappling with deficit reduction, to come up with $111 million to build a new arena. (Taxpayers already owned 36 per cent of the team and covered its losses because of a deal negotiated by the Jets with the municipal and provincial governments.) And most memorably, there was the day when 35,000 Jets supporters held a mass rally at the Forks, the conjunction of the Red and Assiniboine rivers in downtown Winnipeg, to culminate a fund-raising blitz in which young and old opened their wallets and piggybanks in hard times, shelling out $13.5 million to keep their team at home.

That's team loyalty. But it wasn't enough. In August 1995, after months of self-righteous public posturing and self-interested back-room finagling, the Jets' old owners wouldn't accept the terms of the would-be new owners—who called themselves the Spirit of Manitoba but sometimes seemed more interested in a huge federal tax deduction than anything else. In October, the announcement became official: the team was moving to the States after all, and not to relatively nearby Minneapolis but to faraway Phoenix. The people's best efforts, as individuals or through their governments, had come to nothing. *Their* money hadn't talked.

At that point, the Nordiques had already been sold from under their devoted fans in Quebec City and sent to Denver, Colorado, where they would win the 1996 Stanley Cup as the Avalanche. In Winnipeg and Quebec City, the interests of the people have not been served by private owners buying and selling franchises like pieces of real estate, instead of regarding them as pieces of the community's identity—and themselves as temporary custodians of that identity. But in these and probably other small-market Canadian cities later, the owners show no such regard. They exhibit little loyalty of their own to the communities that have struggled to sustain them. The result is, or will soon be, mass alienation: not from hockey itself, but from NHL hockey.

•

Not long ago, when the Jets were still the Jets, Winnipeg won the loyalty of an unlikely adoptee with his own exceptionally vivid memories of the '72 series.

In January 1991, Soviet hockey journalist Igor Kuperman arrived in Winnipeg to take up his new job: communications officer with the Jets. Kuperman had already spent fifteen years writing about Soviet and international hockey in Moscow, serving for a time as a statistician with the Soviet hockey league. When he emigrated, his country was not only undergoing immense political and economic upheaval but losing touch with its own vibrant hockey past.

The authorities in charge of Soviet hockey disdained and disregarded the fans at home. For years, they'd been packing the Central Army team with so many star players that there was little real competition in the Soviet first division. Central Army won thirteen national titles in a row. The fans grew bored, insulted and restless, Kuperman along with them. He made his living writing about the sport, but he also loved the game with a passion extending far back into his youth, and hated seeing it ruined.

When Ken Dryden arrived in Moscow with a camera crew in 1989, he interviewed Kuperman for his television documentary series *Home Game*. With characteristic openness, Kuperman (who until *perestroika* had to go by the name Kuprin to hide his Jewishness) asked Dryden if there were any opportunities for a guy like him in the NHL. Dryden put him in touch with Mike Smith, then general manager of the Jets, who had a degree in Russian literature and was more receptive than most NHLers at the time to the idea of employing a Soviet. Lawrence Martin, former *Globe and Mail* Moscow correspondent and author of *The Red Machine,* a fine and authoritative book on Soviet hockey, wrote a letter to the Canadian government recommending Kuperman be admitted to the country. Less than two years later, Kuperman and his wife, Natasha, and daughter, Jenya, were settled in Winnipeg.

"Coming here completely changed my life," he says now.

In addition to his regular duties of compiling Jets statistics, coordinating media interviews and writing news releases, Kuperman acted as a liaison and advisor between the team and its Russian-speaking players, such as high-scoring Alexei Zhamnov. He helped interpret for them and generally tried to make them feel more at ease in an alien culture. His own English became fully fluent, and he was promoted to director of hockey information.

Kuperman loves the city. From the start, he has found Winnipeggers friendly, welcoming, accepting—echoing Vsevolod Bobrov's reaction back in '72, when the Soviet coach remarked, "We are very happy with Winnipeg. We found the people much like our own." Recognizing the slight, dark-haired man with mobile eastern European features on the street, people stop Kuperman to say they've seen him interviewed on television. "Compared to Moscow with ten million people," he says, "Winnipeg is a village."

But then Kuperman was predisposed to like the place—and the life. As a boy in Moscow during the late 1960s, he adored hockey and therefore the idea of its birthplace. He avidly followed the World's hockey championships, feeling a fascination with the Canadian national team. He knew they weren't Canada's best but thought they were the closest he'd ever get to the fabled heroes of the NHL, those titans who, in his vivid boyhood imagination, were all over six feet tall and fought with their opponents all the time.

Young Igor memorized the names and numbers of Father Bauer's players. He can still rhyme them off for you. On meeting Dryden, Kuperman told him about watching him play on television in the

.1969 World's tournament in Stockholm: "You were number 16!"

The day the '72 series was announced, fifteen-year-old Igor was ecstatic. For him, the opportunity to see the Canadians play at last was a dream come true. He ran around the family's small Moscow apartment, reciting the names of the NHL stars to his family: "Father, do you know we can see Bobby Orr, Ken Dryden, Bobby Hull, Phil Esposito, Brad Park . . . !"

Like 99 per cent of his countrymen, he says, he didn't believe the Soviet team had a chance.

On the night of Game 1, the opening faceoff took place at 3:30 in the morning, Moscow time, and the television broadcast was delayed until 10:00 a.m. (Most Moscow homes had television sets by then, usually black and white with small screens.) Igor avoided listening to the radio that morning so that he could be surprised when he watched the game; he forbade his father and mother to tell him the score. He was so excited that, half an hour before the game started, he was shaking. And when it was all over, "I was shocked."

His heroes had lost. In 1989 Kuperman haltingly explained to Dryden, "The maple leaves fall from ice and legend of professional is gone."

And yet the young Kuperman stood up for his tarnished legends in the schoolyard, telling the other boys that the Canadian professionals would still win—a perilous and probably foolhardy position to take in the circumstances. His friends taunted him with the words of Nikolai Ozerov, the Soviet Foster Hewitt, who had criticized Team Canada's rough play; Ozerov had told his viewing audience, "We don't need the Canadian type of hockey."

Even after the first half of the series was over, Igor continued to believe. He was sure Team Canada would win all four games in Moscow. He was almost right, too.

In May 1995, at the age of thirty-eight, Igor Kuperman became a Canadian citizen. By then he and Natasha had made a good life in Winnipeg for themselves and Jenya. Kuperman felt at home in Winnipeg. He admired his fellow citizens' civic-mindedness. He was impressed by the way they loyally returned to watch the Jets play the shortened 1994-95 season after the long NHL player lockout. And he enjoyed trying out the phrase "my country"—as in, "I don't like it when Canada sends a non-serious contender to the World's championships. I think it's embarrassing for my country."

At virtually the same moment as Kuperman received his citizenship came the news that the Jets might actually leave the city—his city. And the country—his country. The panicky, nervous-making, on-again, off-again rumours about the franchise never stopped flying. Once again, just as in '72, Igor Kuperman stopped listening to the radio. It was all too much. But finally, the seemingly endless suspense was over, along with Winnipeg's NHL dream. In its place, the city would be receiving a minor-league franchise called the Minnesota Moose from the International Hockey League. It wasn't exactly what Igor, or any other Winnipegger, had had in mind.

EIGHT

GAME 3: THE WIN THAT WASN'T

"Someone once said that a tie is as exciting as kissing your sister.
Well for the last ten minutes tonight that hockey game . . .
looked like Raquel Welch to me."

— HARRY SINDEN, *Hockey Showdown*

●

On September 5, the day before Game 3, terror strikes the Olympic Games in Munich. Eight Palestinian guerrillas attack the Israeli team headquarters at dawn. A wrestling coach is killed, another team member lies dying. Nine Israeli athletes are taken hostage. West German troops besiege the Olympic Village, turning it into a terrorized encampment, and the Games are suspended. A few hours later, the bloody dénouement at Munich airport: as troops try to save the hostages, a storm of gunfire erupts, and all the Israeli hostages, five terrorists and a policeman are killed.

It's a grim reminder there are more deadly conflicts out there in the world than a hockey series. Another, although less dramatic, reminder are the demonstrations outside Canadian arenas protesting the Soviets' refusal to let Jews leave the USSR. In the Canadian media, the Olympic tragedy temporarily displaces the series as the number-one story.

Game 3 will be refereed by the same Americans who handled Game 1, Gord Lee and Len Gagnon. Having experienced success when these two officiated, the Soviets vastly prefer them to Steve Dowling and Frank Larsen. In Winnipeg, Soviet hockey boss Starovoitov and coach Bobrov phone Sinden and Ferguson to say they want Lee and Gagnon for Game 4 in Vancouver as well. The call comes around midnight, and Sinden affably agrees—unaware of Starovoitov's tantrum in the referees' dressing room at Maple Leaf Gardens: "We let them have their way because they kept telling us in a nice way that if we truly wanted to play this series in the spirit of sportsmanship and friendship, then we should play the part of the perfect hosts and consent to their wishes." Unsuspectingly, Sinden assumes the Soviets will reciprocate his flexibility in Moscow.

The Canadian coaches don't want to tamper with a winning formula. They'll stick with their game plan from Game 2: dump, chase, and hit, hit, hit. The only personnel change they make is Jean Ratelle for Bill Goldsworthy. For the time being, the original promise to play everybody has to be set aside.

Ratelle's regular linemates are still out of the line-up, with decidedly mixed reactions. Asked by Sinden how he feels about sitting out the third game, Rod Gilbert replies, "Listen, Coach, do what you think is best." But before leaving for Winnipeg, Vic Hadfield has told Sinden, "I'm not going out west to sit around."

As remembered by Alan Eagleson, "Hadfield was very sour with everybody." Hadfield's disgruntlement has already hit the media, and Sinden even wonders if Hadfield will be on the flight from Toronto; he is. But the first cracks in Team Canada's unity are becoming plain for all to see.

Having told his players to savour their victory but not to gloat, Sinden finds the savour fading fast. For him, winning Game 2 rivalled winning the Stanley Cup two years earlier, yet now he can't help wondering which of his teams will show up in the Winnipeg Arena: the one that choked so pitifully in Montreal, or the one that battled so implacably in Toronto.

It's generally assumed Game 3 will tilt the series decisively in one direction or the other. But so many assumptions about this series have turned out to be wrong. Why should this one be any different?

•

Whereas Team Canada is standing pat, Bobrov and Kulagin decide to gamble and shake their team up, add some fresh legs. They make five changes to their line-up, and the average age of the newcomers is 21.5. The Soviet coaches are starting a youth movement; Team Canada will soon discover its promise.

Out come long-in-the-tooth Ragulin and Vyacheslav Starshinov, as well as defenseman Liapkin, blamed for Canadian goals in Game 2, and Paladiev and Zimin, both injured. Into the line-up go defensemen Valery Vasiliev and Boris Shatalov, forward Vyacheslav Solodukhin, and linemates Alexander Bodunov and Yuri Lebedev. The latter pair will be centred by Vyacheslav Anisin, who dressed for Game 2 as a spare; a year earlier, Anisin, Bodunov and Lebedev dominated the World University Games at Lake Placid. The media dub them "the Kid Line." Bobrov says, "We want them to learn."

Before the start of Game 3, the crowd stands and observes thirty seconds of silence—not a full minute, critics point out—to remember the slain Israeli athletes. The most conspicuous figure standing among the 10,600 spectators is the man every Canadian wishes were out on the ice: Bobby Hull, next to the man who has made him wealthy, Winnipeg Jets owner Ben Hatskin. Earlier in the day, Hull received a standing ovation from everyone attending a federal government luncheon honouring the two teams—everyone, that is, except Clarence Campbell, whose hands stayed in his lap.

•

Starting Tony Esposito in goal again, Sinden goes with brother Phil's line for the opening faceoff, White and Stapleton on defense. Immediately they come on strong. Jean-Paul Parise, a natural resource of Smooth Rock Falls in northern Ontario, whom some said shouldn't even make the team, resumes his mission of patrolling the corners. Barrelling into the corner on his wrong wing, to the right of the Soviet net, Parise makes two adroit moves to set up a goal of his own in the second minute. He takes a Soviet defender into the boards, freeing up the puck for Esposito, who passes back to White at the right point. White lets go a high rising slapshot right on the net, and Parise, cruising past the crease, waves his stick at the puck, trying to tip it in, and obscures Tretiak's vision. The goaltender blocks the shot with both gloves in front of his face but bobbles it, and Parise swiftly golfs the rebound into the left corner.

Barely over a minute later, the Soviets get the goal back on a gift from Team Canada while Vasiliev is off for elbowing. Frank Mahovlich falls into a fit of forgetfulness. Standing stationary at his own blueline, he makes not one but two careless passes back into his own zone instead of looking ahead for linemates Mikita and Cournoyer. Centre Vladimir Petrov, forechecking to kill the penalty, deftly blocks Mahovlich's second blooper with his skate blade. Kicking the puck onto his stick, Petrov strides into the open at the top of the right faceoff circle. He confronts Esposito moving far out to challenge him in a triangular crouch, and blasts a lightning slapshot past Tony's right elbow and into the net.

Ironically, Ken Dryden has been musing from the sidelines that Esposito has been successful against the Soviets because of his goaltending style—staying back in the net, instead of coming out to challenge. Dryden has resolved to change his own style accordingly, the better to defend against the Soviets working the puck in deep. But against Petrov, Esposito elected to do a Dryden and try to cut down the angle, and it didn't work.

Both beaten once, Esposito and Tretiak put on strong exhibitions to keep the game tied for most of the period. Team Canada is just as aggressively physical as in Game 2. Cashman goes off for a dumb, nasty slash at Valery Kharlamov; later he'll complain the referees followed him around all night.

In the nineteenth minute of the first period, Henderson is forechecking fiercely when an interrupted line change leaves him out with Ratelle and Cournoyer. Henderson's hip check sends Lebedev flying off the puck at centre ice, leaving it for Bergman, who fires a long lead pass to Ratelle going in over the blueline. Ratelle tips it over to Cournoyer on his right wing, who feeds it right back to Ratelle to spring him loose behind the Soviet defense. Home-free against Tretiak, Ratelle takes two fluid strides and with a graceful left-handed shot buries the puck up high on the stick side—a very pretty goal. The wisdom of playing Ratelle with new linemates suddenly seems indisputable.

In the second period, Parise and Cashman combine on a different kind of goal—a textbook example of Bruins-style tactics in the Soviet end. Both body-slam the Soviet defensemen up against the boards, mucking for the puck in the left corner. They just keep scrabbling until Cashman gets possession and flips a centring pass to Esposito in the high slot. Phil's reflexes are getting sharp: one-timing the pass, he drills it into the upper right-hand corner, literally blowing Tretiak over.

Esposito is maintaining a goal-a-game production. And at this point, with a 3-1 lead, Sinden thinks to himself, "We have their number."

We do have their number—for another eight and a half minutes. But with Lebedev off for tripping, and the Canadians seeking only their second power-play goal of the series, something happens. It's something Sinden and Ferguson have warned their players against—a favourite Soviet ploy when they have a man in the penalty box—but it catches the Canadians napping all the same.

Frank Mahovlich is in the corner to the left of the Soviet net, fighting for possession with the defenseman Gennady Tsygankov, when the puck spurts out to Boris Mikhailov. Instead of simply icing it, as his opponents would have, Mikhailov with practised precision threads a 130-foot pass diagonally across ice to the far side. It's the kind of pass you'd seldom if ever see in the NHL. It banks off the boards just inside the red line and onto the stick of Kharlamov, who's been allowed to float dangerously deep by the Canadian point men, Park and Stapleton. Kharlamov transforms into a blur flying up the left side. He cuts in on the net with Park in hot pursuit. Launching himself at Kharlamov's back, Park slides on his chest and very nearly succeeds in tripping the Soviet player, first with his stick and then his glove, but Kharlamov is too well-balanced on his skates. He draws the puck to his back-hand and veers across the goal mouth, extending his reach as far as he can before sweeping the puck around the falling Tony Esposito and into the net.

Although Tsygankov is officially credited with the only assist, watching the replay shows Mikhailov should most certainly have received one too. With the score 3-2, the disheartening fact is that Team Canada has now allowed two short-handed goals in two periods.

Sobered but not submitting, the Canadians fight back. Less than a minute later, White passes up to Clarke at centre, who back-hands a quick pass to Henderson digging for the Soviet blueline. The pass caroms off Victor Kuzkin's skate in the direction of the net. Henderson, the quicksilver opportunist, outraces the Soviet defensemen to pounce on the puck and, before Tretiak can twitch, whacks a fifteen-footer straight into the left corner. The Canadians' two-goal lead is restored.

The next five minutes mark a psychological turning point whose impact will carry over into Game 4. Quite simply, the Soviets come back yet again to steal our win away. Their depth and conditioning kick in, while Team Canada's reserves of energy prove too shallow, their legs too heavy with pre-season fatigue. The Canadians start losing the battle in the trenches. They start missing their checks, and on two separate shifts, the Kid Line tears their defense to shreds.

Consistently outfighting the Canadians for possession, Anisin, Lebedev and Bodunov set up Vasiliev for a shot from the point—a position the Soviets aren't supposed to like shooting from. The defenseman's quick wrist shot ricochets through a tangle of players in front of Tony Esposito to Lebedev, who tips it in: a typical NHL goal, on view any night of the week at Maple Leaf Gardens. The kids are learning.

Their next time out, the young line maintains pressure on the Canadian zone, moving the puck around relentlessly until Anisin sees Bodunov in the clear and passes out to him in front of the net. Unhesitating, Bodunov beats Esposito cleanly over the right shoulder with a flick of his wrist, and the game is tied 4-4. On the CBC, Brian Conacher rechristens Anisin and Co. "the Headache Line." They skate to the bench, grinning from ear to ear and cuffing each other like pups—decidedly unrobotic behaviour.

Canadian fans begin wondering where our own promising youngsters are—Gilbert Perrault, Richard Martin, Marcel Dionne, Dale Tallon, Jocelyn Guevremont. Could they be doing some damage out there too? But with a whole period remaining, Team Canada has arrived where it was at the beginning of the third period of Game 1: out of gas, with miles to go. Sinden sees it and despairs. His men have nothing left to give.

Yet miraculously, give they do. Anguished over the prospect of victory slipping away, they skate for twenty minutes on empty, on sheer gut instinct, desperate to hang onto a tie—the best, it seems, they can hope for when being so clearly outplayed and even out-muscled. After outshooting the Soviets 32-17 in the first two periods, they manage only six shots on goal in the whole third period; Phil Esposito has none.

But as Pat Stapleton will observe many years later, if the Soviets are so good, why aren't they now wiping the floor with Team Canada? Having seized control of the game, why can't they exploit the opportunity and put it away? Cashman even awards them a golden power-play opportunity: after being repeatedly warned by the officials, he raps Shatalov over the head with his stick and receives two minutes for slashing, then gets himself ejected from the game—just as his coaches had feared—for yapping at the referees.

But some killer instinct, some obsessiveness around the net, is lacking in the Soviet players. Tony Esposito certainly deserves credit for his strong goaltending, especially a key save on Maltsev with thirteen seconds to play, and yet it's as if the Soviets, having demonstrated their power, having flexed their muscles and proved their capacity to come from behind, are somehow reluctant to finish off. They get scoring chances they don't use. When they should be shooting ruthlessly on the net, they pass off unselfishly to a team-mate. On a couple of excellent chances, they shoot wide. Sinden can't believe it. He thanks his lucky stars for his opponents' Achilles heel: placing so much importance on collaboration and teamwork, not individual success.

At one moment, it seems Canada may pull unlikely victory out of the jaws of a tie after all. Henderson, who does have that obsessiveness around the goal, sees Clarke going for a loose puck behind the net. Henderson sprints into position in front of the crease. Shoving Anisin out of his way, he readies himself for the pass-out from Clarke that comes a split second later. Henderson one-times the puck, scooping it high and straight for the exposed upper right-hand corner of the net—he sees it rising true on its trajectory, homing in on glory—he raises both arms above his head in the stance of celebration that will become so familiar in twenty-two days: *He Shoots, He Scores!*

But this night, glory is not to be. Henderson's mouth gapes, his arms drop lifelessly to his sides, his eyes close in the very image of grief. Tretiak's left glove has darted out, equally true, and snatched the goal away.

Henderson is shaken. It was *in*. In the NHL, it *would* have been in. Henderson recovers and, almost in spite of himself, skates over and gives Tretiak a tap on the pads. Tretiak responds with a stick salute and nod of his head, an acknowledgement of their growing adversarial connection. And also, perhaps, in consolation.

After the game, there is little consolation in Team Canada's dressing room. Henderson remembers the mood as painful and puzzled, as "confused unhappiness." The disappointment of blowing two two-goal leads cuts deeply into the Canadians' spirit and self-confidence. They thought they had it won. What do they have to do to beat these guys? The answer is still a few games away. But they don't know that yet. They don't know if they'll *ever* have an answer.

Only Henderson, blaming himself for not scoring the winner, still acts resolutely convinced we're going to win the series: "I mean, we've got better hockey players," he says. He tells it to everybody.

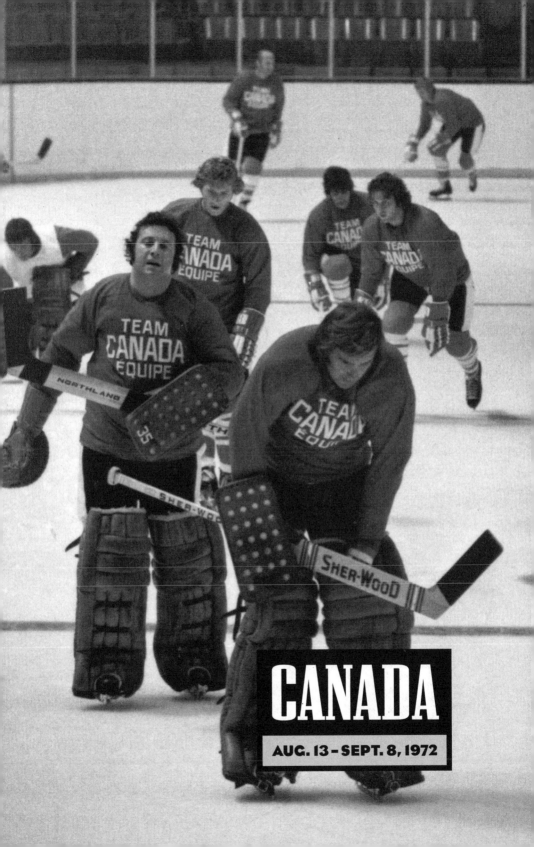

CANADA

AUG. 13 – SEPT. 8, 1972

Overleaf: Expecting victory over the Soviet Union, Team Canada begins working out less than three weeks before Game 1. Goaltenders Tony Esposito *(left)* and Ken Dryden lead their out-of-shape teammates around the ice at Maple Leaf Gardens. BARRIE DAVIS/ THE GLOBE & MAIL

Right: Training camp was never this exhausting, and never this early in the year: *from left,* Team Canada defenseman Pat Stapleton, goaltender Eddie Johnston, forward Frank Mahovlich. BRIAN PICKELL

Below: Coaches' corner: Soviet coaches Vsevolod Bobrov *(left)* and Boris Kulagin *(right)* sit with unidentified Soviet official observing Team Canada practise. Canadian coaches Harry Sinden and John Ferguson *(smoking cigar)* watch the Soviets work out. BRIAN PICKELL

Above: Opening ceremonies, Game 1, Montreal, September 2: Soviet captain Victor Kuzkin, *left,* exchanges gifts with Canadian captains Frank Mahovlich and Phil Esposito, while Prime Minister Pierre Elliott Trudeau looks on. Behind Trudeau are Hockey Canada president Charles Hay and Canadian assistant coach John Ferguson. BRIAN PICKELL

Top right: The empire strikes back: Evgeny Zimin *(far left)* scores the first Soviet goal of the series. Alexander Yakushev *(out of picture at right)* uses Vladimir Shadrin (19) as a screen and feeds Zimin, who slips the puck past Rod Seiling (16) and Ken Dryden. CANADA WIDE

Right: Fog shrouds the Forum ice as Soviet players hug after another goal on their way to a stunning 7–3 upset in Game 1. The dejected Canadians *(from left)* are Phil Esposito, Dryden and Seiling. BRIAN PICKELL

GAME 1

USSR 7 · CANADA 3

Bottom left: The flags of both nations billow high over centre ice at Maple Leaf Gardens during playing of the national anthems. HOCKEY HALL OF FAME

Bottom right: Early in the third period of Game 2, Yvan Cournoyer takes a pass from Brad Park and bursts in alone on Soviet goaltender Vladislav Tretiak to put Canada ahead 2–0. BRIAN PICKELL

Sequence at right: Peter Mahovlich puts Canada ahead 3–1 in Game 2. Mahovlich carries the puck over the Soviet blue-line *(top)*, one-on-one against Evgeny Paladiev. Faking him out, Mahovlich bulls in on Tretiak *(middle)*, feints him to the ice and scores on his backhand. At right, Mahovlich celebrates with Phil Esposito. BRIAN PICKELL

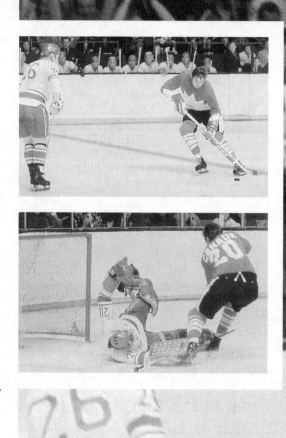

GAME 3

CANADA 4 · USSR 4

The Soviets know how to lay on the lumber too. *Left:* In Game 3 in Winnipeg, defenseman Gennady Tsygankov slashes Phil Esposito on the hand. *Below:* Evgeny Mishakov hooks Frank Mahovlich. The Soviets come from behind to tie the game 4–4. BRIAN PICKELL

GAME 4

USSR 5 · CANADA 3

Right: Before Game 4 in Vancouver, Team Canada players receive gifts of wooden Russian dolls. Looking bemused, *from left,* Rod Gilbert, Phil Esposito, Ron Ellis, Brad Park and Pat Stapleton. BRIAN PICKELL

Below: Yvan Cournoyer, "The Roadrunner," known to the Soviets as "The Train," makes a move on defenseman Vladimir Lutchenko in Game 4. In the background, Frank Mahovlich and Boris Mikhailov. Booed by the Vancouver fans, Team Canada loses 5–3. BRIAN PICKELL

Overleaf: No Team Canada player takes the booing—and ongoing media criticism—more to heart than Frank Mahovlich. His doctor orders him to take a rest from the series' unrelenting pressure. BRIAN PICKELL

NINE

THE SOVIET WAY

"If the stakes are placed on brute force, frightening the opponent . . . it only retards and dampens the ingenuity of a player; it means giving up the opportunity to play wise hockey, to outplay the enemy tactically. The principle 'brawn not brains' is a poor and primitive one."

— ANATOLY TARASOV, *Road to Olympus*

●

Harry Sinden grits his teeth. For the second time in five nights, he has to go and face the media to explain why his team didn't beat "the Russians," as journalists insist on calling them—a term that, despite its inaccuracy, at least ranks above another media favourite, "the Comrades."

By the end of Game 3, Sinden was praying his men would just hold on for the tie. In his heart of hearts, he thinks the Soviets could easily have won. As it is, the series is still far from the way it was supposed to be. At one win, one loss and one tie, it's a dead heat. What will happen in the remaining five games is anyone's guess.

John Ferguson is already playing spin doctor, confiding folksily to the assembled hockey reporters, "Half a loaf is better than none." Ferguson had to calm Sinden down after their team lost their second two-goal lead. Sinden went running down the bench and yelled at Fergie, "What the hell is going on here? They're all over the place!", then flung down a towel in disgust and paced agitatedly back and forth. But now he's composed himself. He steps up to the phalanx of microphones in the packed Winnipeg Arena media room, shaking his head to signal his admiration of the Soviets' come-from-behind poise, and clears his throat. "Gentlemen," he tells the room. "Aren't we all glad to be alive to see a hockey game like that?"

It's a clever ploy. It takes the coach off the defensive right away. Not to be put off the scent of finding fault, a suspicious reporter challenges, "In what way?"

"You saw it," Sinden snaps back. "Super hockey. Both teams had ups and downs. Some mistakes both ways. We could have won it when we were ahead 4-2. But Tretiak made a great glove save on Henderson."

Determined as he is to accentuate the positive, Sinden lets his disappointment show just a bit: "I was a little upset at the way we let them get the puck out of their end. . . . The Russians dig the puck out from behind their goal quickly, which led to them getting a short-handed goal tonight. They break awful fast when they get the puck."

Finally the reporters' questions about his players and tactics push Sinden to a defense of both teams. "Look, give the Russians some credit. They're darned good. And we're playing about as well as we can this early in the season. In midseason we'd be somewhat better, but even this all-star NHL club wouldn't beat these all-star Russians every time out. They play as good in the last thirty seconds as they do in the first thirty seconds, while we tend to let down."

"Do the Soviets compare with the best in the NHL?" Sinden is asked.

"Absolutely," he replies.

"As good as the Boston Bruins?"

"Yes sir. As good as the Boston Bruins."

In the kingdom of Orr and Esposito, there is no higher praise.

Finally, Sinden uses the occasion to throw out a challenge of his own, putting the rhetorical but thought-provoking question that, at this stage of the series, is so clearly crying to be asked: "After all, whoever told us that we in Canada know all about hockey, except ourselves?"

•

Sinden's question was the first "official" Canadian acknowledgement, outside of a maverick such as Billy Harris or John Robertson, that Canadian and NHL hockey wasn't omnipotent after all.

The media were still dwelling on the brilliant performances of individual Soviet players. Kharlamov. Yakushev and Maltsev. And, above all, Tretiak. Everyone was talking about Vladislav Alexandrovich Tretiak. "He's only 20 and he's doing this to us!!" screamed one headline after Winnipeg. Everyone, even Punch Imlach, was fumbling for superlatives to do justice to Tretiak's thwarting of the NHL's biggest shooters. The awesome quickness of his glove hand was compared to a striking cobra. His lightning reflexes were knowingly attributed to a training exercise he'd shyly explained to reporters: throwing two tennis or rubber balls against a wall and trying to catch both at the same time.

Journalists were infatuated with him. They loved portraying Tretiak as a modest, clean-cut young Adonis, with his fresh good looks and tall gracious bearing, who—like all his teammates, but unlike the pampered NHL stars—carried his own sticks and equipment into the arena. When somebody asked Bobrov what Tretiak would do with the two game MVP rings he'd already won (for Games 2 and 3), the coach replied he'd probably keep one and give the other to his new bride. What if he won a third? "I think he also has a girlfriend," Bobrov quipped, and Red Fisher of the *Montreal Star* wrote, "Can you expect anything less from the man with the fastest hands in the West—or East?" In fact, Tretiak had to skip his honeymoon to play in the series; later he'd say, "My honeymoon was spent with the Canadian hockey players."

In capitalist Canada, it had taken Tretiak less than a week to start creating his own legend. But as Sinden had suggested at the news conference, Tretiak, Kharlamov and the rest weren't just individual aberrations or freaks of nature—they were products of a whole hockey system. It was a system possessed of its own particular outlook, expertise, even genius, a system that had been evolving for twenty-six years, far beyond the ken of the NHL.

Since the NHL had never had to compete with Soviet hockey, it had never bothered learning anything about it. Now Team Canada's players and coaches were on the front lines of the learning process. John Ferguson said after Game 3, "If I was starting a new [NHL] expansion team today, I'd go out and buy Anatoly Tarasov's whole collection of books on hockey. The Russians know so much

95

about this game it isn't funny. If the NHL doesn't sit down and ana-lyze what's happened in this series, they're really missing the boat."

The physically and egotistically bloated Tarasov must have been chuckling in his vodka over that one. It was so ironic: he had cre-ated Soviet hockey, and yet instead of coming to Canada to coach or even watch the series, the first test of his system against the NHL, he was back in Moscow, missing out on his greatest moment of glory. His system was pitted against its inspiration, its alter ego and its ultimate antagonist—and winning. Whatever else might happen in the rest of the series, the Soviets had already proved they could match and sometimes outmatch the Canadians. It was a victory far more significant in terms of world hockey, and surely in Tarasov's own mind, than any of his numerous international championships.

•

In his book *Road to Olympus,* Tarasov had called Canadians "the hockey fanatics." By that he intended not a slur but a compliment. He too was a hockey fanatic; his entire purpose in life was to forge superior hockey teams playing a superior style of hockey.

Anatoly Tarasov was that rare animal, a hockey intellectual. He was a theoretician and a tactician; a disciplinarian and an authori-tarian; a psychologist and a Communist. He loved the sport of hockey and admired Canadian hockey tremendously, yet believed he could improve on it—greatly.

A man of convictions as vast as his girth, Tarasov was an innova-tor in a collectivist state. Just because Canadians had invented the sport, he reasoned, and had been playing and practising it in certain ways for seventy or eighty years, didn't mean there weren't other, better ways to play and practise it. There was a Soviet way, and he would invent it. In the process, he reinvented our game.

Tarasov looked at hockey differently. Unimpeded by a hockey tradition, he was able to see tactics and training afresh. Unencum-bered by nay-saying experts at home, he was—paradoxically—free under Soviet Communism to be inspired, to start at ground zero, to experiment with new, untried methods that would have been laughed out of the rink in Canada. He was also encouraged by Soviet pride at having survived and overcome the terrible ravages of the Second World War: a spirit that proclaimed, whether it came to nuclear weapons, the space race or ice hockey, that the USSR had little to learn from the West and must follow its own path.

In reality, isolated from hockey mentors, Tarasov had little choice but to innovate. He wasn't as influenced by Canadian hockey as he might have been chiefly because the Cold War discouraged state-to-state sporting contacts between the two countries. Consequently, he didn't even see a Canadian hockey team play until the 1953 World's championships, one year before his own Soviet national team exploded onto the international scene, shocking the East York Lyndhursts and all of Canada.

When Soviet hockey began in 1946, the players at least knew how to skate—they'd played a traditional game called bandy, which Ken Dryden likens to field hockey on ice, using a ball instead of a puck. But they lacked not only hockey experience and decent equipment but the necessary ice time to learn the sport thoroughly. In the entire Soviet Union, there wasn't a single indoor artificial rink. If they'd remained confined to practising on natural ice during the cold months, Soviet hockey players would have taken many, many years to make up their deficits of knowledge and skill.

To close the gap with hockey-playing nations more quickly, Tarasov resorted to having his athletes play other sports in the off-season: gymnastics, running, swimming, rowing and weight-lifting for strength and conditioning; soccer, basketball and volleyball for tactics and teamwork. To hammer his lessons home, he'd have them play soccer and basketball by hockey rules. For the summer months, he devised a form of floor hockey that his men played with a rubber ring on Moscow's tennis courts and playgrounds. Eventually, they even took up water polo, high diving and ski jumping—the latter two to develop courage, a quality that Tarasov valued highly and always emphasized, knowing how physically and psychologically intimidating hockey can be.

But there was no substitute for getting out on the ice and putting theory into practice. Tarasov wrote that he and his "boys," sequestered at the Central Army sports club in the Lenin Hills, could hardly wait till winter came: "Every morning we would look out the window to see if frost had set in. And we were in no great hurry to part with winter. And in the spring when the ice turns to slush, we trained in the wee hours of the morning while the ice was still a bit hard."

With careful flooding and grooming of the ice, they were able to keep skating until late in the spring. All it took was a willingness to train in the chill of night, while the rest of the world was asleep. But, wrote Tarasov, "we had to stop training as soon as the first rays of the sun came over the pine trees; we really came to despise the hot summer sun." For hockey fanaticism, that's hard to beat.

The Soviet guru exercised nearly absolute power over his players' lives and careers. They were in his charge day and night, living virtually a military existence at the Central Army sports camp, restricted to visiting their families or friends only on Sundays. Tarasov even organized their leisure time and recreation: a little table tennis, a little billiards, good clean fun watching Soviet plays or screen comedies, meetings with the Young Communist League.

Tarasov writes that he and his boys were ecstatic when they heard about plans to create a small experimental patch of artificial ice in a Moscow children's park. They hustled over to the construction site and pitched in to help build the mini-rink. It was intended for the rising Soviet figure skaters, but Tarasov wangled permission for his team to use it between two and six in the morning. Now his players could practise hockey year-round—even though the ice surface was less than a tenth the size of a regulation-size hockey rink. In the summer months, they erected a big army tent to keep the sun off the ice and went right on playing in soccer shorts.

Such experiences led to a new understanding of how to play Canada's game. Ironically, however, one of Tarasov's greatest influences was a Canadian. Tarasov read everything about hockey he could get his hands on, and he was especially influenced by the Russian translation of *The Hockey Handbook* by coach and physical fitness expert Lloyd Percival. Percival's book became Tarasov's Bible. It propagated ideas ignored by the NHL: systematic, scientific training, year-round conditioning, better nutrition, dryland training, precision passing drills. Tarasov didn't slavishly copy these ideas but adapted and embellished them, just as he adapted and embellished lessons in coaching and playing the game from the neighbouring Czechs, who'd been proficient in international hockey for many years. He passed it all through his rigorous, analytical intelligence—and his Communist value system.

Like Percival, Tarasov used logic and science to design a better hockey player, a better hockey team. It stood to reason, for example, that if you imposed physical burdens on a player to make him work harder in practice, but removed those burdens for a game, his powers would be greater in the game itself. So Tarasov designed a thirteen-kilogram rubber belt that his players wore in practice; a later variation was an elasticized tether attached to the boards, which the player had to strain against while skating. These devices developed stronger leg, back and upper body muscles, and improved the sense of balance on skates. Similarly, running in sand built up strength in the ankles.

In terms of strategy, Tarasov called his approach the "creative" or "attacking" style of hockey. It was built on speed, mobility, teamwork and passing. He contrasted it to the Canadian style, which he termed "power hockey" and considered built on bodychecking and intimidation. Although simplistic, these are the terms Tarasov himself used—with all the hauteur of the theorist who knows he's right. "The attacking style of hockey actually eradicates power hockey," he wrote, "because it requires speedy manoeuvres, it requires profound thought, decisions which contain more craftiness, common sense, coordinated actions, superior technique than brute force. And the future is with this type of hockey."

Tarasov's attacking style could take different forms, depending on the strengths and weaknesses of the opposing team. One version he described as his "sea wave" tactics. These were employed successfully against the Canadian national team in the 1967 World's championships in Vienna. Such tactics were also on display in the '72 series, and would find their way into the offensive style of NHL teams in the 1980s, after further exposure in Canada Cup tournaments: "It resembles an incoming and outgoing tide, when the players do not stop anywhere, when the whole team is constantly in motion, skating from one net to the other at a blistering pace."

Tarasov's philosophy of coaching both the individual player and the team as a whole meshed seamlessly with his political philosophy, reflecting his—and the state's—understanding of how society itself ought to function. He saw "real teamwork" as the cornerstone of collectivist thinking in hockey, as in every other human endeavour. In a passage headed "A good player learns from life," Tarasov wrote: "Real teamwork (including in hockey) envisages a common aim, a common idea, a common will, a common discipline. And the sportsman who has greater talent, who knows more, must carry a greater responsibility for the whole team. . . . Real teamwork, comradeship and readiness to help a teammate is cultivated, first of all, by the very atmosphere of our life. . . . such relations have become part and parcel of our daily life, [so] that any deviation from them is a violation of one of the main principles of Communist morals."

In Tarasov's system, every player must play—and train—for the greater good of the team, not for his own glory. In some ideal sense, he must actually play for the greater good of hockey itself. These were higher goals than that glittering prize of NHL hockey, individual stardom.

Tarasov considered training even more important than game experience for his players. In an interview near the end of his life, he said, "I taught them that hockey is the essence of their very lives. And accordingly I explained that everything, absolutely everything I judged about them would come from their behaviour during training, not during the game."

Setting himself up as the sole judge of his men, Tarasov could be indifferent to their individual welfare. His perfectionist demands broke the spirits of some. He, of course, claimed the uncompromising application of his high standards was for their own good. He succeeded in persuading many players of this: Vyacheslav Starshinov, a top Soviet star of the sixties, a leading scorer who played not for Central Army but for its archrival Spartak, acknowledged Tarasov's training methods could be cruel but still produced "unprecedented success" in winning World's championships.

In late 1962, when Tarasov had already coached the Central Army and Soviet national teams for many years, his nationals were preparing for the 1963 World's championships by touring Canada. They were a young team, and although they had won nine out of ten games against Canadian amateur clubs, Tarasov couldn't pass up an opportunity to teach them a moral lesson. When he learned that three of his best forwards, Alexander Almetov, Victor Yakushev (not Alexander, who played in '72), and the captain Konstantin Loktev, had been violating his ban on smoking, he called a team meeting to punish them.

The tactic at such meetings was to have the other players indignantly denounce their teammates. "All three pledged that they would never break the sports rules again," according to Tarasov. But that didn't go far enough to suit him: he expelled Loktev from the team, on the grounds that he'd abused the trust vested in him as captain and should have been setting an example for the younger players.

Morris Mott, formerly of Canada's national team, says that when he and his teammates heard about this later, they were incredulous: Loktev was one of the Soviets' star players, and here he'd been kicked off the team just for smoking. But Tarasov felt amply justified: "In this decision I see a true reflection of collectivism. Rigid and demanding, but direct and honest! . . . After all, punishment is aimed at educating a person."

And after all, the Soviets went on without Loktev to win the first of their, and Tarasov's, ten consecutive international titles in 1963. Loktev was allowed back on the team eventually, and in 1966 he was voted best forward at the World's championships.

In the late sixties, when Valery Kharlamov had arrived on the Central Army and Soviet national teams, Tarasov hadn't mellowed one bit. Like the tyrannical Jack Adams of the Detroit Red Wings in the fifties, Tarasov still liked to knock his star players down a peg or two, just to show them who was boss. Igor Kuperman relates a story Kharlamov once told about a night he'd played a poor game for Army. Tarasov put an arm around Kharlamov's shoulder and asked, "What's the matter, my dear? You weren't playing so well tonight." Kharlamov replied he was just too exhausted from all the practices—there had been one that morning and another in the afternoon. "No, no, my dear," said Tarasov, "you're wrong about that. The problem is you're not practising *enough*," and he sent his star back out on the ice then and there to skate some more.

Early in Kharlamov's career, as cited in Lawrence Martin's study of Soviet hockey, *The Red Machine*, Tarasov had decided the young hopeful "skated like a hunchback" and had little to offer the Army team. So Kharlamov was packed off to a second-division team in the Ural Mountains. A cosmopolitan Muscovite by upbringing, Kharlamov hated living out in the sticks, but he performed so brilliantly on the ice that he earned back his place with Army after all. Of course, Tarasov took the credit for pushing the young player to realize his true potential.

Interestingly, these two very different men shared a passion for the arts. Tarasov had studied theatre and was a follower of the renowned stage director and teacher Konstantin Stanislavsky; he used to quote Stanislavsky's precepts to his players, insisting they applied to hockey as well as acting. Kharlamov's mother had emigrated to the USSR from Spain after the Spanish Civil War and had imbued her son with a love and gift for dance; he liked to hang out with the outspoken young bohemians at Moscow's experimental Taganaka theatre, precursors of perestroika. For both coach and player, hockey was an art as much as a sport.

In *Road to Olympus*, published in English three years before the Canada-Soviet series, Tarasov turned the sights of his judgement on a Canadian player. Former Toronto Maple Leafs defenseman Carl Brewer had been reinstated as an amateur to play on Canada's national team in the 1967 championships. As a former NHLer, Brewer attracted a lot of attention in Vienna from the international hockey world, not least from Tarasov, who itched to test his athletes and his ideas against a bona fide "professional." After the Soviets defeated the Canadians 2-1 and won a fifth consecutive title, Tarasov pronounced Brewer "a natural defenseman . . . an outstanding player—the crowds notice him immediately. His manner of playing is beautiful, even artistic—it is pleasant to watch and yet it is powerful."

Still, Tarasov insisted, he would not pick Brewer for his national team. The reasons? First, he believed Brewer wasn't enough of a team player and had "a very high opinion of himself." Second, Brewer overdid the body and didn't always check cleanly. Finally, Tarasov disapproved of a quality for which Brewer had been much praised in Vienna, his economy of motion. The Soviet coach considered this approach selfish: morally unacceptable and tactically unwise. In his view, it failed to "distract the enemy" with motion: "We are always on the lookout for fast and big-hearted sportsmen who constantly distract the enemy, who help their partners, do not spare themselves, do not economize their energy, who are ready to give everything they have for the game, for the team, for victory."

Tarasov, in other words, objected to Brewer ideologically. If we find it a little absurd that Canadians saw the '72 series not merely as a test of rival hockey systems but of rival social and political systems, nonetheless Tarasov and his countrymen clearly saw it that way too. In a real sense, they'd been working all along to exemplify the superiority of the Soviet way of life through hockey. In a society accustomed to tackling major national objectives with an analysis backed up by a five-year plan, Tarasov had used the authoritarian levers of the state to transform his charges into international champions in record time—all for the state's own glory.

When it came to identifying players who lived up to his ideal of a hockey player, Tarasov naturally chose two of his own. Vitaly Davidov had been voted best defenseman over Brewer at the 1967 tournament. Tarasov applauded this choice, citing Davidov's modesty, dependability and team play: "For him hockey, first of all, means carrying out the coach's orders, performing the functions which have been assigned him."

Tarasov's other model player was the man considered the Soviet superstar before the 1972 series, Anatoly Firsov. For Firsov's strength, speed, agility and stamina, Tarasov called him "the player of tomorrow." Tarasov attributed those qualities to Firsov's tireless love of training. Firsov had actually attracted the admiring interest of NHL teams such as the Los Angeles Kings, and Tarasov made the following comment: "There is no doubt about it, I think Firsov could be one of the best on a professional team, but I hardly think he would adapt himself to that kind of hockey. By his style, by his understanding of and approach to the game, Firsov is worlds away from the pro who wants to play first fiddle. He is kind both in life and on the ice."

And yet, both Davidov and Firsov were absent from the team that travelled to Canada in '72. Although injuries were said to be involved, there were darker political complications, too. Davidov and Firsov were Tarasov men; and Tarasov was no longer in charge of the national team. The Soviet hockey authorities had replaced him with his old adversary, Vsevolod Bobrov, six months earlier.

●

Tarasov and Bobrov had played together on the same line in the pioneering days of the late forties. Bobrov was the individualistic, high-scoring offensive star, Tarasov the unsung plugger who fed him passes and set up his goals. After Tarasov became coach, Bobrov continued to get the credit for the national team's success. Tarasov admitted he'd been particularly bitter when, at the last minute, the Soviet authorities vetoed the team's international debut in the 1953 World's tournament: Tarasov believed his team was ready to take on the world, but Bobrov had fallen ill, and the authorities feared the USSR would show poorly without their big star. Their attitude was diametrically opposed to Tarasov's insistence that no player was bigger than the team.

For years, the two rivals followed separate but parallel paths. Bobrov was also a soccer great and eventually coached the Soviet national soccer team, while Tarasov was establishing his extraordinary coaching record in hockey. But Bobrov coached hockey too, taking over the Spartak team in the elite league for three years in the mid-1960s. In 1967, Bobrov's team performed the unusual feat of defeating their arch-adversaries, Tarasov's Central Army club, for the league championship.

While with Spartak, Bobrov enthusiastically encouraged the more individualistic offensive styles of players such as Starshinov, Evgeny Zimin and Alexander Yakushev. He permitted his athletes greater freedoms both on and off the ice, while Tarasov continued to rule his own charges with an iron fist.

Egomaniac that he was, Tarasov inevitably ran afoul of the Soviet system. The most blatant incident occurred in 1969. In the crucial game for the league championship between Army and Spartak, fought in the same Luzhniki Arena where Team Canada would play, Tarasov blew up when a tying goal by his star centre, Vladimir Petrov, was disallowed. He marched his team off the ice and refused to bring them back from the dressing room until the goal was reinstated. The stoppage of play lasted half an hour, until an intervention from above, as it were, brought the teams together. The most important spectator present, Communist Party General Secretary Leonid Brezhnev, an inveterate hockey fan, decreed that the officials must be obeyed and the game must go on. Anything less would disrupt the absolute rule of authority.

After his insubordination, Tarasov was temporarily removed as national team coach. But he was allowed back and was still coach by the time of the 1972 Olympic Games at Sapporo, Japan, where his team collected its tenth consecutive international championship.

Just before that moment of glory, however, Tarasov sealed his fate as national coach. In defiance of the Kremlin's rules, he allowed his players to compete in two exhibition games in Japan for money—the princely sum of $200 each. Breaking his own commandments about team play and obedience and unselfishness, Tarasov was treading too close to the paths of capitalist damnation. After the gold medal was safely won, the all-powerful Soviet Sports Committee stripped Tarasov and his assistant coach, Moscow Dynamo boss Arkady Chernyshev, of their long-time positions, replacing them with Bobrov and Boris Kulagin.

The Bobrov-Kulagin team was quickly tested. In an unusual move, the International Ice Hockey Federation had scheduled a World's championship in an Olympic year, and Bobrov was behind the Soviet bench for the April 1972 tournament in Prague. "My plan," he announced, "will be to make the maximum use of the individual style of the players."

Heading a team moulded in the Tarasov style, of whom a majority were Central Army players, Bobrov experienced a clash of temperaments and expectations. It wasn't a good fit at first; the team's long streak of international victories was snapped by their hosts and former hockey mentors, the Czechs, who were jubilant over taking symbolic revenge on their country's oppressors. Hockey Canada officials, in Prague to negotiate the series for later in the year with Soviet officials, came away unimpressed with Bobrov's team.

Thus started the notion that Soviet hockey was in decline. In actuality, its next era was just beginning. With a few more months to refashion the team in his own image, Bobrov shook up the roster, dropping Firsov, who was still at the top of his form but sowing discord by speaking out against his new coach, and adding new young blood. Bobrov also had his players take boxing lessons in preparation for playing the Canadians. He remembered all too well the roughing up he'd received from the Penticton Vees seventeen years earlier. This time, the Soviet hockey players would be prepared to handle themselves with their fists, if need be.

Three games into the series, fists hadn't been necessary. Tarasov's boys were now Bobrov's, and they were playing hockey as if they'd invented the damn game.

TEN

GAME 4:
INTO THE PIT

"This Phil was really something. If he felt like complaining,
he complained. If he felt like yelling, he yelled. It was new
to us, this childlike attitude. He didn't hide
his emotions, as *we* were taught."

— BORIS MIKHAILOV, "Summit on Ice" TV documentary

●

A new sound is heard as the greatest hockey series in history moves westward. It's the sound of over-confidence—from the Soviet side. As the teams arrive in Vancouver for Game 4, scheduled for September 8, an unidentified "spokesman for the Soviet hierarchy" states unguardedly that his team can't lose now. "The series is lost . . . for Canada," the official tells the *Montreal Star*'s John Robertson. "We have now reached our objective, which was a win and a tie in the four games here. We'll wrap it up in Moscow, no matter what happens in the Vancouver game."

This is a highly plausible possibility: many Canadians fear the Soviets have taken control of the series already, even though it's tied. If the Soviets lose Game 4, they'll still be only one game down, with all the remaining matches to be played in Moscow—where, coach Bobrov says, he naturally expects his team to be stronger. There is speculation that the two absent Soviet stars, Firsov and Davidov, may rejoin the team there. Tretiak mildly contributes the observation that Firsov has a harder shot than many of the Canadian forwards he's been facing.

The Soviets' boasting seems out of character, yet the visitors are growing bolder and more confident as they go along. Perhaps they're elated their team is performing so much better than expected; perhaps it's the unaccustomed freedom of being able to speak their minds to the press; perhaps it's the streak of bravado and theatricality in the Russian personality, an athletic equivalent to Premier Khrushchev banging his shoe on the podium: "We will bury you."

Even the tactful Bobrov permits himself to say, "We thought the Canadian team would be stronger." He quickly adds, "But they'll be very popular with our Moscow fans, who admire their style of play." Yet the point is made.

Assistant coach Boris Kulagin is blunter. At a news conference after arriving in Vancouver, he comments, "We came to Canada with illusions about the Canadian hockey pros. After the three games that have been held so far, we've discovered they are ordinary people like ourselves." Kulagin then makes an extraordinarily prophetic remark, given this early point in the Canada-Soviet rivalry: he predicts the two styles of play—which he terms "the rigid Soviet style and the rough Canadian style"—will give birth to a new conception of hockey in the future.

The Soviets have always maintained they're playing the series to learn, so it's no surprise that, on a hockey level at least, they remain open to influence. On a human level, the same thing can be said about the players. During the flight from Winnipeg to Vancouver, they pore over North American magazines provided by Air Canada, lingering over seductive colour photographs of home furnishings and advertisements for luxury cars and hotels, stealing a peek at the forbidden fruits of free enterprise. One of them tears a page out of a magazine and scribbles a note on it, intended for someone back home. They ogle the female flight attendants—all of them chosen for this flight because they speak some Russian—and enjoy what a journalist describes as "one of the all-time outstanding airline meals."

A brief stopover in Edmonton is a disappointment. The Soviets, who love cowboy movies, are excited when told they'll be presented with ten-gallon Stetsons by civic officials; but all they receive are little envelopes containing a tourist pamphlet and a ballpoint pen. As the aircraft drifts over the Rockies, however, they relax and laugh and chat with passengers who come aft seeking autographs. They seem to feel right at home in their new surroundings. Being veterans of international competition, they are seasoned travellers—considerably more worldly and cosmopolitan, in fact, than their highly paid NHL opponents, as will become obvious later in the series.

At this point in history, the Soviet conception not only of hockey but of sport and life itself is very different from ours. Take aging (at thirty-two) star Vyacheslav Starshinov, former scoring champion of the Soviet Union and holder of the title "Honoured USSR Sport Master," who is now a doctoral candidate at Moscow's Institute of Sports and Physical Culture. Starshinov has a few arcane questions to put to his NHL counterparts concerning "the moral and spiritual qualities of hockey." He has assembled them in the form of a written questionnaire, translated into English back in the USSR. Starshinov, whose rugged bad-boy looks resemble a cross between James Dean and Guy Lafleur, plans to use the survey as research material for his thesis. He hopes all the members of Team Canada will assist him by completing it; as an inducement, he's offering them anonymity.

"To what extent," Starshinov wants to know, "do you think yourself morally responsible before society?"

"In what extent is your understanding of moral responsibility before society influenced by moral traditions of your social-economic society?"

For the convenience of the Canadian players, who might have other concerns on their minds at the moment, making them disinclined to write detailed answers to his questions, Starshinov has asked them to answer on a scale from 1 to 5—1 representing "no sense of responsibility" and 5 representing "an intense sense of responsibility."

Over breakfast, Ken Dryden examines the document with the seriousness of a law student; he reads the questions aloud to Pat Stapleton and Bill White. "Now here's a toughie," suggests Dryden. " 'To what extent is your attitude to people influenced by feelings of thanks shown for your person by the spectators; gratitude for measures which were put in your sport training; duty to a legal contract with a sports organization; or anger against accepted moral interrelations?' I'd like time to give this more thought."

"Geez, Bill," Stapleton says to White, "do you suppose Starshinov doesn't realize we're defensemen?"

Phil Esposito announces he's ready to cooperate: "The way I see it," Espo declares, "here's a guy who's spent twenty-six years going to school, right? If there's anything we can do to help him get what he's after, I think we should do it. Right?"

Harry Sinden agrees. He wants to help out but has a little difficulty with some of the questions. "The trouble I see with Starshinov's questionnaire," Sinden remarks after studying it on the way to Vancouver, "is that something was lost in the translation."

•

Bemused as they are by Starshinov's questions, the members of Team Canada have to admit there's more than one way to play this game after all. With only one match left in Canada, the NHLers still haven't solved the puzzle of Tretiak and his teammates. Whatever impact the series may have on future conceptions of hockey, they have to get their own conception together in the here and now.

They haven't much time. The Vancouver game will be their fourth in seven days. When Sinden studies his team's disappointing finish in the Winnipeg game, he sees they just couldn't keep up with the fast and furious pace set by the Soviets. He decides to shuffle his line-up again: "In the last two games, the team that came on with fresh legs had the best of it." In all, he makes eight changes.

Forwards Dennis Hull and Gilbert Perreault will have their first opportunities to play. Cashman will sit this game out, since the referees seem to be on his case; Bill Goldsworthy will fill the tough-guy role instead. Hadfield and Gilbert will get another chance, but without Ratelle. With these changes to his forward lines, Sinden hopes to address both the fatigue factor and the discontent of players who haven't dressed much.

Defense continues being a problem. Orr still isn't ready. Injury-plagued Serge Savard, a tower of strength in Games 2 and 3, has just suffered another stroke of bad luck: during practice the morning after the Winnipeg game, a shot by Red Berenson cracks his right ankle. Without Savard, Sinden considers going with only five defensemen again, but the defensemen themselves talk him out of it, and he has the good sense to listen. Awrey and Seiling go back into the line-up, along with the Park-Bergman and Stapleton-White pairings. Guy Lapointe will get a rest to cope with a minor injury.

In goal, Sinden and Ferguson elect to change their original plan, which was to start Dryden in the first game, Esposito in the second, whichever of them played better in the third, and Ed Johnston in the fourth. But they hadn't expected to have only one win by Game 4. Since Johnston is definitely their third goalie, they decide it's time to try Dryden again, hoping he's ready to play a stronger game than before, perhaps eager to prove what he can do after being upstaged by his number-one NHL rival. Dryden shares their thinking: "I now have something to prove to Harry, to Fergy, my teammates, the Russian players and everyone else." The rap on Dryden is that he plays poorly in international competition. To beat it, he's put his mind to work analyzing, with the help of his brother, fellow-NHL netminder Dave Dryden, how to defend more successfully against the Soviet attack. The Dryden brothers' thinking is that Ken will get caught out of position if he plays his usual game of moving out to narrow the shooter's angle, since the Soviets will simply pass the puck to set up a new angle, and he won't have time to react. Hence Ken will change his style, staying deeper in the net, hoping his six-foot, four-inch, 210-pound frame will block enough of the goal mouth while he contends with their wingers coming in from the corners. He'll also try to remember not to kick out rebounds towards the corner, as he does in the NHL, because they'll end up on the sticks of Soviet forwards stationing themselves at the side of the net.

Dryden himself has written tellingly of the "spasm of self-hatred" that shook the country after Team Canada's staggering loss in Game 1. Given how much embarrassment and downright humiliation Canadians felt, Dryden's extravagant phrase is entirely apt. By exposing the crudeness of our version of hockey, Game 1 exposed us—and we did not like what we saw.

By Game 4, the feverish spasm has passed. After victory in Toronto and near-victory (or near-defeat) in Winnipeg, self-hatred has cooled to something more objective—a realistic understanding that this is going to be a long and exciting and exceptionally historic series between two excellent, very different, yet evenly matched teams, easily the two best hockey teams in the world. Yet as the teams warm up before the game in Vancouver's Pacific Coliseum, a baffling and disturbing noise reaches the players' ears: some of the fans are booing. The Soviets know the boos are not for them. And the Canadians can't believe their ears.

But then this is the West Coast, where residents breathe a different air, and national trends and attitudes don't always survive past the formidable barrier of the Rockies. Some suggest the object of the booing is the game's inconvenient starting time: five o'clock, scheduled to match prime time in the east. Or are these Vancouverites just franker and more prescient hockey fans than those in the rest of the country?

In truth, few fans anywhere are expecting the debacle of Game 1 to repeat itself. And yet that's exactly what they're about to witness.

•

From the game's early moments, the tough-guy nonsense gets Team Canada into trouble. Goldsworthy, under orders from Sinden to rough up the Soviets without taking penalties, goes out on his first shift and gets two minutes for cross-checking at 1:24. Talk about starting the game behind the eight ball!

The penalty-killing efforts of Esposito, Frank Mahovlich, White and Stapleton begin well enough. Then the Soviets emerge out of their zone on one of their well-organized rushes. Efficiently they control the puck, Kuzkin to Lutchenko to Blinov to Petrov, who carries it over the Canadian blueline on the right side. Petrov passes across to defenseman Lutchenko at the left point. Directly facing the net, Lutchenko blasts a low slapshot destined for the left corner. With White backing in on him, Dryden cranes his neck and spots the puck just in time to kick out his right leg for a pad save—but Mikhailov, standing unmolested on the doorstep, gets his stick-blade on the ice to tip the puck in, high over Dryden's gangly sprawling form. A second after the two-minute mark, it's already 1-0. A few scattered boos are heard from the cheap seats.

The demoralizing thing is that, almost right away, the same situation develops all over again. After assuring Sinden he won't take another dumb penalty, Goldsworthy pointlessly throws an elbow and gets the gate. Again White and Stapleton go out to kill the penalty, this time with Clarke and Ellis. Again the play develops on the right side with some swift and accurate short passing, Petrov to Mikhailov to Kharlamov, who slips it across to that same Vladimir Lutchenko.

The defenseman skates into the left faceoff circle for a closer shot. This time White doesn't back in but moves up to challenge Lutchenko, crouching to block his shot. Lutchenko's wrist shot eludes White but not lucky number 13, Mikhailov—who duplicates his earlier feat by holding his stick on the ice at just the right angle, so the shot deflects off the blade and over Dryden's arm. Two-nothing.

As Mikhailov grins gleefully all the way to the bench, the booing swells to a chorus throughout the arena. Team Canada, it seems, will not be allowed to get away with allowing goals. And yet the period ends without any further scoring: with two periods left, there is more than enough time for the Canadians to salvage the game.

Indeed, they cut the Soviet lead in half by scoring the first goal of the second period. One of Sinden's fresh pairs of legs comes through—albeit for a flukey sort of goal. Having tried it unsuccessfully before, twenty-one-year-old Gilbert Perreault manages to complete an end-to-end rush. He seems to think beating the Soviets depends not on passing to his more experienced wingers, Frank Mahovlich and Cournoyer, but on one-man heroics. Perreault leaves his linemates standing around looking underemployed as he flies over the Soviet blueline. Trying to sail through the Soviet defense, he loses the puck momentarily but recovers it. As he roars past the net, Perreault throws out a centring pass in the direction of Mahovlich, hitting the skate of defenseman Valery Vasiliev, who has come sliding into the crease to block a shot. The puck deflects off Vasiliev and past Tretiak into the goal.

Canada's sails fill with wind—but not for long. Now comes the ultimate frustration: for the team, for the fans and for that already frustrated pair, Vic Hadfield and Rod Gilbert.

Park starts a rush out of his own end. He hits Esposito with a pass at the Soviet blueline. Keeping possession long enough to draw the Soviet defenders towards him, Espo slips the puck behind them to Hadfield breaking in on left wing. With a poor angle to shoot from, Hadfield centres the puck perfectly to Gilbert as he rushes the net, and it ends up behind Tretiak. But the Soviet defenders are waving their arms frantically; the referee signals no goal! As Gilbert moved into the goal mouth, the pass struck his skate and bounced in—and although he didn't appear to kick it deliberately, the ruling is that it was kicked in illegally.

So instead of tying the game up, Team Canada remains a goal down. Calling this the turning point, Sinden will speculate later it would have been a different game if the goal had been allowed. But then, it would have been a different game if the Canadians had played well enough that they didn't have to count on flukey goals.

It takes the Soviets less than a minute to exploit consecutive Team Canada miscues and restore their two-goal advantage. On a faceoff in the Soviet zone, Clarke gets the puck back to Henderson, who lets Mikhailov knock it off his stick. Stapleton makes a desperate bid to keep it inside the blueline, but his pass hits Petrov on the leg and rebounds out to centre. Petrov keeps right on going to create a two-on-one. Carrying the puck up the right side with Yuri Blinov on his left and only White back between them, Petrov slides it cleverly under White's stick, putting Blinov in all alone on Dryden. Blinov's shot hurtles between Dryden's pads, making the score 3-1.

While he's had little chance on the Soviet goals, Dryden looks shaky even on some of his saves. More than once he gloves the puck only to have it trickle away from him. Awrey alertly saves a goal on one occasion by keeping the puck from sliding over the line. And, with nearly fourteen minutes gone in the second period, the Soviets score for the fourth time.

The Canadian defenders can't seem to clear the zone against the Soviets' forechecking. Maltsev digs the puck off the boards and passes out to Kharlamov in the slot. Instead of shooting, as an NHLer would from that position, Kharlamov spots his opposite wing Vikulov, left all alone at the right corner of the net, and backhands a quick pass to him. Vikulov coolly one-times the pass between Dryden's pad and the post on the short side. Dejected, Dryden hangs his head.

The crowd's booing is unrelenting, and the next incident only redoubles it. When Tretiak comes far out of his net, Jacques Plante–style, to clear a loose puck before Frank Mahovlich can reach it, Mahovlich plows into him. The collision could be construed as accidental at first, Mahovlich propelled from behind by a Soviet defender. But when that defender peels off to pursue the puck, Mahovlich throws himself onto Tretiak, knocking him to the ice and draping himself all over the goaltender, and the two of them lie in a ridiculous heap thirty feet from the net. Tretiak struggles to rise but can't; Mahovlich keeps him pinned for several seconds like a wrestler going for the count.

Even with this desperate measure, Canada can't score. Kuzkin takes up position in the net, while his teammates keep the puck away from Perreault and Cournoyer. The booing goes on and on. After the game, Mahovlich will express his astonishment at the fans' reaction: "I don't see why they booed me. There's nothing wrong with what I did until the referee calls it. He didn't. Man, I'm amazed. As a matter of fact, this whole darn series has me amazed."

Of course, the Big M is missing the point: it's *losing* that the fans object to, so that everything Team Canada does is suspect. Even Dryden's saves are now jeered. The Canadian public isn't exactly covering itself with glory, any more than the team is.

In the dressing room before the third period, Paul Henderson sits slumped on the bench next to Phil Esposito. By his own admission, Henderson has not played a good game—in fact, it will be his only poor game of the series—and he's feeling not a little upset with himself, and a touch hurt. The booing has set him to wondering what he's doing here, playing a bunch of exhibition games instead of enjoying his summer holidays, and he remembers saying bitterly to Esposito, "Our own people are turning on us."

"I hope I'm picked the star of the game," Esposito replies, "because I'm really going to give them a piece of my mind tonight. I've had enough of this."

When they skate out for the third period, Esposito plays so well that he gets his wish. But it isn't for lack of trying to stop him on the part of Vladimir Petrov. Told by Bobrov and Kulagin to shut Espo down, Petrov follows him everywhere like a lovesick retriever. Petrov gives up a couple of inches and twenty pounds to his adversary, but he's acknowledged by the Canadians as one of the strongest and toughest Soviet players.

A comical moment ensues when Petrov throws a bear hug on Esposito from the rear behind the Soviet net, then collapses on top of him. The referee whistles the play down, calling the penalty—unlike the case of Mahovlich tackling Tretiak. Lying on the ice under Petrov, Esposito looks around in rather obvious disgust. The two stare wordlessly at each other for a moment—the language barrier leaving Esposito, for once, at a loss for words—then the stone-faced Petrov gives him a big goofy grin, spreads his arms wide in a "Hey, man, what else can I do?" gesture, and pats Phil familiarly on the rear end as he gets up and heads to the penalty box. You'd think they've been playing each other for years.

The Canadians don't score on the power play. In fact, although they outshoot the Soviets 23-6 this period, most are long shots "coming from downtown," as Sinden puts it, and only two go in the net. But at least the two are worthy goals, and Esposito has a hand in both of them.

In the seventh minute of the period, Park allows Maltsev to skate right though him and walk in on goal, but Dryden kicks the shot out. Recovering the puck, Park leads a rush to centre and hands off to Goldsworthy on right wing. Goldsworthy crosses the blueline, passes back to Esposito in the high slot and heads straight for the net. His timing is right on: Esposito's rising shot hits the crossbar, and Goldsworthy is there to tap in the rebound. After his first period penalties, it's a redemption of sorts.

With the score 4-2 and over half a period left to play, the Canadians struggle unsuccessfully to mount a sustained attack. The Soviets' fifth goal results from their constant offensive pressure, which produces a Canadian lapse: both Bergman and Park become preoccupied with checking Alexander Yakushev behind the net, leaving Shadrin wide open to take Yakushev's pass-out. Dryden stops Shadrin the first time on a backhand shot, but Shadrin switches to his forehand to pot the rebound.

When Dennis Hull closes the gap to 5-3 after a nice pass from Esposito, beating Tretiak cleanly with a high hard shot on the stick side, only twenty-two seconds remain. The score makes the match appear tighter than it's really been. Harry Sinden will observe years later, "We were never in the game. They just took control, and as hard as we tried, we seemed to get a little worse all the time."

•

With the Canadian half of the long-awaited series now completed, and Team Canada on the wrong end of a 1-2-1 record, disappointment and anger are naturally rampant. The fans pin the blame on Team Canada—as if, somehow, the players could be winning the series if they just wanted to, if they really cared enough. This attitude insults not only the Canadian players but also the Soviets, who are simply so much better than the fans seem willing to admit.

Phil Esposito has decided to confront this attitude head on. After the final whistle, he skates out to accept his honour as the Canadian game star, along with Boris Mikhailov for the Soviet team. Johnny Esaw of the CTV network, little suspecting he's about to broadcast a classic post-game interview, one of the most remarkable and moving in the history of sports, thrusts his mike under Esposito's long-jawed, anguished face. As several fools in the stands shout obscenities and throw debris, Esposito stands in the heat with the blood pounding in his temples and launches into a passionate oration, the words pouring out of him like grief, like the rivers of sweat pouring from his tousled black hair and running down his glistening cheeks onto his jersey:

"People across Canada," he begins, like a prime minister addressing the nation, "we tried, we gave it our best. For the people who booed us, geez, I'm really—all of us guys are really disheartened and we're disillusioned and we're disappointed in some of the people, we cannot *believe* the bad press we've got, the booing in our own buildings. If the fans in Russia boo their players like some of the Canadian fans—I'm not saying all of them—booed us, then I'll come back and apologize to each and every one of the Canadians. But I don't think they will.

"I'm really, really disappointed, I cannot believe it. Some of our guys are really, really down in the dumps. We know, we're trying, we're trying, but hell, we're doing the best we can. But they've got a good team, and let's face facts. But it doesn't mean we're not giving it our 150 per cent, because we certainly are . . ."

When Esposito pauses, Esaw feeds him a little, and he keeps on going: "Every one of us guys, thirty-five guys who came out to play for Team Canada, we did it because we love our country and not for any other reason. They can throw the money for the pension fund out the window, they can throw anything they want out the window—we came because we love Canada. And even though we play in the United States and we earn money in the United States, Canada is still our home, and that's the only reason we come. And I don't think it's fair that we should be booed."

With ample justification after he's played his heart out, Esposito speaks with barely restrained fury; yet his sweaty countenance betrays more sorrow than anger. In Team Canada's darkest hour, it is a noble moment.

ELEVEN

THE LONELY MISSION
OF RON ELLIS

"When we were in Sweden, our party—players and coaches
and others—numbered exactly fifty. And we felt
it was fifty against the world."

—RON ELLIS, 1995

●

Ron Ellis remembers exactly how
bad it felt after Vancouver. Although he played on Team Canada's
best line, already acknowledged as such midway through the series,
Ellis remembers feeling down for days afterwards.

"People might find this hard to understand," he says now.
"When we got booed out of that place, it was very, very disappointing. We did not play well, but we did not deserve to be booed out of
the rink. I know it was frustration on the fans' part, and I understand that. But it took a lot out of us emotionally. All of us."

Ellis is a feeler, a brooder. When he and his teammates flew back
to Toronto, home of Ellis's team, it wasn't easy facing people. Pat
Stapleton says it was far easier for *him* to go home: "I went back to
Chicago, where it was hardly even known the series was going on.
When I went into the supermarket, people knew me as a Black
Hawk but not as a Team Canada member who'd just got trounced."
Not so for Ellis. As Stapleton puts it, "There was far more pressure
on Ronnie or Frank or Paul. In Canada, everyone's emotions rode
on the scoreboard."

Today, Ellis lives north of Toronto in semi-retirement. You've arranged to meet him at Teen Ranch—a Christian youth camp and sports facility just south of Orangeville—to talk about the series and a life moulded, determined, perhaps distorted, by hockey. Set among the gently rolling Caledon Hills, their trees turning russet and bronze, Teen Ranch boasts a state-of-the-art, Olympic-size hockey arena with seating for a thousand. The arena, known as the Ice Corral, is sleekly postmodern in design and set on foundations of pink granite. A CBC production truck stands outside in the spacious parking lot. Inside the front doors, a placard welcomes tryouts to the evaluation camp of the national women's hockey team.

Ellis isn't connected with the women's team, or the CBC crew shooting a feature on it, but his involvement with Teen Ranch goes back a long way as parent, volunteer coach and counsellor. Living in nearby Collingwood, he's driven down for a morning skate before the women, who include goaltender Manon Rheaume, step onto the ice. He's still wearing his blue workout suit as he comes across the lobby to shake your hand.

At fifty, Ellis has grown heavyset. Only when he turns aside does the boy-next-door handsomeness of his playing days emerge in profile, like an optical illusion, from his fleshy face and neck. He ushers you into the office of his friend Mel Stevens, the director and founder of Teen Ranch, who has provided the space to talk. Ellis describes Stevens almost reverentially as "the gentleman who had the vision for this place." On the desk between you rests a Bible with a blue-and-white Toronto Maple Leaf crest embossed on its black cover.

In his measured, earnest, soft-spoken tones, Ellis explains it was Stevens who was responsible for him and his linemate and best friend, Paul Henderson, "coming to know the Lord." After the '72 series, when they were both still with the Maple Leafs, Stevens was chaplain to the Toronto Argonauts football team. He persuaded Harold Ballard to let him present an embossed Bible like the one on the desk to every player on the Leafs.

Henderson and Stevens became friends: "And once Paul made his commitment to live for the Lord, we being so close, we talked about it all the time. Then eventually my wife, Jan, and I came to the same decision."

The Ellis and Henderson families have been close for years. "We've watched each other's kids grow up, and Paul's children are just like my own. I made a lot of good friends in hockey, but Paul's the one I see the most of. We rarely go a day without talking."

In personality, the two could hardly be more different: Henderson ebullient, charismatic, opportunistic, bursting with energy and self-assurance; Ellis shy, hesitant, self-doubting, cautious to the point of pessimism. Ellis admits Henderson's incurable optimism never ceases to amaze him. Paul would come into the dressing room before a game and predict he was going to score two goals that night, and by game end, more often than not, he'd have his two goals. "If you're confident, things happen," Ellis muses. "I'd have been better off to be a little more like him."

On the other hand, he accepts they're just different human beings, and drawn to each other for that very reason. In hockey and life, they've made a good balance. "Paul's a risk taker, which made him a good forechecker. And I was the guy who'd always come back so he could take more chances."

•

Ron Ellis wasn't always so modest and so careful, but he was always a hockey player. When your dad is in the air force and you move around a lot, hockey is what you do—not only for fun but for continuity and peer acceptance and social life in every new town you move to: it's your ticket. So Ellis didn't have much doubt hockey was his destiny. While the family was stationed in Ottawa, and he was playing Cradle League and school hockey (once against the author of this book), fourteen-year-old Ron was scouted by the Leafs, the team he'd always dreamed of playing for.

By his grade ten year, Ellis was in Toronto. He played one season of Junior B and three of Junior A with the Leafs' farm team, the Marlboros. In his last amateur season, 1964, he led the Marlies to the Memorial Cup as their top goal scorer, and Leafs coach Punch Imlach decreed he was ready to move up to the big team.

Ellis was nineteen, with a year of junior eligibility left—practically a prodigy. And he blazed brightly in his rookie season: he added energy and point production to an aging team and finished second in Calder Cup ballotting to Roger Crozier, the Red Wings' rookie goaltending sensation. Then he took a careful, practical, realistic look at his career prospects, and decided what kind of hockey player he wanted to be: the kind who has a long career.

To Ellis, that meant playing both ways, and it meant being consistent. "During my whole career I considered myself a two-way player. Plus-minus was very important to me. That was the way I felt I could be productive and stay in the league. In junior I could score goals, but when you get to the NHL, goal scorers come and go. I made a decision very early in my career that being consistent was more important. That's what the management likes—they know they can count on you for so many goals, they know you can be used in tight spots, to kill penalties, to play the last minute of the game. That's the kind of player I wanted to be, and I worked very hard at it."

By the time Ellis was selected for Team Canada, he'd played eight seasons with the Leafs—already a longer-than-average NHL career—and won a Stanley Cup ring against Montreal in 1967, the last year of the six-team league. For four of those seasons, he'd played right wing on a line centred by veteran Norm Ullman, with Henderson on left wing. Ellis and Henderson found Bobby Clarke fitted perfectly between them. He was a lot like Ullman, only younger, brasher and more abrasive: quick, a team player, deft at winning face-offs and setting up his wingers. Henderson, from Lucknow, Ontario, and Clarke, from Flin Flon, Manitoba, shared Ellis's old-fashioned, small-town work ethic. They also shared a gritty ambition to break into Team Canada's starting line-up, even though they knew they'd been invited to camp as cannon fodder for the team's big-name stars: "If Harry hadn't picked thirty-five players, none of us would have been on Team Canada."

That's ironic, considering that Henderson finished second in team scoring and Clarke third. Ellis himself collected just three assists in the series. After his neck injury in the first game, the restricted movement impaired his shooting ability. But he willingly accepted the defensive mission assigned to him from Game 2 onward: to shadow Valery Kharlamov.

It was a mission Ellis knew well. Imlach had often matched him against the top left wingers in the NHL, such as Frank Mahovlich and Bobby Hull, who gave Ellis the most trouble of all with his speed and power. But Kharlamov was a daunting challenge. He had the moves of a conjurer, moves the Canadians had never seen before, and they knew they had to find ways to stop him. "Kharlamov wasn't a big player like Hull, but he was very strong for his size. He was in very good shape, and tricky. He could shift at full speed. Most players tend to slow down when they want to make a move, but Kharlamov could do it all at top speed."

Since Kharlamov was one of the keys to the Soviet attack, Ellis took the assignment as an honour. And he defensed Kharlamov much as he played his opposite numbers in the NHL; in the previous season, Ellis had taken only seventeen minutes in penalties. "I didn't foul him, I checked him clean, the way you're supposed to."

Lest this seem an excessively Lady Byng approach, it should be noted that Kharlamov scored only one more goal after Game 1—the short-handed breakaway goal in Game 3, when Ellis wasn't even on the ice. So to a considerable extent, Ellis succeeded in neutralizing the Soviet superstar, although Kharlamov was able to set up four goals for his teammates at various times. And yet Team Canada eventually chose another, far less admirable way of dealing with the threat Kharlamov represented, as we'll see in Game 6.

Just as NHL players were discouraged in those days from consorting with the enemy, the Canadian and Soviet players had little to do with each other. Ellis remembers, "You had to be very cautious—we couldn't fraternize with them, and they weren't allowed to say boo to us either. But we'd watch them practise, and Kharlamov would be skating around, and our eyes would meet. I'd give him a nod or a little wave, and he'd give me a little wave back. He knew what I had to do. I think he respected me for the way I did it."

Five years later, they met on the ice again. Ellis was preparing for an NHL comeback in the 1977-78 season after a two-year retirement from the Leafs. A born-again Christian by that time, he revived his hockey career with a baptism at the 1977 World's championships in Vienna, the first time Canada had entered a team in the tournament for eight years, and he squared off there against Kharlamov once more.

At the banquet after the tournament, Ellis had the interpreter approach Kharlamov to ask if they could chat. Kharlamov agreed. For Ellis, the ensuing conversation is one of his fondest memories: "We got together in a corner and recalled the times we'd gone up and down the wing together in '72. As that series went on, you heard more and more about a so-called war, one way of life against another. But we just developed a sense of respect for each other, both ways."

Fifteen years after the '72 series, retired players from the two teams played another, shorter series of "friendly matches": the "Relive the Dream" reunion in 1987, featuring three games in Canadian cities. After each game, the old enemies gathered around the dining table with an interpreter to get to know each other in a new way. Ellis and his teammates soon found the Soviets were a lot like themselves, guys who talked about their work and their families and their kids: "It was a bit of a shock, really. Here we'd been at war with them, and they're just normal guys."

But one not so normal guy, whom many consider among the greatest ever to play the game in any country or any era, wasn't at the reunion: Valery Kharlamov had died in a car crash in August 1981. Although he'd worked courageously to overcome career-threatening injuries from another car accident five years earlier, Kharlamov had not been chosen to play on the new-generation Soviet team in that year's Canada Cup. The fatal accident happened shortly afterwards, on a narrow rain-slicked highway outside Moscow. Kharlamov's wife, Irina, was at the wheel. Both were killed instantly in a head-on collision with a speeding truck. Ron Ellis's gifted adversary, who used to say, "I like to play the game beautifully," was thirty-three years old.

•

For Ellis, as for many members of Team Canada, the '72 series was a watershed. Phil Esposito got a monkey off his back by proving he could excel without Bobby Orr. Bobby Clarke established himself as a star and went on to win the Hart Trophy. Paul Henderson became a national icon. Ellis, in typically self-deprecating fashion, decided he really did belong in the NHL after all. "I'd always questioned my abilities—that's my personality. So it really helped to say to myself, 'Hey, you just played with the best in the world.' "

He was drained physically, but the constantly escalating tension of the eight-game drama had also taken its toll emotionally: "It took some of us a good part of that season to get back on track." Then he started wondering, unable to help himself, whether hockey was what his life was all about.

"I would wonder if chasing this little black puck around was my purpose," he told former Winnipeg Jets GM Mike Smith for his book *Life after Hockey,* "if I was really doing what I was put on this earth to do. This happened even when I was playing well. It was hard to explain."

Ellis's self-questioning led him on a search in various directions, both practical and spiritual. In the summer of 1975, he opted for Christianity; and after his eleventh season, his best ever for total points, playing on a line with Darryl Sittler and Tiger Williams (Henderson had gone to the WHA), Ellis announced his first retirement from the game.

"I was really having trouble. Most players do around the ten-year mark. It's decision-making time: are you going to play another five years or make a change? In those two years off, working for a home-building firm in Toronto, I was able to prove to myself I could do much more than play hockey. So when I made my comeback, I felt like I had a piano off my back. I knew I could survive out there in the world."

Still, more difficulties lay ahead. Ellis enjoyed most of his next four seasons with Toronto. He played with a new serenity, not worrying so much about whether he was scoring goals or the team was winning, just playing and practising as hard as he could, "glorifying the Lord." But midway through the 1980–81 season, GM Punch Imlach told Ellis he wanted to send him down to the minors. Since his junior days, Ellis had never played in the minors, and he wasn't going to start now: he'd sooner retire with dignity. He'd been prepared to retire a year earlier, but the Leafs had asked him to stay.

The problem was, he wasn't ready to go right then. He'd been looking forward to finishing out the season and his career with the team. "This time I knew it was over. The real transition started, but I didn't have any specific plans."

Unlike Pat Stapleton with his farm, or Ken Dryden with his law degree, or Paul Henderson with his missionary zeal, or Phil Esposito, Bobby Clarke or Serge Savard, who would become NHL general managers, Ellis hadn't experienced a call. For a time he floundered. He tried teaching physical education for a year at a Christian school, but it was only a stop-gap measure, not a long-term choice. He took an insurance course and opened a branch office of a friend's insurance business in Orangeville and ran it for three years: "It went very well, but there was something . . . I wasn't at peace. So I went into my own business."

The business was in quality sporting goods, an upscale store called Ron Ellis Sports in nearby Brampton, which he operated with two partners. After five years of running the store, he felt uneasy again, restless. He moved on to corporate work with the YMCA in Toronto for a couple of years, then to a three-year commitment with the organizing committee for the 1991 Canada Cup, then to the Hockey Hall of Fame, where he did public relations and helped to develop the educational program for school groups.

"So I've gone through a lot of things," he acknowledges matter-of-factly, "and I've learned from all of them, I've gleaned a lot of experience. But it hasn't been easy. It hasn't been easy to find that thing that's going to replace—well, you're never going to replace it."

The "it" can mean a lot of things: the sheer kinaesthetic pleasure of playing well, the giddy thrill of victory, the adrenalin rush of the crowd, the ego satisfaction of fan and media attention, the Memorial Cup, the Stanley Cup, the honour and pride and mystique of playing for your country. "It" can be addictive. Or "it" can simply mean the hockey life, which Ellis describes as "a world within itself":

"See, when you're playing hockey, you're told when to get up, when to get on the bus, when the plane leaves—it's all looked after. When that's all over, there's a *lot* of adjustment. A lot of guys have never had to get themselves up in the morning and put eight hours a day into a job, and all of a sudden they've got to do it. It takes a disciplined person.

"And there's adjustment within the family. Dad's at home now. And all of a sudden—in our era anyhow, before the million-dollar salaries—you're on a budget, spending's got to be cut back. And some wives don't like that. It creates a lot of *stuff*. And all of our team alumnis, and the NHL Players Association, are starting programs to help players make the adjustment, and help players who get into trouble. You have to be a pretty unique individual not to have any problems, especially if you played as long as I did."

There have been dark moments in Ellis's troubled transition from hockey to what he calls "real life." Doctors have told him he was close to a nervous breakdown a couple of times; his family, friends and faith have seen him through. Now, not really suffering financially, yet feeling he's still adjusting, still in transition, he's withdrawn from the world a little. With their two children grown up, he and Jan have moved to their condo in quiet Collingwood north of Orangeville, a place on a golf course at the foot of a ski hill.

"We're happy there now," Ron Ellis says, and gives a sheepish little laugh—as if he never expected to hear himself saying it.

TWELVE

TEAM UGLY IN NO MAN'S LAND

"We all knew the fun had vanished from the series.
All-out war stared us in the face."

— PAUL HENDERSON, *Shooting for Glory*

●

The two teams have now completely reversed everyone's expectations of them, including their own. Their contrasting mental states are mirrored in their behaviour at the series' midpoint.

The Soviets are pleased with their performance so far. Preparing to leave Vancouver, they take advantage of a last chance to enjoy themselves in the fleshpots of the West. The team management takes the players for some good clean wholesome fun at the Vancouver Aquarium and the whale pool in Stanley Park. Lest the Soviet athletes become overstimulated, however, they're left behind in their hotel rooms while their officials, accompanied by a chaperone from the Department of External Affairs, go out to sample some nightlife.

They hit a nightclub—which first has to be checked out for security risks by the R.C.M.P. and city police—to watch a floor show featuring strippers and four drag queens known as the Fabulous Fakes. Asked by the Soviets through their interpreter who those "women" are, the club owner replies, "They're Russian draft dodgers." The Soviets crack up. When they depart after midnight, they've knocked back $200 worth of champagne but left only $11 in tips. Perhaps to keep their players in the dark about their little adventure, the officials had told the press they were going straight home after the game because, "There's nothing to do in Vancouver."

For Team Canada, there are neither whales nor strippers: it's a time of bitterness, reproach and martyrdom. Esposito's impassioned speech on national television has given the players heart, a commodity they'll need in abundance in the days ahead, but some of them aren't content to let his eloquence speak for them. They try to ape Esposito in their comments to the media; coming out of their mouths, the effect, to put it politely, is less persuasive: "I'm ashamed to be a Canadian," Bill Goldsworthy is quoted in the papers as saying. "After listening to those (censored) fans, I'm disgusted. You go out on the ice and you're afraid of making a mistake, because if you do, you'll get booed."

The self-pity metre hits heights not formerly associated with tough, tight-lipped hockey heroes. Brad Park lisps plaintively, "Look, I don't need this. I've got a wife and new baby at home, and I could be spending this time with them, but we thought we'd really be doing something playing for Canada. And this is the thanks we get. We have more loyal fans in New York."

Alan Eagleson puts an official Team Canada imprimatur on the whining by condemning the boos during the pre-game warmup and uttering a threat: "If a similar series is played in the future, and I have anything to do with it, no game will be played in Vancouver." He'll make good on it, too: no Canada Cup game is played there until 1984, twelve years later.

When the players go for beers after Game 4, a few of them confront their detractors face-to-face. In a downtown Vancouver hotel, the more foolhardy patrons hurl insults at Phil Esposito, Goldsworthy, Cashman and Jean-Paul Parise. Esposito remembers that serious trouble is narrowly averted when he restrains Cashman and Goldsworthy from going after their tormentors.

But nobody reacts quite as Frank Mahovlich does. First, after checking into the room he shared at the Bayshore Inn with Serge Savard, the Big M began tapping walls and peering behind drapes to look for electronic bugs. Then, according to Montreal *Gazette* columnist Ted Blackman, Mahovlich warned his coach, "Watch it,

Harry. Be prepared for anything. This is a Cold War, you know. A Cold War." Perhaps this explains his own unusual approach to stopping Tretiak.

Mahovlich has another original idea. When Team Canada mounts its assault on Moscow in twelve days' time, he suggests to Savard, the players shouldn't stay in the city. Instead, like Napoleon's soldiers in 1812, they should lodge in a tent encampment outside the capital.

When Savard ventures to inquire why that would be a sound plan, Mahovlich replies, "Don't you think they might just start a construction project outside our hotel room at four o'clock in the morning? Just to ruin our sleep?"

"Most of the guys aren't in by that time," Savard jokes.

"Don't laugh. You don't realize what this series means to them for propaganda purposes. They'll do anything. We should buy some tents."

Savard isn't sure whether Mahovlich is putting him on. But a couple of days later, after the players have dispersed homeward for a break before flying to Sweden for a week of practices and two exhibition games, Frank's doctor decides he shouldn't make the trip overseas.

Eagleson phones Sinden at home in Rochester, New York, to break the news: "Frank is too keyed up about this thing and needs a rest." Reflecting on how personally Mahovlich has taken the series, and how troubled he's been by the defeats, Sinden isn't really surprised. He remembers Mahovlich telling him that if somebody gave the Soviets a football, they'd master the game and win the Super Bowl in two years. Still, Mahovlich's retreat is just another problem the coach doesn't need.

Wishing he'd picked a smaller team, Sinden realizes he should have brought all thirty-five players to camp, then cut them down to twenty for the series; but he didn't want to embarrass any of them by sending them home after they'd sacrificed a month of holidays. However, Team Canada's underachieving means he'll definitely have to abandon his promise to play everyone. To come from behind and win this war on enemy territory, he'll need the best possible troops. And he's ready to take the consequences: "Even though it might hurt some of the other guys' feelings, when we get to

Sweden I'm going to concentrate on the guys who will be playing in Russia, basically the guys who won for us in Toronto last week."

Harry Sinden is hardening. He has bigger problems than a few oversized egos. He has begun to entertain severe doubts about his team's chances of winning the games to come. On leaving Canada, assistant coach Boris Kulagin comments that the Canadians are the equal of the Soviets. "I'm glad he feels that way," Sinden says to himself, "because at this moment I'm not sure I do."

●

On September 12, after three days' rest, the players reunite in Toronto. They fly to Stockholm in two different aircraft: one via Paris, the other via Frankfurt. Ron Ellis remembers their departure as "the lowest point of the series." When the players board the two aircraft to begin the long, unfamiliar journey to lands where they have never been, and which some of them have no desire to visit, only a handful of well-wishers gather at the airport to see them off.

So much in the public eye for weeks, the players feel strangely forgotten now, abandoned. Still rankling in their breasts are charges by Pierre Berton and Charles Templeton on their syndicated radio show that the Canadians played dirty. Still ringing in their ears, like the hollow boos in the Pacific Coliseum, are the words of Eric Whitehead from page one of the Vancouver *Province*: after "this long week of humiliation," Whitehead wrote, "it is already plain that the upstart Soviets play a sounder, better, and more exciting hockey than is seen in the National Hockey League." And the even more searing words of the dean of Toronto sportswriters, Milt Dunnell, in the *Star* after Game 4: "Last night, as the last air escaped from the punctured balloon of a national ego, it had the angry sound of disappointment, disillusionment and—excuse the word—almost contempt."

The players can only shake their heads in bitter bafflement. As backup goalie Eddie Johnston will remark later to Scott Morrison, author of *The Days Canada Stood Still*, Canadian hockey fans might be used to booing when their team doesn't live up to expectations, but this is a different story: Team Canada is representing *them*. To boo your own representatives in this series, Johnston suggests, is like booing your army in wartime.

Somewhat to their surprise, the players feel relieved to be putting home behind them. Even as they fly into the unknown, at least they're getting away from the unrelenting pressure, the unforgiving criticism. And perhaps the fans feel some relief, too. For the next few days, we can all take a break from our mounting identity crisis and come to grips with a sobering fact: not that Team Canada has played so atrociously in the series, but that the Soviets have played so amazingly well.

•

Canadians tend to think we're invisible to the rest of the world. But as Team Canada soon discovers, the Swedish people hold fast to a vividly clear image of Canadian hockey players: an image of violent goons. The stereotype was created years earlier when hardrock senior teams from towns like Sudbury, Kimberly, Lethbridge, Penticton and Trail used to routinely and literally clobber European national teams on their way to World's and Olympic titles, then act like some occupying army when they went on a tear to celebrate. The stereotype has long been fostered and reinforced by the Swedish media, surviving even through the era of Father Bauer's national team of relatively gentlemanly college boys.

At first, the media in Stockholm lay off the cliché while making a fuss about the arrival of the NHL stars. The two exhibition games against the Swedish nationals, to be played back to back on the weekend, are meant as highlights of the fiftieth-anniversary celebrations of hockey in Sweden. For the Canadians, the week-long visit has been planned as a bit of a holiday, combined with a learning opportunity—to acclimatize themselves to the larger international ice surface and to European officiating before resuming the series in Moscow. But Team Canada has no idea yet just how big a learning opportunity it will be.

Adapting to the large ice surface—which Pat Stapleton likens to "Lake Erie with a roof over it"—is only the beginning. In fact, it's the easy part. Although they will cause problems for the slow of foot, the spacious wings and cavernous corners created by the extra twelve feet in width are a godsend for Canadian speedsters like Cournoyer and Henderson, and for a sharpshooter like Esposito.

For the netminders, one of the differences is the European goal crease—a semicircle instead of the (at that time) North American rectangle. Ken Dryden, who is reading the novel *Deliverance* by James Dickey during his off-hours, finds the half-moon shape helpful in keeping him farther back in the net; in a short intrasquad game he doesn't allow any goals. And although Dryden won't play either game in Sweden, the practice will stand him in good stead in Moscow, where at times his team will have to rely on him for deliverance.

In the games themselves, the NHLers find the Swedish style of play almost as repugnant as the Swedes find theirs. Instead of using the body to hit, the Swedes use the stick to spear and butt-end. Instead of dropping their gloves and fighting toe to toe, they make sneak attacks behind an opponent's back. Instead of attending hockey school, they seem to have attended drama school. The Swedes are as irritating as woollen underwear.

In his notes, Sinden terms the host team "sneaks, and dirty hockey players." Watching from the stands, Dryden, as objective an observer as exists on Team Canada, concurs: "It was immediately obvious that the Swedes had not changed one iota since the last time I played against them. They are terribly frustrating to play; indeed, it's impossible not to become emotional. Swedes are justifiably known for their melodrama on the ice, particularly for the way they take dives."

The Canadians repeatedly and foolishly fall into the traps the Swedes set for them. In the two games, Canadian penalties outnumber Swedish ones 19-6. They include ten-minute misconducts to Phil Esposito and Goldsworthy, and a five-minute major to Hadfield. It's a clash between different hockey cultures, and nowhere is this more obvious than in the officiating. The two referees are those same West Germans who will soon cause Team Canada such grief in Moscow: Franz Baader and Josef Kompalla.

It's difficult not to conclude that Sinden has inadequately prepared his players psychologically for what to expect from the officiating, and how to respond to it. Having played internationally, he ought to know the marked differences between European and

NHL standards for sending a man to the penalty box. But he only blames the "incompetence" of Baader and Kompalla for allowing two essentially meaningless, so-called friendly matches to deteriorate into brutality, bitterness and mutual recrimination.

In his diary of the series, Dryden comments with some justification: "It's about time we stop bitching about European referees. . . . We knew that European referees would be handling the games in Stockholm and Moscow, and we accepted that fact. Now we should accept the consequences and adjust accordingly."

But Team Canada doesn't have Dryden's calm rationality or worldly common sense. The bitching won't stop: no more than the hockey culture clash will stop. It will go on until the final moments of the final game in Moscow, and it will originate at the very top of the Team Canada hierarchy and inevitably filter down to the foot soldiers, pushing them to extremes of behaviour that are already causing some observers in Stockholm to dub them "Team Ugly."

At least they win the first exhibition game, 4-1. Neither side plays brilliantly. The Swedes are tentative, perhaps a little awed to be playing the stars of the NHL, even though their roster contains several names that will soon become familiar either in the NHL or the WHA: Borje Salming, Inge Hammarstrom, Ulf Nilsson, Anders Hedberg. Many of the Canadians, meanwhile, are still rusty, needing time to find their legs on the unfamiliarly large rink. But they come on strong towards the end of the game, and Sinden is grateful for that. "We needed the win because we hadn't won since Toronto," he notes realistically, "and it would really put us down to be beaten by Sweden."

Team Canada returns after the game to the Grand Hotel, a stately old building on the water near the royal palace, only to find it surrounded by police vehicles. A local television station has received a threat that a bomb will be detonated at midnight inside the Canadians' hotel. The team has to wait outside with the other guests until the hotel is searched. Resigned to their unpopularity in Stockholm, the tired players hang around in the cool night air for two hours until they receive the all-clear: it was a false alarm.

The next day, Sunday, the Swedish press is back to calling the Canadians animals. And in that night's exhibition match, the two teams are even surlier to each other than before. The nastiest incident occurs near the end of the first period. With Wayne Cashman closing in on him against the boards, Ulf Sterner, Sweden's leading forward, who previously had an unsuccessful tryout with the New York Rangers, jabs his stick blade into the Canadian's mouth and opens up a two-inch gash down the length of his tongue. When coach Sinden sees the team doctor, Jim Murray, examining Cashman's mouth on the bench, "I nearly vomited on the spot. His tongue was just dangling. . . . I couldn't believe there wasn't a penalty." Although he wants to get at Sterner, Cashman is taken off to the dressing room for stitches.

Eddie Johnston plays brilliantly to keep Canada in the game. At the end of the second period, with the Canadians leading 2-1 on goals by Hadfield and Awrey, the two teams converge on the runway coming off the ice. Phil Esposito and the Swedish coach get into a yelling match, questioning each other's manliness quotient, then a shoving match. Cashman, in street clothes by now and unable to speak or swear, tries to get in on the act. Other players follow their coach's lead and ridicule the referees. Finally Sinden and Ferguson herd their charges towards the dressing room.

But the ugliness isn't over. Photographers come swarming along the runway, eager to capture the Canadians living up perfectly to the Swedes' caricature of them. Some of the Canadian players who haven't dressed for the game snatch at the photographers' cameras. The police arrive with leashed dogs. Before the whole thing blows up further into a major diplomatic incident, Sinden and Ferguson hustle everybody inside the dressing room, slam the door and try to calm the players down.

With some of the reserves getting their chance to play, Team Canada blows a one-goal lead three times and eventually falls behind 4-3 in the third period. A little over five minutes remain when Hadfield is run into the boards from the rear. Incensed, he retaliates against Lars-Erik Sjoberg with a high stick, cutting his nose. Sjoberg collapses in a stricken heap. As the fans scream for Hadfield's head, Sjoberg hams it up shamelessly: he waves off the trainer and skates exhibitionistically around the ice, displaying his bleeding nose for all to see. Sjoberg skates past Hadfield, now sitting in the penalty box with a five-minute major, and waves at him while pointing to his nose. For his final act, Sjoberg leaves the ice to wild cheering, brandishing a bloodied towel, and poses heroically for the photographers at the bottom of the runway.

Mercifully, Phil Esposito averts the ultimate embarrassment for Canada: he scores a short-handed goal to tie the game 4-4 in the dying seconds. Sinden calls the whole thing "a nightmare." He also knows Esposito was a mile offside when he took Dale Tallon's pass for the goal, but this time he silently thanks the referees for their incompetence.

The next day, the Swedish newspapers have a field day with front-page photographs of Sjoberg and his prize nose, but none, strangely enough, of Cashman's devastated tongue. The Bruins' bad boy has to be hospitalized overnight. His tongue has swollen so badly that he has difficulty breathing; he can't eat and must be fed intravenously. Other photographs show Canadian players in various postures of assault on their poor defenceless Swedish opponents.

Ulf Sterner actually has a byline story in one of the papers, calling the Canadians by the Swedes' favourite epithet, "gangsters." And to add insult to injury, the Canadian ambassador, Margaret Meagher, who has earlier thrown a reception for the players at her swank residence, now dumps on Team Canada for the way they've been playing. Undeterred by rank or gender, R. Alan Eagleson dumps right back.

It's hard to believe any good could come from all this angst and acrimony; yet it does. The fact is, nothing unites people in a common cause like being attacked. Ask any former Team Canada member today, and he'll point to Sweden as the crucial turning point in the team's evolution—the moment when this motley collection of disparate individuals begin to bond, to transcend their old NHL loyalties and personal rivalries and feel a gut conviction that they're in this thing together, with nobody to turn to but each other. As Ron Ellis will say, it's "fifty against the world."

Some players no longer even feel they represent "Canada"—that abstract and increasingly remote entity that seems to have disowned them. They don't like the rumours they keep hearing from home, rumours that Canadians have begun to agree with the Swedes that they're animals, goons, gangsters. One columnist, Pierre Gobeil of

Montréal Matin, has written of their performance in Sweden, "I am ashamed to be a Canadian." Well, to hell with them all.

The members of Team Canada hang out together in the Grand Hotel, take meals together, go out to bars together. (Sinden tells them not to wear their team blazers: no point further attracting the unwelcome interest of drunks, journalists and photographers.) Many of the players have never travelled outside North America before. Feeling self-conscious and out of place, they build a reassuring sense of security through bonding with each other. Sure, they drink too hard and stay out too late, but the next day at practice they go all out as Sinden and Ferguson drive them through the heaviest skating drills of the series so far. They put their backs into it, leaving the ice an exhausted but happier crew.

Sinden is pleased. He notices the players are actually starting to *like* one another—a definite change, given how they've been conditioned for years to fear and loathe their NHL enemies. Dozens of small grudges and large hatreds have built up over the seasons. It's well known, for instance, that Park and Phil Esposito couldn't stand the sight of each other before now. Not even the coaches are exempt: just about everybody detests "the big bad Bruins," who got that way playing under Harry Sinden; and John Ferguson, who stopped playing only the previous season, had a tendency to beat up everyone who crossed his path. But now that the players are facing hardship and ostracism, they're pulling together.

Or almost together. The malcontents are still malcontented. Getting farther away from home doesn't improve their attitude. Other players, too, even some who will play key roles in the games in Moscow, have come to Eagleson to voice complaints about the way the team is being managed and coached—to the point where they're worried (like Sinden himself) about their prospects of winning the series. Eagleson tells them he understands; he knows they need "to get some bitching out of their system." But after the two exhibition games, complaints are still rife, so Eagleson calls a team meeting to clear the air and put the problems to rest once and for all.

First he lets the players talk—indeed, encourages them to talk, to get all the pent-up frustration and anger out of their systems in a collective catharsis of sorts. Then he adopts a nautical metaphor in laying down the law about their future relationships to each other and the team: "We're in a leaky boat that's going down," Eagleson tells them, in his own paraphrase of the event. "If enough of us get to the goddamn oars and start rowing and the other guys start bailing, we're going to make it. But if we start hitting each other over the head with the paddles, we're going down—and we're all going down together. So if you don't want to get to the shore with us, get the hell out of the boat!"

It's a message they desperately need to hear. Whatever his other excesses in '72 and his later international hockey dealings, Eagleson does Team Canada, and the country, the immense service of demanding the players act like adults. And they, in turn, have a demand of their own: to be treated like adults. They ask coaches and management to leave the room for a few minutes so they can discuss a matter dear to their hearts. There has been talk that plans to have the players' wives and girlfriends meet them in Moscow may be cancelled. So the players confer among themselves and decide they won't stand for this curtailment of their rights: patriotism has its limits.

As Phil Esposito remembers it, they believe they have Eagleson and Sinden over a barrel. This is an issue worth going to the wall for: if necessary, they will simply refuse to continue the series and go back home. "We all stuck together and told Eagleson that that was it. And right then and there is when we became a real unified group."

Two other positive events occur near the end of the stay in Sweden. Frank Mahovlich rejoins the team on his doctor's OK. And, as planned before the trip, part of the team is bused up to Sodertalje, a town just north of Stockholm, to work out in the local arena. Some 4,000 people turn out to watch the Canadians practise—and this after the two exhibition games have left so many raw feelings. There are plenty of kids in the crowd, and the players ham it up for them. Tall Peter Mahovlich kneels down to face off against little Marcel Dionne. Guy Lapointe weaves up and down the ice like a drunk on skates. They scrimmage against a local peewee team, clown around with the kids, give them hockey tips and sign autographs.

As they leave the ice in Sodertalje, the Canadians receive a prolonged, appreciative cheer. It feels like the first time they've been loved in ages.

THIRTEEN

GAME 5: BEYOND HOPE

"We had to play those fellows in Russia now—
someplace where I really didn't want to go."
— PHIL ESPOSITO, 1989

●

Phil Esposito has little appetite for a jaunt to the USSR, he'll tell Ken Dryden years later for the television documentary *Home Game*. But for 3,000 Canadian hockey fanatics, it's the trip of a lifetime. They're raring to cheer the boys on against the Russkies, and they've plunked down hard cash for the privilege.

Dryden will characterize his teammates as "babes in the world," unaccustomed to moving through alien cultures. The same description can be applied to the visiting fans. Twenty planeloads of them arrive in Moscow one day before the team's arrival. From both sides of the great Canadian language divide, most of them are hockey nuts, pure and simple—plain folks from Kamloops and Corner Brook, Chicoutimi and Charlottetown, Trois-Rivières and Toronto, with a few honorary Canadians from Boston and New York thrown in, waving tiny Canadian flags for the occasion.

For most of them, this is their first trip outside North America. At times, when no hockey game or state-sponsored guided tour is scheduled, it will seem they can't find much to do besides frequenting Moscow's "dollar bars"—establishments accepting foreign currency, to which tourists are confined if they want to drink. But in

truth, these hockey tourists are a kind of elite in 1972: not only witnesses to the greatest international hockey series in history, but
adventurers who actually step behind the Iron Curtain and return
home to tell about it.

In 1972, the world is starkly polarized. Communism and capitalism are competing for the souls of humanity. The Soviet Union is a
Marxist nuclear superpower, a source of menacing images and imag-
inings for the West, its missiles aimed at the hearts of our cities—in
our worst nightmares, the potential source of our very destruction.
For decades, we've educated our children to believe in the Communist Threat. So, like any bogeyman, the Soviets have come to
resemble something darkly malevolent, scarcely human. Now a few
thousand Canadians armed only with maple-leaf pins and hangovers
will be the shock troops who stare those Communists square in the
face. The rest of us will make do with television.

In fact, Team Canada's televised invasion of Moscow is a major
breakthrough in the psychology of East-West relations. For the first
time, a mass North American audience will see beyond our stock
images of the Evil Empire, glimpsing something more than the
usual footage of intercontinental ballistic missiles parading past
stony-faced Kremlin leaders on May Day. The largest audiences in
Canada's broadcast history will witness a sustained series of events
occurring within those heavily guarded borders—events being
watched simultaneously by actual Soviet *people*. And even if those
events are confined largely to a hockey arena, at least the experience
will be shared, for once, by Soviets and Westerners alike. Detente
takes many forms. Hockey will provide the common ground on
which two peoples will meet and tentatively begin to know one
another, in however symbolic and fragmentary and fleeting a way.

Of course, the Soviets have already had *their* glimpses into our
own fair dominion—and the full-throated partisan conduct of our
hockey crowds, so much more demonstrative than their own. The
glimpses have been mediated through their state-controlled television and the wry, politically tinged observations of commentator
Nikolai Ozerov, whose custom is to announce the play-by-play
from rinkside. Foster Hewitt, Ozerov's counterpart in Canada,
leaves politics out of it while in Moscow, confining his comments to

hockey. And yet the four games broadcast from the Soviet Union are not without their implicit political subtext.

The games are beamed to Canadians via satellite on the wings of those pervasive messengers of capitalism, television commercials. Detente on Ice is brought to us by the bankers, the car makers and the brewers.

Revisiting the melodic mantras of the '72 telecasts, one realizes how North America's revolution of rising expectations is still rising that year. In the commercials, all is sweetness and light, ease and affluence and upward mobility. The bankers at Toronto Dominion send the musical message, "It's people who make our country grow, People who have a happy glow." Beautiful innocent young "tellers" with fashionably long ironed hair, one blonde, the other brunette, inform us, "There's a new way to borrow at the TD Bank." Other sponsors thoughtfully advise us what to borrow for: Mercury Cougars and Ford LTDs with grotesquely elongated snouts and living-room-sized interiors; or Zenith Chromacolor television sets with massive wooden consoles, altars before which the whole wholesome family—kids included—are served drinks by faithful servant Mom.

The mood is determinedly middle-class, uniformly angst-free and pre-feminist. A housewife gamely hefts paper bags brimming with groceries into the back seat of her Ford Maverick, earnestly observing, "My husband works hard for his money!" And heaven knows, after us guys have slaved away to pay for our suburban toys and mortgages, plus the interest on those helpful loans, we've earned the right to a little fun. Some hot-air ballooning, maybe, since "When you're smiling, Blue smiles right along with you." Or simply tanking up at the lake with some fellow volleyballers and bikini-clad beach bunnies who love nothing better than to soak up the sunshine and "Take five for 50 Ale, my friends, Take five for 50 Ale!" Ah, the Good Life—all here for the taking, no matter what the final score. The Baby Boomers haven't yet learned to worry about the deficit, AIDS, middle age, downsizing or death. Only, perhaps, the Bomb.

But for the moment, hockey is everyone's surrogate for world conflict. Even the brewing giants who share Canada's cozy beer oligopoly come to unseemly blows over sponsorship of the series. It all happens because the Soviets are learning to profit by selling rink advertising. Along with board ads for Heineken, Hitachi, Ski-Doo, CCM, Gillette, Ford, Jockey underwear, Turtle Wax and a product with the unlikely name of Stimorol, the Soviets sell a centre-ice spot to Molson's for $25,000. What they don't realize is that Labatt's has already purchased advertising rights on Canadian television for many times that amount, and the free market isn't as free as the West likes to claim. Labatt's pulls a few strings, and Molson's clever deal to beam its name around the world for peanuts at Labatt's expense is undone. It will take the Soviets a while to learn the rules of playing the capitalist game; they'll get it eventually.

•

As they wander the airports of Europe, Harry Sinden and his band of NHL refugees are more or less oblivious to all this. Having passed through the cleansing fire of Stockholm, they arrive in Moscow on the evening of September 20 with other things on their minds.

They're met at the airport by Canadian ambassador Robert Ford and whisked through customs in record time on order of the Soviet authorities. Sitting in the bus on their way downtown in darkness, the players receive their first, murky impressions of Moscow: grim blank-faced apartment blocks, decrepit truck and car traffic, institutional building complexes—one of which houses Anatoly Tarasov's old haunt, the Central Army sports club.

Team Canada is staying at the Hotel Intourist, a modern twenty-two-storey structure reserved for foreign visitors. The Intourist comes closer to Western standards than any other Moscow hotel, although that's not saying much. It's just easier for the state to keep an eye on foreigners if they're restricted to certain places—another being the less comfortable Metropole nearby.

In the brightness of the Intourist lobby, the players find their wives and girlfriends waiting—their reward for having hung together in solidarity in Stockholm. Sinden notes how excited the guys are "about seeing some 'friendly' faces from home." At least, he adds sarcastically, he doesn't *think* the wives have copped out on the team yet.

Whether proximity to loved ones helps or hinders an athlete's performance is an old debate. It's notable, for example, that the Soviet players travelled to Canada unaccompanied. But on balance, the wives' presence in Moscow will give Team Canada a badly needed boost. By Game 5, the players will have been in Europe for ten days, living under unfamiliar conditions and subjected to intense scrutiny and pressure, which will only increase over the next week. Most are glad to have their wives there to share the stress of living behind enemy lines and adapting to strange customs, hard beds and a shortage of Cokes. Practically speaking, it will work out particularly well: the couples can stay settled and relatively relaxed since, unlike the Canadian half of the series, all four games are being played in one city.

It was initially thought the Soviet part of the series would also be played in different cities, but the Soviets decided playing all four games in Moscow would give them another advantage, since their national team is based there. As it turns out, it's an advantage for Team Canada too. Not only does it give the Canadian players some needed emotional stability and focus, but it also keeps the hockey adjustments to a minimum—confined to the peculiarities of one arena. At their practice on the morning of September 21, the Canadians get their first look inside the Luzhniki Arena, where the games will be played. The 15,000-seat rink is just one of the facilities of the Lenin Sports Complex, a huge development that also contains swimming pools, tennis and basketball courts, a 100,000-seat soccer stadium and two bandy rinks.

While the Soviet team practises, the Canadians are shown to their dressing rooms—not one room, but three small ones connected by a corridor, including a room for the coaches. In a homey welcoming touch, the arena staff has provided apples, grapes and bottles of mineral water. The players pass up an invitation to take a dip in the communal pool; the water doesn't appear to have been changed since Christmas.

Out on the rink, their first surprise is the ice itself. It's much thicker than North American ice, nearly three inches instead of three-quarters of an inch; and the thicker ice is, the harder and bumpier it becomes, with a tendency to chip and flake. The other immediately noticeable difference is at either end of the rink. In place of shatterproof Plexiglas, wire-mesh netting runs above the boards. Immediately the players begin testing the mesh, firing shots against it to see how they rebound. The material is so flexible that it has a slingshot effect; some of the pucks carom all the way out to the blueline before hitting the ice. "You wait and see," Peter Mahovlich remarks prophetically, "that mesh is going to cost someone a goal."

The players take a while to get the feel of the ice. Then the lines and defense pairings that will play in Game 5 the next night work on line rushes. The ones who won't be playing—"the Black Aces"—work out last. When Sinden forms them up into lines, he unaccountably leaves one man out, and it just happens to be Vic Hadfield.

Sinden insists it's a memory lapse, not a deliberate slight. But to Hadfield, who has been burning since being left out of Game 2 in Toronto, and has now been further displaced on left wing by Frank Mahovlich's return, not being assigned to a line in practice is the last straw. He stands by the boards in a deepening funk. Finally he asks John Ferguson to intercede with Sinden for him. Realizing what he's done, Sinden tells Ferguson to tell Hadfield to take turns with the other spare left wings, but by this time it's too late. Ferguson returns bearing Hadfield's reply: "I don't have to take this crap."

Sinden leaves Ferguson in charge of the practice and skates over to deal with Hadfield, who is now sitting on the bench, ostentatiously reading a newspaper. The ensuing dialogue, as reported by Sinden, is worth quoting for what it shows about Team Canada's coach. An NHL coach today would be likelier to use a little psychology in persuading one of his millionaire superstars to cooperate. But Team Canada isn't paying Hadfield's salary, and Sinden doesn't have a long-term relationship to nurture with him, just a simple, short-term job to do: win for his country.

Sinden: "I think you should be out there practising. Your sitting there like that seems kind of silly."

Hadfield: "I'm not going to."

Sinden: "Then you might as well take your stuff off. There's no point in you just sitting there and making all of us look foolish." [The Soviet players are watching attentively from the stands, along with coaches from all over the USSR attending a coaching clinic scheduled to coincide with the visit of "the professionals."]

Hadfield: "Why did you bring me here?"

Sinden: "Like everyone else, I brought you to play hockey. Like everyone else, Vic, the players decide who plays on this team."

Hadfield: "You mean the players voted, or something?"

Sinden: "No. I mean a player determines who plays by the way he plays."

With those plain words, the last he'll exchange with Hadfield, Sinden skates back to the practice. Quite deliberately, he hasn't made it any easier for the Rangers' star to swallow his pride.

Hadfield turns to Eagleson with a request to return home. Eagleson relays this to Sinden. "Fine," the coach replies. "Get him on the first plane out of here."

After practice, Rick Martin, who has seen action only in one game in Sweden, tells Sinden he wants to get back to the Buffalo Sabres' training camp. He's worried about not working himself into shape soon enough. Sinden knows this is a phony excuse: Martin is in far better shape for having practised with Team Canada for the past six weeks. So the coach says simply, "We'll have you on the first plane out of here."

And when Jocelyn Guevremont says the same thing later that day about returning to the Vancouver Canucks, Sinden is in danger of repeating himself: "I'd be happy if you get out of here as quickly as you can."

No ambivalence about Harry Sinden.

Instead he feels, along with anger, a powerful sense of relief and vindication. The defectors are not only rats leaving a ship they fear is sinking but rats carrying "a potentially fatal disease which could spread through the whole squad if I let them stay around." Hadfield has been griping to his good buddy Dennis Hull, for instance, but Hull has hung in there and says he's staying. If only Sinden can rid his overblown team of all the naysayers infecting their teammates with the virus of doubt about their ability to win, Team Canada still has a chance.

Others among the Black Aces take a very different attitude. Ron Ellis remembers some of the players who don't get into the series at all, such as Brian Glennie or Dale Tallon, as being "100 per cent behind the team the whole time." Backup goaltender Eddie Johnston tells his teammates after Hadfield's decision, "We've got one guy who's quitting, some other guys talking about quitting. Why don't you all quit right now?" Johnston believes the team doesn't need any more problems; they need to be drawing closer together as the series progresses, not drifting apart.

With the malcontents falling away, those who remain will be the loyalists: charter members of a renewed, tighter, tougher, more ruthless Team Canada, preparing for the battle—and the glory—of their careers. Most of them feel as Ken Dryden does when Hadfield, Martin and Guevremont come around to say good-bye later that day at the hotel: "I don't understand how a player can leave. Sure, I'm certain some people are hurt and disappointed that they have not been playing, but at the same time what can they gain by going home? . . . To me it seems incomprehensible."

●

The Soviets, meanwhile, are basking in the familiarity of home. After their return to Moscow, coach Bobrov allows his players the unprecedented liberty of taking a break from training to visit their wives and families. This would never have been permitted under Tarasov. It suggests a degree of freedom, and of confidence, that's only possible after the team's performance in Canada.

Indeed, some of the Soviets have begun to indulge the giddy feeling that they can bring off a coup after all: dethroning the monarchs of hockey on their very first attempt. Having prepared so thoroughly for the series, having secured every possible advantage for themselves in the negotiations, having kept a book on every Canadian player and tactic, now further documented by the experience of four games, and having lost only one of those matches, the Soviets wonder how they can possibly do any worse playing on home ice before their home fans and with European referees. The Soviets cannot escape their own logic: they will be even stronger now, whereas the prima donna professionals will be at an even greater disadvantage so far from home.

As Vladislav Tretiak has said, "We knew that in Moscow, in our own rink, we could not lose. This was our fatal mistake." And Tretiak cannot help but defer longingly to the wisdom of his wily old mentor: "If Tarasov had been our coach, he would have noticed our over-confidence. But Bobrov wasn't very experienced as a coach and he didn't see that our team was 'swimming in glory.' We weren't training as hard as before."

This is not apparent to the outside world. The Soviet public itself looks forward to the next four games with huge anticipation, all the more so since their team's successes in Canada; many doubted they could win against the famous professionals, and the hockey authorities were careful to keep expectations low, to avoid political embarrassment. An estimated fifty million people across the fifteen republics of the vast USSR will watch the games on television. Those viewers number more than twice the population of Canada at the time, and over 20 per cent of the Soviet population of 242 million. Allowing for the fact that there are fewer TV sets per household, this makes hockey almost as popular per capita in the USSR as in Canada, where the viewing audience for the different games runs from a third to over half of the population.

The visiting Canadians are far from unknown to Soviet hockey fans. Like fifteen-year-old Igor Kuperman, many were keenly aware of big-name NHL stars even before the series started. The Soviet hockey public also knows Team Canada is missing the talents of two of its best players. The Russian program prepared for the series mentions that "the great player Bobby Orr" has had a knee operation and "the great player Bobby Hull" has moved to "a new division."

Tickets for the games are at a premium. People line up all night to buy them, just as housewives queue up in the daytime for bread or meat or sugar. At first, scalpers get ten rubles a seat, but as excitement over the series mounts, the price rises to twenty-five and finally a hundred—the better part of a month's salary for an average worker. At the Canadian embassy, Gary Smith finds himself receiving phone calls from senior Soviet bureaucrats whom he normally has difficulty reaching: does he happen to have a pair of tickets for any of the games? He does; and these prized items turn out to be useful pawns in the chess game of international relations.

The Canadian public, meanwhile, is at last rallying behind its team. Telegrams and telexes and postcards bearing thousands upon thousands of names arrive almost hourly from all across Canada, addressed to Team Canada or Harry Sinden or particular players, wishing them well. Some of the mail is delivered in potato sacks tied with baling twine. One wire reads: "Team Canada: We're with you, all of us. Get in there and win. On est vingt-deux millions à vous épauler au fond, Equipe Canada. Pierre Elliott Trudeau."

The effect on the players is heartening. It reinforces the growing resolve they've discovered in Sweden, dissolves some of the bitterness they've been hoarding against their homeland. Phil Esposito reads out to his brother all three hundred names on a telegram from Sault Ste. Marie: "Hey Tony, listen to these! Luigi Bertolli . . . hey, the Frank Corsa trio . . . the guys at Angie Petrella's furniture store . . ."

•

By the evening of September 22, as they pull on their gear for their first game in Moscow, the Canadians have papered whole walls of their dressing rooms at Luzhniki with those messages from home. The sheaves of paper run up and down the corridor, too. And when they skate out onto that alien ice, they can scarcely believe their ears.

In place of the boos of the Pacific Coliseum, in place of the hoots and jeers of Stockholm, the dominant sound of Moscow is the roar of 3,000 Canadians giving tribute: fans hollering encouragement with trumpets blaring, cowbells clanging, noisemakers rattling, maple-leaf flags large and tiny waving, banners unfurling. One banner intended for Pat Stapleton reads "Sarnia's here, Whitey." Another says simply "VANCOUVER." Circling the ice with a wonderfully familiar sensation fluttering in their chests, the Canadian players feel strangely at home.

Tretiak will say it sounds as if he's in a Canadian arena, not a Soviet one. This is partly because Soviet hockey spectators are under orders to behave sedately and circumspectly, partly because so many tickets have been snapped up by Moscow's elite, who aren't necessarily knowledgeable about the game. "Our most passionate hockey fans were not present," Tretiak will tell Ken Dryden. "We felt we were losing to your team as far as the spectators were concerned, even at home. And it was very sad for us."

The teams line up at their bluelines. "O Canada" is belted out with greater volume and emotion than the Soviet anthem. Then Olga Berenova, a lovely young star of the Moscow Ice Ballet, skates out in Russian folk dress and presents tall and handsome Jean Ratelle, one of the Canadian captains, with a freshly baked loaf of rye bread sprinkled with salt—the traditional gift of welcome to visitors from another land. Ratelle leans down and kisses her on the cheek. His spontaneous gesture brings smiles to the stoical Soviet faces in the crowd.

To the jazzy strains of "Midnight in Moscow," forty-four even younger figure skaters, age six to fifteen, file onto the ice, one to each player and coach, and peel off to present both teams with carnations. The individual player introductions begin, visitors first. When the announcer reaches number seven for Team Canada, Phil Esposito—so nervous he's absentmindedly snapped his carnation stem in half—steps forward onto the broken stem, feels his feet going out from under him, and lands flat on his behind.

The Canadian fans cheer Esposito wildly. With gracious aplomb he rises onto one knee, rests his stick on his arm like the lance of some rakish Don Quixote, and makes a sweeping, grandiloquent bow to the crowd. Everyone loves it. The Canadian fans rise in their seats and applaud more loudly. Even the Soviet players crack a smile.

Someday Tretiak will say, "You know, if *I* had fallen down, or any of our players, we would be humiliated and confused. We would never have reacted as Phil Esposito did—like an artist, with such elegance."

And someday Esposito will say that, as he raises his bowed head to the crowd, his eyes run all the way up to the top row and settle on none other than Communist Party boss Leonid Brezhnev, sitting surrounded by militiamen next to Soviet President Nikolai Podgorny and Prime Minister Alexei Kosygin: "And I looked up and he's looking down at me, no smile or anything. And that's when I blew the kiss to him. Like I was saying, 'Up yours, baby. I hate you.' " But all that the crowd in the arena see, or the millions of people watching on television, is the unflappable Esposito grin. And, as Tretiak says, the elegance. Team Canada will need exactly such grace under pressure to win this series.

During the introductions of the Soviet players, the hometown fans cheer each of their stars equally—until they come to number seventeen, Valery Kharlamov, the only one to get an ovation louder than the others. And when the puck is dropped, the Kharlamov-Maltsev-Vikulov line against the Clarke-Henderson-Ellis line, the battle is joined. The hard part begins.

Physically and psychologically, the toughest hockey of the series starts now. Every one of the four remaining games will be too close to call. Every one will be decided by a single goal, and every outcome will hinge not only on skill and strategy but on a witch's brew of hunger, anger, passion and plain old ornery luck.

In this game, at least, officiating will not be an issue. The referees are Uwe Dahlberg of Sweden and Rudy Bata of Czechoslovakia, and they preside with competence and consistency, letting the players play. The teams respond with exciting offensive hockey and without excessive violence. The first period is scoreless for over fifteen minutes. Both sides set up excellent scoring chances, both goalies are superb. Tony Esposito comes up big against Kharlamov and Vladimir Shadrin, receiving on one occasion a crucial assist from the post, and on another some major help from overachieving Stapleton and White, who both end up in the net behind him to block a loose puck. The Canadians stave off intense Soviet pressure while killing off a penalty against Ellis for tripping Maltsev; they stay in their defensive box but keep it looser than usual because of the extra twelve feet of ice between the boards.

As for Tretiak, he doesn't seem to have suffered by being permitted home leave. The young bridegroom commits theft successively on Henderson, Ellis and Frank Mahovlich, who for the moment is playing on a line with Ratelle and Cournoyer. From the start, Henderson is particularly dangerous. Twice in the first period he breaks a play open and feeds Ellis for near-goals, but Ellis can't put the puck past Tretiak.

Team Canada is working hard, applying the lessons learned in the first four games, and especially in the tough workouts in Sweden. Every line and defense pair is putting out. And yet the Soviets are clearly more in control of their game—more confident and self-possessed than ever on this rink. The Canadians are still scrambling, still finding their legs.

Then gradually, they begin loosening up, utilizing the wide-open spaces. They make longer lead passes up ice, forcing the Soviet defenders to stay back, to be more cautious about moving onto the attack. And the more creative Canadian attackers start using the extra space to make some moves.

Inserted late in the period to spell Esposito, Gilbert Perreault takes a pass from Rod Gilbert over the Soviet blueline. Stickhandling masterfully, Perreault carries the puck in deep, keeping it away from the big defenseman Vladimir Lutchenko and two other Soviet defenders, singlehandedly preoccupying them so long that they forget about J.-P. Parise in the slot. Perreault finally passes the puck back to Parise, who bangs it between Tretiak's pads for the first goal.

Although outplayed during the period, Team Canada takes the 1-0 lead into the intermission. "They're going to have to get better," Howie Meeker warns the TV audience back home.

And they do. In the second period, they play as Harry Sinden expected them to play just before the game, when he found his players all fired up and ready to win. In the third minute, Clarke wins the faceoff to the left of Tretiak. The puck goes to Henderson, who gives it right back to Clarke. Using the referee as a post, Clarke bulls in ferociously on goal, shrugs Maltsev off his shoulders, and drills a backhander between Tretiak's skates—a triumph of will as much as skill—for a 2-0 lead.

When Ellis treats Kharlamov a little more rudely against the boards than he recalls today, and Kharlamov retaliates, the pair of them go off with simultaneous penalties. The Soviets prove more adept at playing five a side. For the next two minutes, it's as if they actually have a man advantage, and the Canadians make like penalty killers, even though they're at even strength. Then they have to penalty-kill for real when Bergman goes off for throwing a punch at Kharlamov—the first sign that Team Canada has targeted the Soviet player for a fate nastier than Ellis's close checking.

By the game's midpoint, there has been no more scoring. Battling like underdogs, the Canadians take the play to the Soviets. Their persistence pays off in the twelfth minute. As they press the attack, Gennady Tsygankov manages to block Guy Lapointe's slapshot with his stick, but the puck comes on the rebound right back to

Henderson, and he fires it unerringly between Tretiak and the right post to widen Canada's lead to 3-0.

Henderson is in his element on the big ice. More than once he dashes into the clear behind the Soviet defenders. On his next shift, he outraces the Soviets to the puck and breaks over the blueline with a full head of steam. Just as he's about to get a shot away, Maltsev slashes him from behind, then trips him, and Henderson is spun onto his back. Helplessly, sickeningly, he slides backwards past the net, his velocity carrying him straight into the boards with terrible force. His shoulder blades absorb some of the shock, but his neck and the back of his head take the rest. His head snaps back; he rolls over and collapses onto his face in a heap, unconscious.

Play is halted. The Canadian players converge on Henderson. There's a long, disturbing silence while trainer Joe Sgro tries to bring him around. After Sgro breaks the third ammonia capsule under his nose, Henderson finally comes to. He lies there a minute longer. When it's determined he can stand, Frank Mahovlich takes one arm, Rod Seiling the other, and they skate him down the full length of the ice to the ramp at the far end. At first, Henderson's legs don't move of their own accord; finally they start to shuffle a bit, recovering the memory of skating.

Canada's 3-0 lead stands up till the end of the second period. Between periods, Henderson is crying. Dr. Jim Murray has told him he's suffered a slight concussion and should stay out of the game. Henderson knows all too well how much worse the injury would have been if he hadn't been wearing a helmet, but he doesn't care. He pleads with Sinden, "You've gotta let me play!" Ignoring the doctor's orders, Sinden tells Henderson he can play if he wants to. Then he calls the players into the coaches' room. He instructs them not to sit back in a defensive shell during the third period to protect their lead, but to keep attacking and forechecking; if they hang back, they'll get murdered.

"Let's go out there and score more goals," he exhorts them. "We've just played our best period since Toronto. And you can see they're starting to falter. They're not as sharp as they were."

Not even Harry Sinden can be right all of the time. It takes the Soviets just three and a half minutes to get on the scoreboard.

Canada is pressing in the Soviet zone, the defensemen staying well up as Sinden has ordered, when Vladimir Petrov steals the puck from Stapleton at the blueline and breaks out to centre. Petrov passes up to Yuri Blinov on the left wing, putting him in alone on Esposito. Tony gambles by coming a long way out to challenge Blinov, but as he slides to the ice, trying for a pad save, the Soviet forward simply steps around him and shoots it into the net.

Still, 3-1 isn't a bad lead to enjoy. And just over a minute later, Team Canada reestablishes its three-goal margin. Although Paul Henderson will score some extraordinary goals in this series, the next one, his second of the game, is as extraordinary as they come.

Consider how recently Henderson was knocked out, nearly missing the rest of the game, if not the series, which certainly would have changed the way events unfolded. Yet now he repeats his feat of racing in behind the Soviet defenders—difficult enough at the best of times, much less when you've just suffered a concussion. Clarke spots Henderson streaking up ice and threads a perfect long lead pass diagonally between the two defensemen. Henderson has them beaten; he catches up to the pass at the red line. Harassed from behind all the way, but not tripped this time, Henderson cuts swiftly in on Tretiak and triggers a lightning-fast wrist shot that catches the goaltender backing in, beating him cleanly on the stick side. It's a classic goal—one that Kharlamov and his teammates seemed to have trademarked a couple of games ago.

With only fifteen minutes remaining, Canada's 4-1 lead appears insurmountable. But in fact, it takes the Soviets less than six minutes to demolish it. Their perseverance is never more indefatigable, their consistency never more daunting, their knack for scoring in rapid-fire clusters never more awesome or demoralizing.

First it's Vyacheslav Anisin at 9:05, scoring the kind of goal it would be very difficult to duplicate. With his back to the net, he cleverly redirects Yuri Liapkin's shot from the point between his own legs and past a screened Esposito, making the score 4-2. A mere eight seconds later, before Team Canada has a chance to recover its poise, they strike again: Shadrin firing home a loose puck from right in front. The normally sedate home crowd roars lustily. They're learning from the Canadian fans.

The teams exchange ends at the ten-minute mark. Without pausing for breath, the Soviets just keep on coming. At 11:41, Alexander Gusev stands at the left point, takes a cross-ice pass from Alexander Ragulin at the other point, and aims a high rising slap-shot at the left-hand corner. It hits someone and caroms straight past Esposito, who is again heavily screened. In scarcely more than two and a half minutes, the Soviets have moved from a three-goal deficit to a 4-4 tie.

The game is up for grabs. But there's no question who has the momentum. Team Canada gets a chance for the tie-breaker when Frank Mahovlich zips a centring pass to Ratelle to put him in all alone, but Ratelle hits the post. And although Tony Esposito will fault himself afterwards, he has turned in two periods of outstanding goaltending until now, when he just isn't receiving the protection he needs.

After Esposito makes one more save, Bobby Clarke commits an inexplicable error in judgement. Closely checked against the boards as he comes out of his own zone, Clarke passes back over his own blueline. Rod Seiling steps up to the puck, but Vladimir Vikulov picks his pocket in the blink of an eye. Coming from the left of the Canadian net, Vikulov skates unhindered straight across the goal mouth, drawing Esposito out, and slips a nifty backhander around him for the go-ahead goal at 14:46.

Esposito slams his goalie stick on the ice in disgust—whether out of self-recrimination, or anger at being left so exposed, or just plain frustration at the Soviets' skill. Nothing like this ever happens in the NHL. Sinden will make a telling observation later: he's never seen a team as good as his so completely outplayed.

With five minutes remaining, the Canadians have to go all out for the equalizer. But at this point, they don't have a whole lot left to give. They receive the gift of a man advantage when Yakushev goes off for hooking at 15:48, but their power play fails to exert much pressure.

The Canadians' best opportunity occurs in the final minute. On the ice are the same three forwards who will make history six days later: Cournoyer, Esposito and Henderson. Cournoyer steals the puck from Kharlamov; he zooms in on Tretiak and fires from point-blank range, but Tretiak gets his glove hand on the shot and knocks it away. Recovering the rebound, the Soviets take it all the way back. Petrov almost gets around Tony Esposito, but Esposito, sprawling, stretches his stick out on the ice to block the shot and gathers the puck in to safety. A memorable save: but sadly, too late to make a difference.

By this time, Harry Sinden can feel himself losing control.

As the clock ticks down, it's obvious his players have blown the game and will go down to defeat 5-4. After the lead they had, Sinden fully expected them to win. It's too much. Trembling with anger, he's never felt so helpless in his life. "We're just not destined to win this thing," he'll write later. "No matter what we do, these people beat us."

Sinden goes into the coaches' room. He shuts the door behind him, sees the tray of coffee in little demitasse cups which the arena has provided. He raises a cup to his lips, takes a sip and smashes the cup against the wall.

John Ferguson comes in. The game has ended. There's shattered china on the floor and splattered coffee on Sinden. Sinden doesn't care. He doesn't mind Ferguson seeing him like this, because Fergie shares his frustration, his fury, Fergie understands. But Sinden doesn't want any of his players to see him, and he sure doesn't want to see them: "I would have said the wrong thing. There wasn't any right thing to say after this. I've said all I could for six weeks. They've listened to me enough. Now they've got to come up with their own answers."

FOURTEEN

THE CANADIENS CONNECTION

"The Stanley Cup is something you've dreamt about all
your life, and when you win it for the first time, it's like a
dream come true. In '72, it was like the country come true."
— YVAN COURNOYER, 1995

●

In his hockey classic, *The Game,*
Ken Dryden describes his former coach with the Montreal Canadiens, Scotty Bowman: "He starts each season with a goal—the Stanley Cup—and he has no other. . . . A good season is a Stanley Cup; anything else is not."

That rather simple philosophy—so difficult for most other teams to espouse and still be taken seriously, even before the advent of a twenty-six-team NHL—was second nature to coaches and players in Montreal. If it wasn't, they didn't last long. This was the legacy passed down from Frank Selke, Dick Irvin and Maurice Richard, to Sam Pollock, Toe Blake and Jean Beliveau, to Bowman, Guy Lafleur, Dryden and their teammates in the 1970s. It was a legacy embellished by Blake's five consecutive Cup victories between 1956 and 1960, Bowman's four straight between 1976 and 1979.

Around the time of the '72 Canada-Soviet series, the Canadiens' dominance of the NHL can be measured by the ten Stanley Cups they captured out of a possible fifteen between 1965 and 1979. The series was played at exactly the midpoint of that period. So it isn't surprising that of all NHL teams, Montreal contributed the largest contingent of players to Team Canada—six. They were Dryden, Cournoyer, Lapointe, the Mahovlich brothers and Savard. All were key figures in the core group that accomplished Canada's big win in Game 2, and that stayed more or less intact for the crucial matches in Moscow. Not to mention the role played by their old Montreal teammate, Team Canada assistant coach John Ferguson.

By comparison, Boston, Chicago and New York contributed five players each; Detroit four; and Toronto three. But in all cases, these included one or more who saw action only sparingly in the series, or not at all.

The Habs' prominent presence in Team Canada's line-up ensured that the series was followed as fanatically, and covered as voraciously by the media, in French-speaking Quebec as in English-speaking Canada. The series did more for national unity than a dozen royal commissions and any number of constitutional conferences.

When Canada fell disastrously behind, as it seemed, after Game 5, the team desperately needed to call on the Canadiens' spirit of indomitable pride and dedication to victory. Two carriers of that spirit would play critical roles in the remaining three games: Yvan Cournoyer and Serge Savard, who, between them, own twenty—count them—Stanley Cup rings.

In the last three matches, the margin of victory was one, and therefore every goal rare and precious. Cournoyer would use his speed and dexterity to score two especially big ones—the go-ahead goal in Game 6 and the tying goal in Game 8. Just as significantly, he'd intercept a careless Soviet pass to initiate the play that resulted in the biggest goal of all.

For his part, Savard would solidify Team Canada's defensive wall with his mobility, strength, reach and savoir-faire under pressure, his knack for controlling the pace of the game and settling his team down. Bobby Clarke would call him "our best defenseman." Savard would assist on two goals in Game 7 and accumulate the distinction—of which he remains unobtrusively proud today—of being the only team member to play in all of Canada's wins, plus the tie, and none of its defeats.

In a film documentary of series highlights, "The Canada/Russia Games 1972," the pair discuss the public's low estimation of their team's chances after the loss in Game 5 put them behind 1-3-1. "At that point, not too many people believed we were going to come back," Savard observes. Nodding, Cournoyer replies: "Nobody except our guys."

•

On an overcast morning in September 1995, the Montreal Canadiens are about to start their final season in their hallowed home of three score years and ten, the Forum. It will not be a full season; in March, the Canadiens will leave the building forever for the Molson Centre, still under construction, which at this point everyone calls, out of a natural human yen for continuity, "the new Forum."

On Ste. Catherine Street, Montrealers dash into doorways out of the rain. Some of them duck into the lobby of the old Forum, which in six months will be unceremoniously dismantled and auctioned off piece by piece to the highest bidder, from the scoreboard to the penalty benches. But for the moment, the building still serves its time-honoured function at the heart of popular culture. In the lobby hang grainy photographic blowups of Céline Dion, Tina Turner, Paul Anka, Aretha Franklin, Leonard Cohen. Roller hockey has just ended. NHL hockey will soon begin. Upstairs, the Canadiens' front office is deep in preparation for this transitional season, hoping it will be memorable for something more than just moving to a new building—certainly more memorable than last year, the miserable lockout-shortened season, when the team finished out of the playoffs for only the second time since 1948.

In the second-floor waiting room of le Club de Hockey Canadiens, the walls are lined with vanished heroes—and not so long vanished, either: not Joliat or Lach or the Richard brothers or Geoffrion, but cover boys from the team's fan magazine between the late eighties and early nineties. Bob Gainey, Larry Robinson, Mats Naslund, Stéphane Richer, Bobby Smith, Chris Chelios, Claude Lemieux, Guy Charbonneau: all gone now, to retirement or coaching or other teams, which they're busy imbuing with the Canadiens' win ethic. The only one still with *les Glorieux*—for the moment—is Stanley Cup–winning goaltender Patrick Roy. Through the glass partition, the man who will "punish" Roy for insubordination by trading him to the Colorado Avalanche in a couple of months, Canadiens' dapper president Ronald Corey, can be seen disappearing down a corridor. Suddenly looming in the doorway is a much bulkier figure in a dark suit: a familiar-looking figure with plenty of still-dark hair and plenty of nose—the Canadiens' long-serving general manager Serge Savard.

In his office, Savard checks the calendar and sighs. "Yeah, looks like we're set to open the new building Saturday, sixteen March against the Rangers. It's too bad, maybe we could've gone against Toronto—but there's nothing we can do about the schedule. The last game here in the old building will be against Dallas."

Dallas? Savard doesn't comment further. His peeved frown and the Gallic shrug of his large well-tailored shoulders say it all. Tradition doesn't count for much in the newborn, New York–based, NBA-influenced NHL.

Guarded and deliberate in speech, Savard seems a worried man, stressed by the continuing weight of his responsibilities: weary, even a touch morose. This will be, after all, his thirteenth season as the Canadiens' GM, a job he's held ever since he retired as a player in 1983. But when asked to think back to '72, he relaxes visibly. Actually, he recalls, his acquaintance with the Soviets goes back even farther—to his junior days in 1965, when the Soviet national team came to play some exhibition games against reinforced Junior A teams. The Toronto Marlboros added four young stars from other teams, including Savard and Bobby Orr, and lost. The next night, Savard and his own team, the Montreal Junior Canadiens, played the Soviets and won: "Jacques Plante played for us, and we beat them 2-1. They had some great athletes then, too, but we were so high emotionally we played our best game against them."

Savard moved up to the big team in 1967. His playing proved he belonged, but he had a terrible time with injuries. In 1970, he broke his left leg crashing into a goal post. A year later, he broke it again and had to undergo a bone-graft operation. He got back into action in 1972, only to end up in the hospital yet again: when fire broke out in a St. Louis hotel where the Canadiens were staying, Savard and his teammates helped rescue guests trapped in their rooms, and he severely gashed his ankle while kicking open a window.

By the '72 series, Savard hadn't played for several months, but his old buddy Fergie called to ask if he was well enough to attend Team Canada's training camp: "I said, 'I think I'm just about 100 per cent.' He said, 'Come anyway.' I still wasn't supposed to play, but after that 7-3 loss here, they changed the line-up for Toronto and put me in, and that was a real big win." He also played Game 3 in Winnipeg, but his ankle was fractured the next morning in practice, and he didn't return to the line-up until Game 6.

Unlike some players, Savard acknowledges he was upset by the defection of his teammates in Moscow. Ron Ellis avers that he couldn't be sure what he himself might have done in their place, but Savard says, "I felt bad about it. Everybody on the team was really, really mad. Well, Vic Hadfield had to live with that—he was booed in every city when he came back. Other players felt he was a quitter. It was such an emotional time. I haven't talked to those guys about it, but I'm sure every one of them feels he made a mistake today."

One thing Savard knows for sure: the defections had the positive impact of rallying and solidifying Team Canada. "We became one unit after that. Often something like that has to happen to bring players together." And once Team Canada became unified, Savard found there was no life like it. Contrary to Phil Esposito, for example, who insists he'd never want to repeat the experience, Savard enjoyed playing the Soviets. Defending against their great skating and puck handling required great mobility, and Savard was a mobile defenseman: you had to be on the move all the time, and that's how he liked to play. "That's why a defenseman like Donny Awrey, who loved to block shots, had a tough time against those guys. I don't want to take anything away from Awrey, but he wasn't the right style of defenseman to play the Russians."

Who played most like the Soviets? The Montreal Canadiens, of course. Playing the Soviets, Savard says, "was like playing against ourselves." The true test of those two "attacking" styles, as Tarasov would term them, emphasizing speed, teamwork and artistry, would come in the famous 1975 New Year's Eve exhibition in the Forum, when the Canadiens played Central Red Army to a 3-3 draw.

For Savard, part of the pleasure of playing the Soviets was relief from the brutal toll of "goon" hockey, taken to its heights, or depths, in the 1970s by the Philadelphia Flyers. "The Flyers brought a style to the game," Savard contends, "that we had a tough time to get rid of. For a player like me who hated to fight, who believed fighting has nothing to do with sports, it was hard. We were forced to fight. We had a brawl every time we played the Flyers. So it was really refreshing to play against the Soviet style. That's what hockey should be."

And yet in '72, Savard admits, Team Canada won not with artistry but with the diggers and grinders. And with emotion, another factor in Montreal's Stanley Cup mystique—and a factor whose dark side is the very brutality that Savard dislikes. "I've been on ten Stanley Cup teams, eight as a player and two as a manager, and none of them brought your emotions to the same level as we were in the '72 series. The Russians were better prepared than we were, but they couldn't bring themselves as high emotionally. They still can't."

In some strange way, Savard believes, the Soviets were expecting, perhaps unconsciously, to lose the series. Not that they wanted to: "Seventy-two was really a battleground between two systems. It wasn't just about hockey. I think *they* saw it that way too. They wanted to shock the world—and they came very close to doing it." But they lacked that one crucial ingredient. Savard noticed the same thing fifteen years later when the two teams staged the 1987 "Relive the Dream" reunion, playing three games, all of them won by Team Canada: "They were the same players, and they were ready to be beaten again. They didn't *care* the way we did."

You tell Savard you're off to see Yvan Cournoyer at the new St. Raphael golf club. "That's a beautiful course, I hear," he remarks, a wistful note creeping into his voice, suggesting he doesn't get much time for golf these days. "Now, Yvan played a key role in '72. He's a character player, and his character really showed. He had a great series. Henderson was the hero because he scored those goals, but a lot of other players played extremely well, and Yvan was one of them."

Neither of the old teammates can know that, in a few short weeks, they will switch places. On October 17, Ronald Corey will bring Savard's thirty-first year in the Montreal Canadiens organization to an abrupt end. With four losses in the first four games of the

1995-96 season, Savard, his assistant GM, and coach Jacques Demers will be fired. After a brief interval, a brand-new managerial and coaching team will be brought in. Among them will be assistant coach Yvan Cournoyer.

•

In Frank Lennon's timeless photograph of Paul Henderson with arms upraised, joyously celebrating The Goal, Yvan Cournoyer is the invisible man. He's the short guy, number twelve, his face obscured by Henderson's elbow and armpit, his arms flung rapturously around Henderson's chest. But at le Club de Golf St.-Raphael in the northwestern suburbs of Montreal, Cournoyer is very visible indeed.

He's appearing as a celebrity guest at a tournament, courtesy of Molson-O'Keefe, with whom he's had a promotional contract for six years. The tournament, however, has been pretty much rained out. Only a few die-hards remain out on the lush green tree-fringed fairways. Wearing a canary-yellow golf shirt and a faint but permanently expectant smile, Cournoyer takes his ease at a table in the clubhouse's gleaming, spacious dining room. Golfers stop by to kibitz with him, club employees cater to him. Fellow celebrity Gaetan Boucher, the Olympic gold medallist in speedskating, passes with a cheery wave.

Cournoyer orders a bodum of coffee and warms to a discussion of '72. Like Savard, he's well-tanned and somewhat over his playing weight—but with a relaxed, boyish bonhomie that's missing in Savard. In Cournoyer's round full lips and cheeks, there's a touch of the Buddha. On his left hand, there's a Stanley Cup ring—this one from 1979, his final season—and on his right, a ring from the Hockey Hall of Fame, into which he was inducted in 1982.

Cournoyer has no trouble agreeing with Savard's assessment of the series as bigger than the biggest thing in hockey: "I've won ten Stanley Cups, but after twenty-some years we're still talking about that series. The Cup is always there. The '72 series was unique, one of a kind. Only afterwards do you realize how big it was."

You can tell Cournoyer has thought a lot about the whole experience: what it meant, where it belongs within an honour-studded life in hockey. Despite the title of the fifteenth anniversary reunion, the series doesn't represent to him a "dream" to relive: "We'd never dreamt of a series like that. It just happened. The Stanley Cup is something you've dreamt about all your life, and when you win it for the first time, it's like a dream come true. In '72, it was like the country come true."

An extraordinary statement: the series as this country's self-actualization. Dryden isn't the only Montreal Canadien with a gift for words—and for Cournoyer, in his second language at that. At the same time, Cournoyer's seasoned, pragmatic hockey sense knows full well what it took to win. His formulation is that "We played more for ourselves, to win as individuals. For the Soviets, the system was more like everybody works together, and you do your little part." In a sport like hockey, when everything is on the line, our approach usually works better—other things, such as talent, being equal. But on the emotional level, according to Cournoyer, it wasn't a matter of desire alone: fear was also essential.

It was the fear of losing, and it took hold after the shock of Game 1. Sinden and Ferguson didn't even have to say anything, Cournoyer insists: the players were all professionals, they realized what was at stake. "People were saying, 'The Russians are going to beat you,' and that really scared me. And when you're scared, you're a good player. I've always been afraid to lose. Maybe that's why I won so much."

Consequently, the most important game in the series as far as he's concerned, the real hinge-point, wasn't Game 5 or 6 or even 8 but Game 2. Team Canada had something to prove, and right away: "If we'd lost that game, that was it. We had to show those guys they had to respect us. 'We're not that team you beat the first time. We're a new team with a new attitude, new thinking, new mentality.' That second game, my mind wasn't like the first one: just, 'We're going to beat them, we're going to beat them, we're going to beat them.' " His words recall the image of the twenty-eight-year-old Cournoyer in Maple Leaf Gardens, staring trancelike at the ice for half an hour before Game 2 got underway.

Winning in Toronto gave Cournoyer and his mates their first taste of confidence that they could defeat the Soviets. "In Winnipeg, they had to come back and tie us. In Vancouver, we lost by our own mistakes—we beat ourselves with those early penalties that gave them two power-play goals. We thought, 'That one's lost, no big deal.' The big deal was Toronto."

That belief operated even after the loss in Game 5 in Moscow: "We could look back to Toronto and remember we could beat them."

At that point, says Cournoyer, the other big change was that Team Canada had actually become a team. In the Canadian half of the series, they played under the enormous handicap of not being a team at all, just a pickup squad of random all-stars, most of them badly out of condition. "Don't forget, we had too many players, too. We tried to please everybody, so every game there were a few new guys on the ice." By the time they reached Moscow, not only were they in better shape physically and mentally, but Sinden and Ferguson had settled on their core team: "We got to play regularly with the same guys. And that's why we came back."

Several golfers, their shirts slicked flat to their backs, pass by and rib Cournoyer about staying out of the rain. For a long time, these people knew him not only as the retired Canadiens hero and Hall of Famer but as a restaurateur-proprietor of an establishment in suburban Lachine known as "Le Douze, Chez Yvan." He ran it for twelve years, selling out three years ago. "It was time for me to do something else. I was going to be fifty."

Something else turned out to be roller hockey: the new sport that has become, for the moment, Cournoyer's big new passion in life. He's just completed his second season as coach and general manager of the Roadrunners, the Montreal entry in the nineteen-team professional league, Roller Hockey International. The sport itself he terms "fantastic": far more exciting for the spectators than today's NHL hockey, with its fast but oversized players clogging up the undersized ice surface and interfering with each other so much that nobody, not even a Mario Lemieux or Jaromir Jagr, can get anything going.

"I'll tell you something," he enthuses. "I don't want to put hockey down—for me it's always going to be the best game—but if you go to see roller hockey a couple of times, you'll find regular hockey very boring! Watching our game, you can't get up for a hot dog because you're going to miss a two-on-one or a breakaway or a big save, even a goal or two. The NHL has all these promotions and commercial breaks and the game isn't over till after eleven o'clock. It's tough if you're with kids who have to go to school next day. Our game is two hours, one intermission—four quarters, like basketball. It's really great, very fast, with shootouts to decide the winner."

And yet, and yet—a few weeks later, there's Yvan Cournoyer back in the Forum again, back where they play that other, boring, old-fashioned sport, wearing a suit and tie, behind the Montreal Canadiens' bench. There he is helping new coach Mario Tremblay and new GM Réjean Houle, both former teammates, try to inspire in a new generation of Canadiens the will, emotion and guts to live up to the formidable Montreal mystique—and, just maybe, to recreate a little of the equally potent spirit of '72.

FIFTEEN

GAME 6: STAYING ALIVE

"I told them that the only thing that really counts is winning. That if we won this game, and went on to win the series, we would vindicate ourselves and all that we stand for."

— HARRY SINDEN, *Hockey Showdown*

●

Team Canada could not possibly face a more formidable challenge. With three games remaining, they've dug themselves a pit so deep that it could soon be their grave. They must now win every single game or lose the series—and lose far more than that: in coach Sinden's words, "all that we stand for."

If the Canadians do not win Game 6, the last two games will be beside the point. Even if they win two out of three and tie one, for a 3-3-2 draw in games, the Canadians will have lost, given their expectations of themselves. The Soviets, on the other hand, will have won a clearcut moral victory.

The odds are unquestionably against Team Canada. Most Canadians find it hard to argue with those odds. We're preparing ourselves for defeat, looking for rationalizations to explain it. But don't tell that to the 3,000 hardcore loyalists who've travelled to Moscow to be there with—and for—their team.

At the disappointing conclusion of Game 5, *they* didn't boo or jeer or sulk away into the damp chill of the Moscow night to trade excuses. They did what true fans everywhere do, rose in their seats to give their team a lusty standing ovation as the players skated off the ice, sending them the only message that in the circumstances is likely to do them any good at all: You're still our boys, you're still great, we still love you.

For Team Canada, it's morale-boosting and inspiring to know this very same gang of horn-blowing, banner-waving, slogan-chanting, hockey-crazy Canucks, so conspicuous because of their gaudy clothing amid the uniformly sombre greys of the other spectators, will be in the stands for the next game too, and the next, and the next, until the bitter end.

One person who will not be there until the bitter end is Gilbert Perreault. At practice the morning after Game 5, the young Buffalo Sabres star tells his coach he's joining the Hadfield Express. He gives the same unconvincing reason as his teammate Richard Martin—he has to get back to his team because he's not in shape. And Sinden gives him the same response—"Don't worry. There's a flight leaving soon and you'll be on it." Perreault also claims he hasn't played enough, even though he was dressed the night before and earned a well-deserved assist on Parise's goal, Team Canada's first on Soviet territory. He isn't satisfied with the role Sinden has assigned him—spelling off Phil Esposito, who sometimes needs a rest after playing an extra shift as a penalty killer or on the power play.

According to Alan Eagleson, the defections by Martin and Perreault are encouraged by their coach in Buffalo, Punch Imlach, who's in Moscow covering the series for the *Toronto Sun*. "I think Imlach did us a disservice," Eagleson later tells Scott Young in *War on Ice*. "I think he should have done what other guys were doing: just saying get the goddam guys glued together." To Sinden, Perreault is simply an immature kid who doesn't know any better.

The other players are all too focussed on Game 6 to take much notice of Perreault anyway. From now on, Sinden will tell them repeatedly, they have to forget about the previous game, in fact forget about the series as a whole. They have to take it one game, even one *period,* at a time.

That's one important concept. At practice on the day before Game 6, Sinden introduces them to another: the Soviets, he and

Ferguson have decided, have a weakness—a major one. If the Canadians can exploit it, they may yet find the edge they need to win.

The Soviets' Achilles heel is poor defensive play in their own end. When Team Canada keeps the puck under control in the Soviet zone, the Soviet defensemen tend to be ineffective, even rather immobile and passive about moving the puck. Curiously, they are not well prepared to defend against the very type of controlled passing attack they themselves use.

Sinden and Ferguson introduce a new drill to take advantage of this perceived liability. For an hour, they send five-man attacking units into the offensive zone, rushing against three defenders and trying to pass as often as possible, to keep control of the puck until forced to give it up. The key to defeating the Soviets may lie not in unloading bombs at the goaltender, nor in intimidating them with goon tactics, but in keeping the puck away from them by exerting maximum offensive pressure. No doubt Anatoly Tarasov would approve.

The Canadian players feel heartened to be given a new offensive weapon and respond well to the drill. Among themselves, they exchange observations and tips about the Soviets' style; now that they've faced them five times, they can assess their opponents' little habits and tendencies and weaknesses. They've begun the essential process of demystifying the enemy. Tactics that were unfamiliar and surprising at first, leaving the Canadians a step behind the play, are becoming commonplace, even predictable: criss-cross pass patterns, attackers weaving back and forth across the ice, the quick pass up centre to spring a man free. The Canadians are learning to expect these manoeuvres and break them up. The Soviets, in turn, are reluctant to change their style, and that too works to Canada's advantage.

The Canadians are also learning to believe in themselves. They may be alarmingly behind in games, but they feel positive about how far they've come in battle readiness: Game 5 was theirs for two periods until the roof caved in. What they need now is to put three strong periods together.

Most Team Canada players claim they still believed they'd take the series after Game 5. Ron Ellis remembers, "I could sense the feeling afterwards, 'We're okay.' We let them off the hook, but at the end we felt good about how we played. And I just sensed this thing isn't over." Phil Esposito insists, "I never thought we'd lose another game." He remembers saying so to his brother while consoling him after the loss, reassuring him it wasn't his fault.

There is some evidence of such positive thinking from the time itself. Red Berenson, after watching Game 5 from the stands, rushes into the dressing room to tell his teammates, "Boys, we can beat this team!", then goes out to play inspired and inspirational hockey in Game 6. This time, Team Canada's confidence has a quiet, private quality, grim and determined, darkly tinged with—as Cournoyer has attested—the stark fear of losing. The old arrogance has been displaced. In fact, it has been appropriated by the Soviets. Boris Mikhailov has stated, "After the first game at home, we came back to win, and we were all very certain we would win the series then. Maybe the team had become overconfident."

Essentially, the teams have exchanged roles. Team Canada is the underdog now, and the Canadians kind of like it that way. In Paul Henderson's retrospective view, "It was probably the best thing that could have happened to us." Game 6 will emerge as the series' true turning point. Exposing once and for all the niceties of "friendly matches" and "sports diplomacy" as shams, this game will charge an already charged atmosphere with a bitterness that persists until Team Canada's aircraft leaves Moscow. From the moment the puck is dropped in the Luzhniki Arena on the evening of September 24, nothing about the series will be quite the same—on the ice or off—again.

•

That morning, Ken Dryden is nervous as a cat. He hasn't felt so shaky since the very first time he played the Soviets as an amateur. To his surprise, Sinden and Ferguson have picked him to start the sixth game. After playing in both the team's losses in Canada, after sitting out both exhibition games in Sweden, after compiling a career goals-against average of 7.00 playing the Soviets, Dryden has figured he'll be playing cheerleader for the duration of the series.

Not so. In this all-important game, the coaches have decided to take a chance on him. They're gambling he'll recover the championship form that amazed the hockey world in the 1971 Stanley Cup playoffs. That year, with only six regular-season NHL games to his credit, Dryden came out of obscurity to flummox all comers, starting with the defending champion Boston Bruins, prompting veteran Johnny Bucyk to say, "For a big man, he's got incredible reflexes." Phil Esposito described one of Dryden's moves in that series as "the greatest save that's ever been made off me in my life. My God, he's got arms like a giraffe." Espo's biology was a little off, but you get the point.

Now the giraffe is recovering from a rotten cold, product of a midnight stroll around Red Square with his wife, Lynda, when he wore only a sports jacket against the freezing temperatures. On top of that, Dryden suspects his teammates have lost confidence in him; probably they'd prefer to have Tony Esposito in goal again. But on the positive side, he's been preparing mentally, which is always Dryden's way, just in case. He's been progressively adjusting his goaltending style to deal with the Soviets' strengths. Now he believes those adjustments will stand him in good stead: under pressure, he'll stick with his new method, not revert in panic to his old one. Moreover, the team in front of him will be playing better than it did in Canada.

As his teammates warm Dryden up before the game, they pepper him with shouts of encouragement and bouquets of lavish praise, even after he blocks the easiest shots. He finds it embarrassing that they know his confidence needs bolstering, yet at the same time rather comical. Three other players have been inserted into the lineup, and all will make a decisive contribution tonight: Serge Savard in place of Rod Seiling, Dennis Hull for Frank Mahovlich, and Red Berenson for Gilbert Perreault.

On the Soviet roster, two surprising absences are the experienced defensemen Alexander Gusev and Victor Kuzkin. Bobrov is going with youth again, playing the Anisin-Bodunov-Lebedev Kid Line, Yuri Shatalov on defense, and a brand-new forward, Boris Volchkov. His changes make him appear very confident indeed.

The Canadian fans are back in force, supplying their own brand of confidence, roaring "GO TEAM GO" over and over. The Soviet authorities in charge of the series have held back the Canadians' tickets until late in the afternoon; when they take their seats, they find that instead of sitting all together as last time, they've been dispersed to various locations around the arena. The Soviet motive is to break up the foreigners' concentrated roar, which the authorities found so unsettling in Game 5. But all this does is make the Canadians cheer louder, as if to unite their voices with their brethren across the ice. When the time comes to sing "O Canada," they are 3,000 open throats.

On air, Brian Conacher remarks wonderingly, "To hear those 3,000 Canadians singing the national anthem is really an emotional experience!" To which Foster Hewitt simply replies: "I've never heard anything like it." And when Hewitt tells the viewers back home, "It's do or die tonight," he's describing the cross Team Canada will bear every game for the rest of the series.

The referees signal the faceoff. They are those two Canadian favourites from the games in Stockholm, the West Germans Franz Baader and Josef Kompalla—variously dubbed by Team Canada wags "Baader and Worse" or "Baader and Wurst."

Right from the start, the Soviets swarm into the Canadian zone, and Team Canada swarms right back. For five minutes straight, the teams mount an exceptionally exciting display of wide-open, end-to-end hockey, changing lines repeatedly without a single stoppage in play. For now the two referees are invisible, letting the teams play; the only whistles to be heard come from the Soviet crowd, disapproving of the teeth-rattling jolts administered to their players by Bergman and Park. "This is going to be a different game!" Hewitt exults. "The Canadians are really hitting, right off the bat!"

Tretiak is tested, but Dryden even more. In those five minutes, he kicks out Liapkin's hard slapshot from the point, makes a pad save on a dangerous drive by Maltsev from in close, and plucks Vikulov's rising shot out of the air. Dryden's reflexes are back, his instincts sound, his anticipation acute. With each save, he feels his confidence building; and along with it grows his teammates' confidence in him.

Ellis muffs a scoring chance when Clarke feeds him right in front and he shoots wide. The same thing happens when Dennis

Hull can't convert a set-up from Ratelle. But the Canadians are demonstrably pumped, over the top, a team possessed, playing with more reckless physical abandon than at any previous time in the series. They're also clearly sharper on defense, intercepting Soviet passes with seeming foreknowledge and swiftly making the transition to offense.

At 10:21 of what has been a superb hockey game, problems with the officiating start. Lebedev does a triple-gainer over Gary Bergman's ankle, and the Canadian defenseman is sent off for tripping. Bergman's sweet disposition forsakes him. During his penalty, he takes exception to an icing call and stands up in the box to protest. When a rinkside official tries to make him sit down, he furiously throws off the man's restraining hand. The official recoils from Bergman as from a madman.

Dryden, meanwhile, continues steady, making saves while his teammates kill off the penalty. But no sooner is Bergman back on the ice than Esposito cross-checks the new player, Shatalov, behind the net, taking an obvious penalty, then cross-checks him again for good measure after the whistle. Esposito receives a double-minor for charging. Canada must play short-handed for four minutes.

Fortunately, Savard's steadying hand keeps the lid on the Soviet cauldron. Savard turns and wheels with the puck, shielding it with his large frame, moving it out of the zone, slowing the flow of play with the effortless aplomb of a latter-day Doug Harvey. In the dying moments of the period, Dryden comes up big, robbing Maltsev again on a play that would have been a sure Soviet goal a few games ago: Maltsev, standing alone at the left corner, tries to stuff a pass from Vikulov inside the post, but Dryden lunges across the goal mouth with that immense reach and sweeps the puck aside with his stick.

Eventful as it is, the period ends scoreless. Hewitt says it reminds him of Krefeld in 1955, "when the Penticton Vees hammered away at the Soviets in a rough-tough tussle." But on that occasion, Soviet militiamen were not stationed throughout the arena to control undesirable behaviour by the public. During the first period, Alan Eagleson had his first run-in with those militiamen as he sprang to the defense of a lady. Mrs. Joe Kryczka, wife of the CAHA chairman, was being bothered by the antics of a spectator in front of her, who kept leaping up and blocking her view. When Mrs. Kryczka tapped the man on the shoulder and asked him to sit down, he threatened her with his fist. Eagleson intervened and was accosted by several soldiers, who seemed intent on ejecting the unruly foreigner until they got the idea he was someone important. The spectator turned out to be an unidentified member of the Soviet team.

In an intermission feature, Johnny Esaw interviews Sharon Seiling, Nancy Ratelle, Gerry Park and Lynda Dryden. "Now girls," Esaw chirps brightly, "everybody's wondering what it's like to have your husband playing in a series like this."

Lynda Dryden answers instructively: "During the Stanley Cup the team doesn't live at home. But this time we're actually the guys' roommates, so it's a much different experience living with them and the pressures of the games, day in and day out." She is too tactful to mention that the players are being fed juicy steaks and milk imported from Canada, whereas their roommates have to make do with Moscow hotel food, which they sometimes find inedible.

Very early in the second period, Dryden faces a two-on-one. Big, hawk-nosed Yakushev, skating like a predator in a low, lunging forward crouch, foreshadowing Wayne Gretzky, breaks out with Volchkov. In a switch from Soviet routine, Yakushev shoots instead of passing, perhaps lacking faith in his new linemate. His shot is wide, but Shadrin, trailing on the play, picks up the rebound and gets it back to Liapkin at the left point. Heavily screened, Dryden doesn't see Liapkin's slapshot until it's in the net. The Soviets 1, Team Canada 0.

The next penalty goes, for once, to the Soviets—veteran Alexander Ragulin, long ago christened "Rags" by Canadian opponents, going off for interference at 2:09. Team Canada's power play, stuttering so far in the series, is still tongue-tied. The short-handed Soviets play boldly, more like the team with the man advantage. Canada's best opportunity comes when Henderson centres to Esposito, who one-times the pass with a blistering blast; but Tretiak's save makes the spectacular look easy.

A minute or so after the Soviets kill the penalty, a new Canadian line combination presses hungrily in the Soviet zone. Double-shift-ing Esposito, Sinden now has him centring Dennis Hull and Rod Gilbert (in addition to Parise and Cournoyer). Gilbert shoots from the top of the right faceoff circle, hits a defenseman, then outfights him for the rebound. Persevering, Gilbert manages two more shots on goal, a forehand and a backhand. Although Tretiak stops them both, Gilbert's fusillade has him flat on the ice as Hull, correctly anticipating the direction of the last rebound, arrives in front to smash the puck up and over the fallen goaltender and tie the game at one.

During the next minute, Red Berenson is out spelling off Esposito between Parise and Cournoyer—Perreault's role if he hadn't left for home. The Roadrunner pounces slyly on a stray Soviet pass in his own end and flies up the right wing on a two-man break. He centres to Parise right on top of Tretiak, but Parise can't control the puck. The Soviets come right back, and Dryden makes the save.

Berenson leads a return rush. Five Canadian attackers put the previous day's practice drill to good use, controlling the puck, maintaining relentless pressure on the Soviet zone. Berenson one-times Parise's pass right on Tretiak. Recovering the rebound, Parise throws it out to White at the right point, who hands it back to Parise, who wires it cross-ice to Stapleton at the other point. Tretiak blocks Stapleton's slapshot, and the puck bounces behind the net. Bird-dogging Berenson centres it right out to Cournoyer streaking in, who simply taps the go-ahead goal past Tretiak.

After two Canadian goals in scarcely more than a minute, the Soviets are reeling, disoriented. Seconds later, the normally steady Lutchenko makes a blind back-pass out of his zone to centre ice. Henderson intercepts it, takes three strides to cross the blueline and penetrates the small space between Lutchenko and his defense partner, Tsygankov. Henderson releases a quick snap shot, low to the ice. Taken by surprise, Tretiak doesn't even move on it. Henderson, unassisted!

With that burst, the Canadians have struck, Sovietlike, for three goals within one minute and twenty-three seconds. The Canadian contingent is ecstatic over the 3-1 lead.

The goal parade having passed, the penalty parade begins. First, Lapointe and Vasiliev go off together for roughing. At 10:12,

Clarke ends up on his knees beside Kharlamov at the whistle; as he stands up, Clarke tauntingly rubs the knuckles of his glove against Kharlamov's nose. His temper aroused, Kharlamov retaliates with a quick short jab, Clarke with a counterpunch.

Not content to let Clarke take care of himself, Bergman runs at Kharlamov. He bumps him provocatively, once, twice, trying to goad him into losing that temper completely, then hounds and harasses him all the way back to the Soviet bench. Only Baader's intervention keeps the pair from fighting. Bergman then yammers at coach Bobrov like a junkyard dog, and it takes Peter Mahovlich's bulk looming over him to calm Bergman down and steer him back to his own bench.

Clarke receives, mysteriously, a slashing penalty, as well as a ten-minute misconduct for fighting. Kharlamov receives nothing. Bergman receives nothing. Bizarre calls. But the war on Valery Kharlamov has begun.

Brian Conacher puts a polite interpretation on it: "Team Canada is certainly showing a lot of respect for Kharlamov. They're giving him a lot of attention tonight. Every time they get a chance, they're taking him for a rough ride along the boards."

And sometimes elsewhere. Peter Mahovlich elbows him at centre. A moment later, the gutsy Kharlamov, half Mahovlich's size, cruises by and dumps him to the ice. Kharlamov can hand it out as well as take it. He can't be intimidated. He can only be stopped by plain outright premeditated viciousness.

In a manoeuvre somehow missed by both the television cameras and the referees, Bobby Clarke homes in on Kharlamov while the Soviet star has possession of the puck. Just after Kharlamov releases a pass, Clarke swings his stick back over his shoulder with both hands like a lumberjack felling a jack pine and slashes Kharlamov's left ankle as hard as he can. Kharlamov gasps, winces, stumbles; the play goes on. Kharlamov will continue playing the rest of the game, his traumatized ankle in a state of shock. Only afterwards will it be discovered that Clarke has fractured it.

At 17:02, Dennis Hull gets the penalty Clarke should have received and goes off for slashing. Nine seconds later, Yakushev scores a power-play goal on a goal-mouth scramble as Dryden, Park

and Bergman all kneel in attitudes of prayer. Canada's lead narrows
to 3-2.

When Esposito receives a five-minute major for cutting Ragulin
with a high stick, thirty-five seconds after Yakushev's goal, the
Team Canada bench freaks out. Sinden and Ferguson are convinced the officiating is biased in favour of the Soviets. "Fergie and
I were yelling so much," Sinden admits, "some of the players
thought we had lost our minds. I remember Berenson telling me
once to calm down. I just looked at him. Another time Dryden
skated over and looked at me like I was nuts."

What Berenson and Dryden would tell their coach, if he were
willing to listen, is the same thing another player with international
experience, Brian Conacher, is telling the folks back home: Team
Canada would be better off to come to their senses, accept there's
nothing they can do about European officiating, and save their
energy to play hockey. All their out-of-control rage will have no
effect except to throw them off their game.

That's not how Sinden sees it. He believes that by screaming and
throwing towels and holding the referees up to ridicule, he and
Ferguson can embarrass them and force them to make the right
calls. But it's hopeless: European and North American officiating
standards are too different. The only people Sinden and Ferguson
embarrass are themselves, their players and their fellow citizens.
Ferguson's mouthing-off draws a bench penalty on top of
Esposito's, and his team must play two men short. No more penalties will be called against the Soviets all night.

With only three defenders in front of Dryden to cover that big ice
surface, Canada's penalty-killing is truly put to the test. Led by
Savard and Berenson, cooler heads among the Canadians take com-
mand. The Soviets are kept off the scoresheet despite their two-
man advantage—but possibly by the grace of a goal judge's faulty
eyesight.

At this point, Kharlamov is still mobile enough to go out on the
power play. The Soviets quickly work the puck around the wheel
clockwise, Lutchenko to Liapkin to Petrov, until it's relayed to
Kharlamov standing all alone by the right corner. His one-timer
ends up in Dryden's glove. But did Dryden catch the shot, or did it

hit the back of the mesh first and bounce out into his waiting mitt? Even Dryden doesn't know for sure. Later he'll write that it might have rebounded into his glove from hitting the post, or from inside the net. The Soviets think the latter. Kharlamov and Petrov remonstrate with the referees, but mildly, compared to the Canadian style. Even Alan Eagleson thinks they're right.

Foster Hewitt and Brian Conacher think the shot hit the side of the net. But from the video replay, it all happens far too fast to tell—that's how swiftly Kharlamov accomplishes the act. And in the end, the only judgement that matters is what the goal judge and referees think, and they rule no goal. For once, the Canadians defer politely to authority.

As the teams are leaving the ice after the second period, Sinden is worried his players are so incensed they'll do the referees some harm. Baader and Kompalla have to leave by the same runway as the teams. Sinden and his former protégé Bobby Orr want a word with the referees themselves. It's hard to fathom why they think that will help, but here is how Sinden himself describes—and rationalizes—the next extraordinary scene:

"We chased them up the runway screaming. We shouldn't have been behaving this way but they didn't give us any choice. If they were going to do a job on us, we weren't going to let them off the hook. Just before they got to the dressing room one of them stopped in his tracks to answer us. Orr was right on his heels, and when the referee—Baader—stopped, Bobby ran into him. Bobby gave him a shove, and faster than you could yell 'cop,' the Soviet police and officials were all around us. We looked like clowns once again, but at this point we were beyond caring. We're not going to sit around and take the shaft any more."

In the meantime, there's one more period to play. Sinden somehow has to persuade his players to cool down and recover their poise. After his own performance, he has understandable doubts about his credibility on that score, so he tries a novel tactic: keeping his team sitting quietly in the dressing room for an extra five minutes after they're supposed to go on the ice. "This could be our last act," he'll say later, "and we were going to play it our way."

Sinden sends Stan Mikita, in civilian clothes, out to inspect the condition of the ice surface. As suspected, the arena people have applied too much water, just as they did earlier, and the surface is still wet. Sinden uses this excuse to keep his players where they are until they can get focussed enough to play the last period at their best.

And they do. Their play is acute and purposeful, both defensively and offensively. They intercept the Soviets' passes, poke-check the puck off their sticks, break up their attack patterns. They carry the play to them, unlike the third period of Game 5. And they don't let up on their physical game. Foster Hewitt calls it "the hardest-fought game I've seen in years," and Brian Conacher's reply gives a vivid picture of the action:

"Foster, I can't believe it—down there on that ice it's just sheer war. These two teams are going at it, they're not sparing the lumber, they're not sparing the body, but is it tough down there. . . . But Team Canada are giving, I feel, their best effort in this whole series."

Indeed, the Canadians play their best third period so far, finishing up as strongly as the Soviets. Each team is a match for the other. Team Canada has to kill off a late penalty to Ellis, but neither side scores. Canada stays alive with a 3-2 victory—with perhaps a little help from an anonymous goal judge, but also under the conspicuous handicap of thirty-one minutes in penalties against the Soviets' mere four minutes. The Soviets may be marginally more saintly than Team Canada, but not *that* much.

It's the first time since Toronto, twenty days earlier, that the Canadians have put three good periods together—and the first time since Toronto that they've beaten the Soviets. This time, unlike the end of Game 5, Sinden attends the post-game news conference. The Soviet journalists want to know how he could possibly act so crudely towards the referees, who in Europe are always held in reverence. Sinden replies that Baader and Kompalla are so incompetent, he won't permit them to work the series again. He'll meet with the Soviet officials tomorrow to guarantee it.

Maple Leafs in Moscow: Brian Glennie, Barbara Glennie, Ron Ellis and Jan Ellis take a break from hockey to sightsee in the Soviet capital. BRIAN PICKELL

USSR

SEPT. 20 – 28, 1972

Right: Hitting the ice for Game 5 in the Luzhniki Arena, Moscow, Jean Ratelle, Eddie Johnston, Gary Bergman and Pat Stapleton skate past the 3,000 "Good Sports" in the voluble Canadian cheering section. BRIAN PICKELL

Above: In Game 5, Team Canada roars into a 4–1 lead with some robustly physical play. Here defenseman Bill White puts the collar on Alexander Yakushev. But the Soviets roar right back to win 5–4. BRIAN PICKELL

GAME 5

USSR 5 · CANADA 4

GAME 6

CANADA 3 · USSR 2

Left: Game 6 is the turning point: the Canadians must take all three final games. Erupting for three goals in quick succession, they win 3–2. Phil Esposito gets five minutes for cutting veteran defenseman Alexander Ragulin with a high stick. FRANK LENNON But Ragulin *(bottom right)* is no slouch with a stick himself. BRIAN PICKELL

Bottom left: In Game 6, Team Canada targets Soviet superstar Valery Kharlamov for elimination. Here Bobby Clarke *(left)* pursues Kharlamov (17, *with puck)* before hunting him down and fracturing his ankle. CANADA WIDE

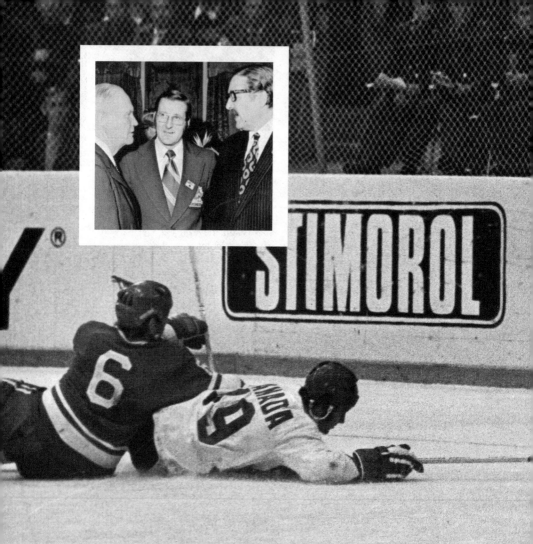

Above, inset: The evening before Game 7, the Canadian embassy in Moscow hosts a huge reception for Team Canada and the Canadian fans. *From left,* Hockey Canada president Charles Hay, NHLPA executive director Alan Eagleson, Canadian ambassador Robert Ford. **BRIAN PICKELL**

Above: With an extraordinary effort, Paul Henderson bursts through the Soviet defense and gets hauled down from behind by Valery Vasiliev (6), but still beats Vladislav Tretiak to win Game 7 for Canada, 4–3. **FRANK LENNON**

Right: Game 7 sees the biggest brawl of the series. Gary Bergman and Boris Mikhailov tangle against the boards, Mikhailov kicks Bergman with his skate, and both teams converge. *From left,* Vladimir Petrov (16), Jean-Paul Parise (22), referee Joseph Kompalla, Brad Park (5), Vladimir Lutchenko (3), Alexander Gusev (2), referee Franz Baader between Bergman and Mikhailov, Phil Esposito (7) and Alexander Yakushev (15). **CANADA WIDE**

GAME 7

CANADA 4 · USSR 3

GAME 8

CANADA 6 · USSR 5

Facing page: Anticipating disorderly conduct from the Canadians in the crowd, Soviet militiamen mass at rinkside during Game 8. Later they intercept Alan Eagleson on his way to remonstrate with a goal judge. FRANK LENNON

Above: Canadian defenseman Guy Lapointe sends Alexander Yakushev into orbit in front of Ken Dryden during hot and heavy action in Game 8.
FRANK LENNON

Left: Having predicted the greatest hockey game in history, Harry Sinden, shown behind bench, is furious at early penalties against his team. To protest what he believes is biased officiating, Sinden throws two chairs onto the ice. BRIAN PICKELL

Left: The most famous photograph in Canadian sports history: Paul Henderson leaps into Yvan Cournoyer's arms as Vladislav Tretiak sprawls on his back after Henderson's series-winning goal with 34 seconds to play. The stricken Soviet defender is Yuri Liapkin.
FRANK LENNON

Below: Like thousands of school classes and millions of Canadians, these students at Niagara Public School in Toronto watch Game 8 on television and erupt in jubilation as Henderson scores.
CANADA WIDE

Overleaf: Moment of triumph: Peter Mahovlich (20) hoists his arms in the air at the conclusion of Game 8 as Victor Kuzkin (4) salutes him.
BRIAN PICKELL

SIXTEEN

BUTCH AND SUNDANCE

"I have come to believe that hockey never leaves the blood of a Canadian. You like to think you're more mature than that, that a game shouldn't mean that much, but it does."
— HARRY SINDEN, *Hockey Showdown*

"I don't care how we win, as long as we win."
— JOHN FERGUSON, 1972

Etta: "They said you were dead."
Sundance: "Don't make a big thing out of it."
— *Butch Cassidy and the Sundance Kid*

●

There is a special hell reserved for coaches. They can school and mould and encourage and threaten and exhort and discipline their players; they can never *do*. Like parents raising adolescent children, managing the best they know how, then sending them out into the world to live their lives, coaches have to let go of their players once the game starts; they have to leave them alone to make their way against the opposition. That means watching them make their own mistakes, as well as create their own triumphs. It means watching them win or lose on the strength of their own efforts, no matter how well or inadequately you've prepared them.

And yet in professional sports, unlike parenting, coaches are still judged *entirely* by their teams' success or failure. There's the rub. In the National Hockey League, coaching is by far the most precarious and short-lived job. You're only as good as this year's won-lost record. Coaches considered brilliant one season are expendable another—in the 1995-96 season, you only had to ask Jacques Demers or Pat Burns—no matter how much it's their players who've let them down.

In 1972, Harry Sinden and John Ferguson bore the ultimate responsibility for the success or failure not merely of their hockey team but of their country. They felt the pressure any NHL coach experiences, multiplied by ten. Make that a hundred. If their team lost the series, Canadians would hold Sinden and Ferguson personally responsible, no doubt about that. The pair of them would be condemned to that special coaches' hell, not just for a season but for the rest of their lives, forever to be known as those jerks who lost our hockey supremacy. Their futures would be blighted.

By the team's arrival in Moscow, Sinden had already experienced a bitter taste of that kind of treatment. Looking back today, he recalls how it felt to become suddenly the brunt of Canadians' contempt, the scapegoat for our loss of illusions, after the first half of the series ended: "People treated us like we'd committed treason. It's evidence of how passionately Canadians feel about hockey. But we felt we had no friends left back home. Our reputation, the aura of who we were and where we came from, were no help to us then."

Sinden believes the mental toughness of Canadian hockey men, their ability to overcome adversity and fight back when they're down, is what equipped him and his team to handle the problem. "In Sweden, we came to grips with being on our own. So we were able to play better after that. In Moscow, we were a different team—like a cornered animal with nowhere to go but inward."

From that inward journey they brought forth new resources to throw at the Soviets. Even after they'd let Game 5 slip through their fingers, they neither despaired nor surrendered. "Players know if they're committed to winning or not. They sensed we were onto something good in Game 5. We'd been in danger of losing the series before then, but after Game 5 they felt a lot better about themselves. What held us together then was that we *had* played so well."

Significantly, it's these intangibles of mind and spirit that Sinden emphasizes, so many years later, as the keys to defeating the Soviets, not the tactics and techniques he instilled in his players at practice, not even the Bruins-style physical intimidation. That emphasis is rooted in the experience of a long and distinguished lifetime in hockey. Soon after the series ended, Sinden was appointed Boston's general manager and has been in the job ever since. Today there is scarcely a more respected figure active in the NHL. As early as '72, his unusual background, combining international experience as a player and a Stanley Cup victory as a coach, made him peculiarly qualified to lead Team Canada.

•

Harry Sinden's hockey career goes back nearly half a century, to a Montreal Junior Canadiens' tryout camp in 1948—right around the time Anatoly Tarasov and his colleagues were getting hockey going in Moscow. Sixteen years old at the camp, Sinden skated alongside a teen-aged Dickie Moore and Bernie Geoffrion. He was an offense-minded defenseman, and he impressed the Canadiens enough that they signed him to play junior in Oshawa, not far from his family home in York Township, north of Toronto.

After four good but unspectacular years in Oshawa, Sinden was invited to Boston's training camp. He declined. A working-class boy whose family had struggled through the Depression, he was highly security-conscious; he already held a day job with General Motors and he was about to be married. In those days, he wasn't really sure he was good enough to make the NHL. If he stayed put, he could play Senior A hockey with the Whitby Dunlops, based right next door to Oshawa, and keep his GM job.

Playing it safe agreed with Sinden back then. Over the next several seasons, the Dunnies won an Ontario championship, two Allan Cups, and of course the big one, the World's championship in Oslo in 1958. Sinden's memory of the Soviets in '58 is that they didn't skate or shoot as well as in '72, and played a far more mechanical, predictable game: virtually all their plays started in the corner, with the aim of working the puck within close range of the net before shooting, as in soccer.

He got another chance to play the Soviets two years later, as one of the reinforcements added to the Kitchener-Waterloo Dutchmen, who represented Canada in an amazing tournament of upsets at the 1960 Winter Olympics in Squaw Valley, California. There were five strong, evenly matched teams that year: the Canadians, the Soviets, the Czechs, the Swedes and, surprisingly, the Americans. Canada soundly defeated the Soviets 8-5, but the victory was good enough only for the silver medal; Sinden's team lost the gold to the U.S. in a 2-1 heartbreaker. He has described that loss as "the most disappointing thing in my hockey career. It stayed with me a long time."

The next season, at the age of twenty-eight, Sinden left security behind to gamble on a full-time career in pro hockey. He became playing assistant coach with Kingston in the Eastern Professional Hockey League, where he was voted the league's most valuable player. After several years coaching in the minors, including stints in Minneapolis and Oklahoma City, he jumped at the chance to coach the Boston Bruins in 1966. He was just thirty-four.

In the Bruins he inherited a team that "had been losing for so long, they really didn't know what it was to win." The first year was difficult; the team finished sixth in the final season of the six-team NHL, and the only bright spot was the play of a much-heralded rookie named Bobby Orr, who completely outshone his teammates. But by the next year, 1967-68, the Bruins had made the crucial trade that brought Phil Esposito, Ken Hodge and Fred Stanfield from Chicago to play alongside Orr, Johnny Bucyk, Johnny McKenzie, Ted Green and rookie Derek Sanderson. They finished third and got knocked out of the playoffs by the Canadiens, who were on their way to another Stanley Cup, but the team began to build their reputation as "the big bad Bruins."

Creating that particular identity was a conscious decision of Sinden's. Every other Original Six team had a distinguishing personality except Boston. Now the Bruins would become a physically formidable club that others had to fight or fear; even their growing reputation helped them win games, Sinden found, because some teams weren't prepared to play all out against their intimidating style.

In 1969, Boston finished the season a close second to Montreal and won their first playoff series in a decade, defeating Toronto, before losing to the Canadiens in an electrifying six-game series. In 1970, Sinden made his reputation as a coach. During the regular season, Orr and Esposito again burned up the league, finishing one-two in scoring; Orr had established his dominance as a rushing defenseman, and Esposito his extraordinarily prolific scoring capacity from the slot. The team then cut a mighty swath through the playoffs, eliminating the Rangers, and running through the Black Hawks and the St. Louis Blues in eight games straight. It was Boston's first Stanley Cup in twenty-nine years; Bruins fans were beside themselves with happiness.

It's characteristic of the man's stubborn pride that Harry J. Sinden resigned three days after his smashing Cup victory. He felt the Bruins' brass didn't value or respect him enough. His evidence was that they second-guessed and criticized him behind his back, and nickle-and-dimed him when he asked to renegotiate his contract: seeking a raise from $22,000 to $30,000, he was offered $25,000, take it or leave it. So after winning hockey's greatest prize, Sinden left the game entirely. He joined a home construction business in Rochester, New York, run by an old schoolmate from Toronto, and became an ordinary fan. Or so he thought.

To stick by his decision to quit hockey, Sinden had to turn his back on no fewer than twelve coaching offers, six from the NHL and six from the WHA; all offered more money than he was making in the construction field. He stayed away for two years. Then came the news that Canada and the Soviet Union had negotiated a best-against-best series to be played that September. Sinden simply couldn't resist: "I sensed right away this series would become the most famous in the history of hockey, and I wanted to be part of it."

Too proud to ask for the coaching job outright, he waited to be approached by Hockey Canada, knowing from news reports that he was being mentioned as a possibility along with Milt Schmidt, Emile Francis, Jean Béliveau and Gordie Howe. When no phone call came, Sinden planted a story with a journalist. The story ran nationally. Still the phone didn't ring.

Finally, Sinden called Alan Eagleson on the pretext of talking about Bobby Orr's hockey camp. Eagleson said he'd been meaning to call, but just hadn't got around to it. The NHL Players Association liked Sinden as Team Canada coach—was he willing to be interviewed for the job?

During the interview in Montreal, Sinden told the Hockey Canada steering committee that he deserved the job because he knew international hockey and had never lost to the Soviets as a player. When they put those facts together with his Stanley Cup victory two years earlier, they decided he was their man. Sinden had some conditions of his own, based on his experiences with the Bruins' front office: he'd pick the team, and he'd run it his way, without interference from the board.

His title would be head coach and general manager, his fee $15,000. It was already June. The opening game of the series was less than three months away.

•

Sinden's first decision was to hire John Ferguson as assistant coach and assistant GM. With so little time to organize Team Canada and prepare it for battle, Sinden needed someone who, like himself, was available immediately.

Ferguson had retired as an active player a year earlier, at the same time as teammate Jean Béliveau—who in his autobiography calls Ferguson "the consummate team man" for his partisanship and work ethic. Ferguson was generally known as the undefeated heavyweight champ of the NHL, but he could also come up with the big play offensively. In his most productive year, 1968-69, he scored twenty-nine goals while playing on a line with Béliveau and Yvan Cournoyer.

Sinden says he didn't know Ferguson off the ice but chose him because he was a rugged battler who had been successful in business and must therefore be "very bright." Ferguson says he was "flattered" to be asked. He accepted without hesitation. At first he thought he might be a playing coach, but he was soon deterred by the Bobby Hull controversy; Ferguson too wasn't under contract to an NHL team. Besides, he'd been off skates a long time. It's doubtful whether his age and conditioning would have allowed him to skate with the Soviets, and his bad-cop playing style would have kept him in the penalty box constantly under international rules. Ferguson was far more valuable on the Team Canada bench. He was closer to some of the players than Sinden and knew how to motivate them.

Although Ferguson had never coached before, the disparity between his experience and Sinden's was far less important than the qualities they shared: a voracious competitiveness and a visceral need for victory, abetted by a readiness to do whatever it takes to win—especially in the service of your country. Each found a soul-mate in the other: someone whose values and temperament coincided symmetrically with his own. When the Soviets stormed from behind to tie Game 3 in Winnipeg, and Sinden screamed at Ferguson, "What the hell is going on here? They're all over the place!", Ferguson looked at him and replied, "I know how you feel. I know just how you feel." That bonding moment made Sinden think of Butch Cassidy and the Sundance Kid, the scene where they're pinned down by a hail of bullets from all directions, and Butch asks Sundance, "Who *are* those guys?"

The two coaches even shared the same superstitious rituals. Sinden had never indulged in superstition before, but after winning Game 6, he vowed to repeat every act that had coincided with vic-tory: wearing his alligator shoes, not watching the team warm up, etc. Before Games 7 and 8, he and Fergie downed two Scotch and waters in Sinden's room at precisely 5:15 before leaving for the arena, just as they had before Game 6, and sat in exactly the same seats on the team bus. Until now, Ferguson had never been a Scotch drinker.

The dark side of their approach to winning was the extra-legal tactics that both coaches not only condoned but occasionally encour-aged. Ferguson could be trenchantly funny on the subject. After Pierre Berton and Charles Templeton objected on air to Team Canada's belligerence in Game 2, he told the press: "I thought it was just another quiet Sunday evening in Boston Garden. Hell, these guys can't know much about the game. That's the way it's been played for the past fifty years, and that's the way it'll be played for another fifty. Has hockey ever been anything else but a street game?

After a century, are we going to change it to suit the fine-arts crowd?"

Potentially more sinister was Ferguson's summing-up at that same point in the series: "I've never played in a series that mattered when the going didn't get rough. My view of it is this: I don't care how we win, as long as we win." In Game 6, that philosophy extended to ordering his players to commit all-out assault on Valery Kharlamov.

Time hasn't mellowed John Ferguson. Today he makes no bones about the instructions he gave Bobby Clarke, recalling in an interview, "What I told Clarke, I told him, 'Kharlamov's hurting us badly, go over and break his ankle. Put him out of the series.' And he did. Kharlamov was the guy who was beating us. There's no friends on the ice, there's never been, for me."

It was no accident that Ferguson chose Clarke. "Nobody else would do it [but Clarke]. That's the way *he* played the game too. You gotta ask the right player. No point in asking [Rod] Gilbert or Ellis or Henderson or even Espo. Clarke had that tenacity about him. He played to win. It was the right thing to do as far as I'm concerned . . . Kharlamov was their most dangerous player. It was very critical that he was put out of action."

Kharlamov missed Game 7 altogether. He was back on the ice for Game 8, but disabled, a hockey artist operating at half-throttle, shot full of Novocain. As Clarke himself has stated, somewhat sheepishly, "I don't know if it broke his ankle or not, but he wasn't a very effective player after that."

The Soviets are quite sure: the ankle was fractured. The act of premeditated violence is widely remembered and denounced in Russian hockey accounts, but little discussed in Canada. In *The Red Machine,* Lawrence Martin refers to the newspaper *Sovyetsky Sport* quoting Clarke as saying he came to feel respect for Kharlamov and embarrassment for injuring him.

Given the closeness of the series, it is entirely possible that, in the final analysis, Kharlamov's crippling is what gave Canada the edge. Ask Harry Sinden, and he replies he knew nothing about Fergie's plan to take out Kharlamov. This seems strange, considering how close the two men were. But Sinden insists the incident came as a surprise to him, and suggests Ferguson's words "break his ankle" were probably just "common locker-room talk."

At the same time, Sinden is completely frank about the consequences of Clarke's slash: "It definitely had a decisive impact on the outcome. You're never as good a team without your star player, and we couldn't contain him as well as we wanted." He pauses, then adds tartly, "I can't say the Soviets were a better team without Kharlamov."

Morris Mott and Herb Pinder both avow that a hockey player does strange things when playing for his country—especially when atrocious refereeing and his opponents' sneak tactics are driving him crazy. It's such an unusual, emotionally charged situation, they say, the rest of us can't possibly know how it feels. Perhaps we can't even judge it fairly. Mott, the history professor, and Pinder, the player agent, remember feeling outraged and disgusted by bad calls and biased officiating in Europe, with the result that they scarcely felt responsible for their actions. Sometimes you just wanted to maim somebody.

This is hardly to justify Ferguson's decision to eliminate Kharlamov from the series, but it does help to describe the psychological context in which the act took place: an act so brutal, it likely would not have occurred even in the brutal NHL. There, a player would have to face the consequences from league authorities and, even more seriously, from avenging adversaries in game after game after game. Team Canada, on the other hand, did not expect to see the Soviets again, ever.

After all, this was war. And come to think of it, Butch Cassidy and the Sundance Kid were outlaws.

•

There is a subsequent, ironic twist to all this: two twists, in fact.

The quarter-century since the '72 series has turned Harry Sinden into one of the NHL's leading opponents of fighting—an advocate for a cleaner game emphasizing finesse rather than fists. Sinden believes fighting will never be eliminated from hockey completely, because of the game's speed and spontaneity, but it should be handled as in other sports: "Players fight in basketball or baseball, too, but they don't play the rest of the game." To illustrate the benefits of his approach, Sinden cites the play of Paul Henderson in '72: "He showed talent we didn't know he had because he wasn't intimidated. He knew the Soviets wouldn't fight him."

The second irony is that, in the same quarter-century, John Ferguson, through his managerial work with the Winnipeg Jets, the New York Rangers and the Ottawa Senators, has become distinguished as one of the NHL's sharpest eyes for European hockey talent—a connoisseur of speed and artistry over brawn and brutality.

After all these years, the two men are still close. In mid-1996, several months after Ferguson quit as the Senators' director of player personnel over the team's mishandling of his most prized discovery, the young Russian Alexei Yashin, Sinden was trying to figure out how to hire Ferguson for the Bruins. Someday, Sinden hoped, Butch and Sundance could be reunited to rob another bank or two.

GAME 7: BACK FROM THE DEAD—AGAIN

"I would have killed to win."
—PHIL ESPOSITO, quoted in *Home Game,* 1989

●

On the morning between Games 6 and 7, Team Canada arrives at the Luzhniki Arena for a 10:30 practice. As the players prepare to go onto the ice, it's obvious there's been some sort of mix-up: the rink is in busy use by a crowd of children, variously described as being in the hundreds or, according to Alan Eagleson, at least five hundred, which seems like stretching it a bit—the international ice surface isn't *that* big. The arena officials inform the Canadians they'll have to travel to a different rink to practise. To which Eagleson responds tactfully, by his own account, "No fucking way!"

The next scene is straight out of the childhood of anyone who grew up contending with the neighbourhood bully on the neighbourhood rink. Eagleson instructs Dennis Hull, whose slapshot rivals his famous brother's, to go out there in full equipment and blast away with a puck. "Suddenly those kids had other things to do," Eagleson has said.

This may be the ultimate Ugly Canadian story. Unable to speak the language, unaccustomed to getting along in another culture, uncomprehending, in the words of Canadian diplomat Patrick

Reid, "that life [has] dimensions beyond the rectangle of a rink and the round of a puck," Team Canada feels justified in resorting to brute force.

Reid has been assigned to Team Canada by the Department of External Affairs as a liaison officer—and less officially, "because the government could see too many possibilities of Murphy's Law coming to pass." Reid's job is to foresee potential diplomatic or other incidents, and to resolve them before they become serious. In his view, at least some of Team Canada's problems are the result of a self-fulfilling prophecy: "A great deal of it was an anticipation on the part of Eagleson and Sinden and others that they were going to get screwed. They were pretty close to paranoid at times. The fact the team was losing didn't help either, so there was a beleaguered attitude. You couldn't say it was just a case of the Soviets being aggressive and the Canadians simply responding. Sometimes it was the other way around."

So the Canadians are feeling victimized, frustrated by alien forces beyond their control. They're victims of fixed officiating, they believe, because the referees are under the thumb of Soviet hockey boss Andrei Starovoitov; the USSR will host the next year's World's championships, and Starovoitov's committee decides which referees will be used in the tournament. And they're victims in an even more vulnerable, personal area: much of the team's remaining cache of steaks, milk and beer transported directly from Canada has gone missing from the Intourist Hotel. The milk they can live without, maybe, but the beer! As Rod Gilbert has said, "That's when we got mad—when they stole our beer after the fifth game."

"They" are, in fact, forerunners of the petty and not-so-petty thieves who flourish in Moscow today under the glories of free enterprise. Steak-thieves on the hotel staff make a tidy profit selling Team Canada's meat to Canadian fans desperate for a decent meal. But in '72, "they" loom larger than life as the faceless Soviet state, the whole diabolical Communist system, which Team Canada feels it is battling symbolically on the ice and literally at the Intourist. At three in the morning, telephones in some of the players' rooms ring mysteriously, disrupting their sleep; when they pick up the phone, the line is dead. Frank Mahovlich, Phil Esposito and Paul Henderson all report getting these calls. So does Brad Park, who also says the intercom in his room crackles with voices speaking Russian in the dead of night.

These real-life problems don't improve the Canadians' state of mind. Before even arriving in Moscow, they've been told to expect to be eavesdropped upon, possibly followed. Phil Esposito told journalist Scott Morrison, "You always had the feeling you were being watched. And there's no doubt in my mind we were." By whom? By "the KGB," in Team Canada parlance—not just some run-of-the-mill plainclothes policemen, but the big-league Soviet intelligence agency.

Patrick Reid, who will eventually become commissioner general of Expo 86 in Vancouver, works closely with Canadian embassy official Gary Smith. Between them, they try to oversee arrangements at the Intourist to ensure that team members and their wives are comfortable. For the benefit of all the visiting Canadians, they set up a trilingual information desk—English, French and Russian—in the Intourist lobby to answer Canadians' questions and concerns about coping with the peculiarities of life in Moscow: the currency, the black market, the atrocious food, the prostitutes, the law, the fearsome "floor ladies"—concierges who tyrannize every floor of the hotel, demanding foreigners surrender their keys whenever they leave their rooms, and generally treating everyone like dirt. The information desk, Reid remembers, is "besieged morning, noon and night."

Told that some players are checking their rooms for listening devices, Reid assures them the bugs are undoubtedly there, but will be ineffective; the eavesdroppers will never decipher their fast-paced hockey patter anyway. As for the phantom phone calls, Reid himself is awakened twice by voiceless rings to his room. He takes the matter up with the hotel manager: henceforth, all calls to Team Canada rooms after midnight are to be routed through the Canadian information staff, who will pass on messages. The calls cease. Reid speculates the reason isn't hockey espionage as much as the notoriously inefficient Soviet telephone system.

But the players, influenced by their own officials and a steady diet of the spy movies so popular at the time, firmly believe "the KGB" is everywhere: watching, listening, plotting. One classic story is said to involve Frank Mahovlich, who later denies it; or perhaps it's Phil Esposito and Wayne Cashman, except that they too have denied it. Apocryphal or not, the story bears repeating, since it's emblematic of the Canadians' perilous journey to the land of the KGB.

Two players are scouting their room at the Intourist. Their thorough inspection includes tearing up the broadloom to search for suspicious-looking devices. Sure enough, they find one planted underneath the carpeting: a metal gizmo secured to the wooden floor with bolts. Enterprisingly, one of the players takes a Canadian quarter from his pocket and proceeds to unscrew the contraption. As the last bolt emerges, the players can hear a distant, oddly musical crash. They have dismantled a glass chandelier hanging from the ceiling below.

Phil Esposito is the source of a more fully documented tale. Esposito remembers his buddy Wayne Cashman convincing himself the mirror in his room is bugged. Cashman rips the mirror from its mountings, carries it to the window and throws it outside. Afterwards, Cashman's wife has to go to the Espositos' room to put on her make-up.

But the Canadians aren't the only paranoid ones. Before Game 7, Patrick Reid takes up a sore point with Starovoitov and his English-speaking colleague Alexander Gresko: there are "far too many uniforms for comfort" in the arena, Reid points out, because of the omnipresent militiamen stationed in the aisles and around the perimeter of the rink. Security guards have been confiscating any horns or noisemakers they see Canadians carrying into the arena.

Starovoitov replies, in Reid's account: "We agree that a decrease in uniformed security guards would be desirable, but there is concern about possible incidents between our citizens and Canadians; both on and off the ice. We are not used to the demonstrations put on by your fans."

Starovoitov goes on to say that in the event of an incident, no action will be taken against Canadians until a senior officer has been called to the scene. What he does not say is that the Soviet authorities are anxious not only about "incidents" and "demonstrations" menacing public order but about the influence these may have on their own populace. A sudden outbreak of free speech is to be prevented at all costs. The Soviets have seldom, if ever, played host to such a large throng of foreigners within their borders, much less televised their behaviour; the Canadians' outspoken conduct, in full view of a Soviet TV audience of fifty million, runs the danger of setting an example. No wonder the authorities are nervous.

The repressive atmosphere doesn't prevent all interaction between Muscovites and foreigners. Out on the streets, Canadians often find a different attitude. Almost to a person, they encounter an inquisitive, hospitable people, at least among those out of uniform. As Pat Stapleton remembers, "I think they wanted to be friendly, they wanted to know what was going on. There weren't a lot of people laughing or smiling, but we'd walk down the street and the children would speak pretty good English to us. Or older people would stop you and tell you in sign language they'd seen you on TV. Then my wife, Jackie, and I picked up on a few words of Russian, and people smiled when we used their language."

Jackie Stapleton enjoys the excursions laid on by the Intourist tourism agency to the Bolshoi Ballet, the Moscow Circus and the Kremlin Museum, and appreciates a chance to get away one-to-one with Nadia, her tour guide. "I wanted to buy a recording of the Soviet national anthem and a song they played at the arena before the games, 'Cowards Don't Play Hockey,' " she recalls. "Nadia took me to a record store, and on the way we were able to talk more freely. She asked me about my family, and when I told her I had five children at that time, she was shocked I would have so many. She said how different it was there—you were only allowed to have two children, and the women worked. The state provided daycare. You could leave your kids there all week, you didn't have to pick them up in the evening. And of course the kids were indoctrinated into their system that way."

At Team Canada's morning practice, Harry Sinden is dealing with yet another apparent mix-up. At noon, Vsevolod Bobrov appears with an interpreter to say it's time Team Canada vacated the ice for the Soviet team practice. Sinden bluntly refuses. He produces an itinerary that states the Canadians have the ice until 12:30, the Soviets for the following two hours. Bobrov doesn't agree with the itinerary.

Sinden replies: "I don't care what you say. We're not leaving until 12:30. If you want to bring your players out on the ice before that, I don't know what might happen to them." This time, brinkmanship seems entirely more appropriate, and it works. Bobrov concedes the point. World War Three is averted.

Perhaps Bobrov feels Sinden owes him one; the Soviet hockey authorities have just decided to accept the Canadian demand that Baader and Kompalla not referee again in the series. After practice, Sinden meets with Karel Romansky, chairman of the Soviet Committee on Sports and Physical Education, accompanied by the English-speaking Alexander Gresko. The pair agree to Sinden's insistence that the West German officials be sidelined—but only after Romansky spends fifteen minutes haranguing Sinden about his team's behaviour the night before.

Romansky enters three official protests against the Canadians. One, their mistreatment of the referees. Two, the aggressive conduct of the players in street clothes, especially Bobby Orr: "I have great respect for Orr," Romansky says, "but you should teach your players to control their tempers." Three, Gary Bergman's taunts to coach Bobrov. Romansky states, "Coaches and officials are sacred in Russia. If your players address our coach in this manner again, we may not be able to control our players."

Sinden tells the Soviets they can expect no further trouble from Bergman or any other Canadian player or official, as long as the refereeing problem is fixed. When they agree, he can feel "the relief pouring out of me."

That night, Sinden and his players relax a bit at the huge embassy bash thrown by Ambassador Ford for Team Canada and all the visiting Canadians. The stage is set for a thrilling Game 7 tomorrow evening.

•

"Do or die" is becoming almost routine. Introducing the telecast for the folks at home, announcer Pat Marsden states, "This may well be the most important game in the history of our national pastime." Team Canada has to reach down and come up with another big game, just two nights after their last one. If ever they needed all that down-to-the-wire, come-from-behind Stanley Cup playoff experience they've accumulated over the years, this is the time.

Game 7 will take a different shape from all the previous games. There will be no goals scored in bunches, never a lead larger than one goal. Although their styles and skills and virtues are still quite distinct, the two teams have become so evenly balanced in strength, and have learned to play each other's strengths so well, that it's impossible to pick a favourite. At the same time, the Canadians have run out of alibis. They have the referees they want, Bata and Dahlberg. Ferguson and Clarke have seen to it that they don't have to contend with Valery Kharlamov. And they're in much better physical condition. It's time not only to do or die, but to put up or shut up.

Sinden and Ferguson continue their practice of alternating goalies; tonight it's Tony Esposito, out to erase the memory of his nightmarish third period in Game 5. The only other change from the Game 6 line-up is Bill Goldsworthy for Red Berenson.

Bobrov and Kulagin seem to acknowledge the need to get more size and experience back into the Soviet game. Gusev and Kuzkin return to the defense, while Anisin's two young wingers, Bodunov and Lebedev, are benched. Yuri Blinov joins the Petrov-Mikhailov line. The wounded Kharlamov is replaced by hard-nosed veteran Evgeny Mishakov, who doesn't back down from a fight. And despite all the talk of spelling off Tretiak with alternate goalies Victor Zinger or Alexander Sidelnikov, talk started in Canada by the Soviets themselves, Tretiak is in the net again for the seventh straight game. His goals-against average to this point is 3.50, which the Soviet coaches clearly consider more than respectable against the Canadian shooters.

The Canadian power play has scored only once in the entire series so far, out of fifteen attempts—a record that would be considered shameful in the NHL. At the two-minute mark, Boris Mikhailov goes off for a somewhat dubious tripping penalty, and Canada fails to score once again; but the power-play personnel are still on the ice a few seconds after Mikhailov's return, and Henderson puts the puck into the right corner. Ellis races after it and centres to Phil Esposito. Taking the pass with his back to the net in a traffic jam, Esposito pivots, shielding the puck from the defensemen, and shoots low and true between Tretiak's pads. The Soviets are having little more success than NHL teams in shutting down Esposito in the slot.

As Peter Mahovlich and Mishakov serve coincidental minors, Sinden paces feverishly back and forth behind his players, while Bobrov gazes meditatively at the ice. With the teams back at full strength, Alexander Yakushev gives Sinden something more to worry about. Esposito loses the faceoff in the Soviet end to Vladimir Shadrin, the Moscow Spartak centre who has emerged as a master of faceoffs, and Shadrin streaks away with the puck, passing up to Yakushev on his left. His lanky legs gobbling up the ice, Yakushev leaves Park and Bergman to eat ice chips. Yakushev hits the Canadian blueline in no time, draws his stick back and blasts a slapshot that literally blows Tony Esposito over on its way into the net.

With the score tied at one, the teams play every bit as physically as in the previous game. Dahlberg and Bata jump on any sign of a violent outbreak but dole out the penalties more even-handedly than Baader and Kompalla.

At 12:39, Esposito is penalized for cross-checking Mikhailov. Ever verbal, Esposito rags Mikhailov, trying to goad him into retaliating, but the Soviet player airily waves him off to the penalty box. From there, Esposito resorts to a more primitive form of communication, a drawn-out charade of hand signals—the finger across the throat, followed by the pointed finger and the raised dukes: "You. Me. Fight." We're back to the old bully-on-the-neighbourhood-rink stuff again. But the Soviets aren't much better. Mikhailov, their designated pest, skates past the Canadian bench and mimics "You're nuts" to John Ferguson, giving him a circular motion of the finger beside his head.

The penalties are three apiece when the Soviets get their next power-play opportunity, Bill White off for interference, and it results in one of the most spectacular goals in the series. Vladimir Vikulov carries the puck to centre ice. Canada has three men back, Ellis, Park and Bergman, but suddenly Vladimir Petrov splits Ellis and Park to catch up to Vikulov's lead pass and burst in alone on Tony Esposito. Petrov draws Esposito out. Sprawling in desperation, Tony lunges with his stick and nearly succeeds in poking the puck away from Petrov, but the Soviet centre recovers it, swirls around the fallen goaltender and backhands a shot into the net before Ellis, literally soaring through the air, can smother it. The Soviets go up 2-1.

They come right back after that goal, Yakushev threatening again. At this point, Team Canada is wilting. But some great forechecking by Phil Esposito—who one way or another manages to be constantly at the centre of things—breaks up the Soviet attack. Then he, Cournoyer and Parise go on the offensive. All three of them move in on Tretiak like wolves on a fallen deer, but Parise can't hoist the puck high enough over the goaltender's body.

Esposito wins the next faceoff, to the left of Tretiak. He passes across to Parise on his left, who sends it diagonally back to Savard at the blueline. Savard fakes a shot, pirouettes to elude his man as gracefully as a two-hundred-pound defenseman can, and moves in closer. Esposito, who has just been dumped to the ice, scrambles to his feet in time to take Savard's short lateral in the high slot and flicks a quick wrist shot between Tretiak and the post for his second goal of the period.

The Soviets 2, Esposito 2. Despite being outplayed, Canada takes the tie into the intermission.

Things heat up further in the second period. There's plenty of stick work around heads and faces. On two occasions, the teams play five a side, and the Soviets generally get the better of it, knowing how to spread out and make better use of the big ice surface. But Tony Esposito just keeps getting stronger and stronger: he needs to. He stops Liapkin's drive, and Yakushev's, and kicks out an excellent chance by Maltsev cruising in for a point-blank shot—Maltsev always a bridesmaid in this series but never a bride, despite being one of the all-time top Soviet scorers and having more shots on goal in the series than any Soviet player.

Miraculously, thanks to the inspired goaltending of one Esposito and the inspired penalty-killing of the other, and the fact that Vikulov shoots over top of the net on a breakaway, the Soviets are kept off the scoresheet throughout the period. The game is still tied 2-2 at the second intermission. In the late moments, Henderson is dumped in the corner by Vasiliev, and Ellis charges in to clobber the big defenseman in retaliation. "It wouldn't take much to cause a real donnybrook in this game," Foster Hewitt observes. "They're getting chippier every minute."

The third period begins with a bang. The remnants of the GAG Line, with Dennis Hull replacing Hadfield on left wing, make their mark. Rushing into the Soviet zone on right wing, Gilbert stretches to intercept Gusev's pass and feeds Ratelle driving to the net. Ratelle is checked; the puck bounces into the left corner. Another careless Soviet pass behind the net ends up on Gilbert's stick, and he strides out to backhand the puck between Tretiak's pads on a smart wrap-around.

Canada's 3-2 lead holds up for exactly three minutes and two seconds. The Soviets are once again on the power play, with Bergman off for holding. Phil Esposito kills time by masterfully ragging the puck in the Soviet end and gets dragged to the ice by Liapkin. There ought to be a penalty, especially under international rules, but the play is allowed to go right on. Setting up in the Canadian end, the Soviets throw the puck around, calmly keeping possession, until Maltsev in the right corner zings it straight across the goal mouth to Yakushev, just when Park is looking the wrong way. Unmolested near the left post, Yakushev skillfully directs the pass past Tony Esposito, who has no chance whatever. Yakushev and Phil Esposito have now both scored twice in the game, confirming their ongoing status as their teams' leading scorers.

Prior to the ten-minute mark and the change of ends, the Soviets come at the Canadian net in wave after wave, exerting tremendous pressure on the power play during a foolish penalty to Gilbert for charging Mikhailov—Team Canada's new target now that Kharlamov is out. Tony Esposito makes big saves on Yakushev and Vikulov. His superb goaltending is unquestionably making the difference, keeping Canada in the game.

Now that both the game and the series are going down to the wire, the mutual animosity between the two teams is more naked than ever. The pressure finally seems to be getting to the Soviets, sowing discord internally. Stapleton notices that, on the Soviet bench, smiles have turned to frowns, and players appear to be jumping on one another, blaming the other guy for mistakes.

With about three and a half minutes to play and the score still 3-3, Harry Sinden is silently praying his faltering team can hold onto the tie: it won't be enough to win the series, but it will be a damn sight better than a loss. Just then the flow of the game, and the Soviets' growing momentum, are interrupted by the biggest fight of the series. Bergman traps the puck against the boards behind the Canadian net. Jamming against him, Boris Mikhailov clamps a blatant headlock on Bergman as the play is whistled dead. Bergman freaks. Struggling and squirming free of the headlock, he goes for Mikhailov with flailing fists, trying to climb over the referee to get at him. Panicking, Mikhailov too loses control and kicks repeatedly at Bergman with his skate blade. Cournoyer, normally a peaceable soul, sees red; he comes in and connects with several roundhouse punches to Mikhailov's head. Yakushev arrives to restrain Cournoyer. Phil Esposito arrives to restrain Yakushev, rapping him smartly on the side of the helmet. Suddenly Soviet and Canadian players are all paired off, clutching each other like long-lost brothers in an orgy of international friendship.

Mikhailov goes off first, a five-minute major for roughing. Bergman discovers his stocking and shin pad are torn and his leg bleeding; he also gets five minutes for roughing. Everyone else, even Cournoyer, is spared. It seems reasonable in the circumstances. Both sides are more or less responsible for the mayhem, and neither side is put at a disadvantage.

The Soviet public and the international viewing audience are now treated to a thuggish display by Bergman. Although understandably upset as he skates to the penalty box to the shrilling of thousands of high-pitched whistles, and justifiably outraged at being kicked, he makes a revolting spectacle as he repeatedly points to Mikhailov in the next box and runs his finger razorlike across his throat.

The teams go back to playing hockey, five a side. Some fire has gone out of the Soviet attack. In such an explosive contest, the 3-3 tie seems more fragile every second. It will be broken by the one player who most believes in his heart he has another goal in him.

With slightly more than two minutes left in the game, Guy Lapointe fires the puck behind the Canadian net to defense partner

Savard. Lugging it up the boards, Savard hits Paul Henderson with a pass as he speeds over the blueline. Henderson zags swiftly through the neutral zone, leaving Soviet forwards scrambling in his wake, and bears down on Vasiliev and Tsygankov. Just over the Soviet blueline, Henderson works some occult magic on both the puck and the two defenders. It's as if he possesses predestined knowledge of the puck's intentions. With a shoulder fake, Henderson makes as if to split the defensemen—but instead slips the puck between them, outflanks them to the left and recovers the puck as it skitters off a Soviet skate and arrives obediently back onto his stick. Sweeping past Tsygankov, Henderson drives in on Tretiak, but Vasiliev starts hauling him down from behind. Falling, Henderson realizes there's only one spot to shoot the puck—high over Tretiak's right elbow, just under the crossbar—and that's exactly where he fires it, winning the game for Canada and making the series dead-even.

The goal is a masterpiece. Later Henderson will say, "When you're totally focussed, you can sometimes do things you never dreamed possible."

•

After the goal, the red light doesn't flash on. John Ferguson thinks maybe the Soviets plan to deny Canada the goal. Immediately he runs along behind the bench, telling the players to get onto the ice and congratulate Henderson. Amid their celebrating, the goal judge belatedly turns on the light.

Although it's Henderson who administers the coup de grâce, others clinch the victory in the final two minutes and six seconds. Tony Esposito makes four more saves, including another on unlucky Maltsev, for a total of twenty-eight. Ron Ellis gets off his best shot of the series, hitting Tretiak with such force that he's lifted right off his feet and turned head over heels. Bill White and Pat Stapleton throw their bodies all over the ice to block Soviet shots in the closing seconds.

At last the horn sounds. Team Canada has walked out of the graveyard.

For 3,000 delirious Canadian fans in Moscow, faith in their team is 100 per cent confirmed. As they file euphorically out of the arena into the chilly night air to board the waiting buses, the Canadians get two surprises. One is that the ground has been transformed during the game by a blanket of snow, a reminder of what will soon await them at home.

The other surprise is less pleasant: they are confronted by a wall of soldiers with bayonets fixed to their rifles. The troops have been dispatched to the scene to deal with some Soviet officer's fantasy of a riot started by foreigners armed chiefly with horns and maple-leaf flags. What follows is best described by a passage from Patrick Reid's recent memoir *Wild Colonial Boy*: "Canadians, wondering and suddenly quiet, moved right up to the soldiers, standing rigidly at ease, and could be seen gazing questioningly into the stolid young faces. A legless Soviet veteran, bemedalled, paddled his way forward on a board supported by ballbearings just large enough to keep him off the ground, made for the officer patrolling in front of his troops and shouted angrily. The officer was taken aback, gesticulating at the Canadians, explaining. The veteran was far from mollified, swung around to face the nearest group of Canadians and shouted again in Russian. Then came three words in English, 'I am sorry,' as he pushed off into the night. He was cheered as he left."

EIGHTEEN

THE INEFFABLE GRACE OF PAUL HENDERSON

"I basically learned how to play on the roads and the ponds."
— PAUL HENDERSON, 1995

●

You have to love Paul Henderson. You have to love someone whose knack for success in life transcends mere ambition and hard work and talent and luck—although all are abundantly present—to acquire a mysterious kind of grace. Whether achieved through his personal determination or some less worldly means, Henderson's blessedness becomes him. It seems his element.

An incident from early in his NHL career illustrates this happy state. Breaking in with the Detroit Red Wings, Henderson got to play nearly five seasons with his idol, Gordie Howe. In that time, he saw plenty of evidence to conclude that Howe was "one of the meanest suckers ever to play the game." Then, on March 3, 1968, the young left winger was involved in a major trade. In exchange for superstar Frank Mahovlich, Pete Stemkowski, Gary Unger and the rights to Carl Brewer, Henderson was sent to the Toronto Maple Leafs along with centre Norm Ullman and right winger Floyd Smith.

At first, Henderson felt "betrayed" by the organization he'd played for since his junior days. But soon he faced a more pressing problem: in his first game against his old team, he had to line up opposite Gordie Howe. The aging but unmellowing Howe had a well-earned reputation for headhunting his former teammates after they'd been traded. "I'd seen Gordie do it a hundred times," Henderson recalls. "He'd just go out and pitchfork them. So I figured he'd be coming after me, and I was more than apprehensive."

As they lined up against each other, Henderson was determined not to say anything, or otherwise to give Howe any excuse for violent retribution: "So Gordie says, 'Paul, how's everything? Family okay?' And I just said, 'Yeah, they're okay.' I was suspicious, I wasn't sure if it was a set-up. But you know? He never, ever gave me a shot. And I have no idea why."

Henderson's exemption from Howe's peculiar code is a mystery. Maybe it was because Howe recognized Henderson was himself a relatively clean and blameless player. Or maybe, just maybe, it had something to do with Howe's recognition of kinship with the younger man. There is a striking series of parallels between these two, both archetypal local heroes who became, in very different ways, Canadian icons.

It starts with their family backgrounds—rural working-class, just this side of poverty—and even the circumstances of their births. Howe's mother delivered him herself on a Saskatchewan farm in 1928; Henderson arrived in a blizzard in January 1943 before his grandfather, driving a horse-drawn sleigh, could get his mother to the little hospital in Kincardine, Ontario. Both boys were close to their mothers; both had fathers who were big, strong, domineering, wrathful and short with praise. Garnet Henderson, a 250-pound station agent for Canadian National Railways who coached Paul in his early years in Lucknow, a small town near Lake Huron, told him always to take his first shot of the game straight at the goalie's head.

Like Howe, Henderson learned his hockey on icy roads and ponds, using Eaton's catalogues for shin pads, and owed his first real hockey equipment to the generosity of neighbours—in Henderson's case, the Chin family, who ran the town's Chinese restaurant. Howe and Henderson shared the dream of starring in the NHL with millions of Canadian boys and practised writing their autographs over and over. But in both cases, their dream was borne out by exceptional skills that attracted the interest of NHL scouts by the time they were fifteen: Henderson because he scored eighteen goals in a single playoff game.

From there, Howe's and Henderson's careers diverged considerably. The older man was by far the more complete all-round player: Howe set a galaxy of NHL scoring records that would stand until Wayne Gretzky came along and established records for career longevity that will likely never be met: Henderson himself calls Howe "the most amazing athlete who's ever played pro sports." Nonetheless, by quite a different route, Henderson became a national hero too—a name and face so instantly recognizable that he can't enjoy the privacy the rest of us take for granted, can't visit a restaurant to this day without being accosted by complete strangers and asked for the autograph he once polished so long ago. Henderson acquired that status through his brilliant performance during the eight games against the Soviets in 1972—and in particular, through one singular, climactic goal, "the goal of the century," the most celebrated instance of Paul Henderson's ineffable grace and good fortune.

And yet some have wondered how fortunate he really was. An old saying among NHLers goes, "Thank God I didn't score the winning goal against the Russians." Dennis Hull gives it this twist in his after-dinner speaking engagements: "Paul Henderson scored the winning goal, but he became a born-again Christian afterwards. So I thank God every night it wasn't me." Henderson has been present many times when Hull says this, and thinks it's "a good line." He also acknowledges his life became easier financially after the series made him an instant celebrity, but in other ways much, much harder. He terms that period his "dark days." Luckily for him, he likes a challenge.

●

The lettering on the door reads: "Leadership Ministries, Campus Crusade, Athletes in Action." The door is the entrance to a low, flat-roofed, one-storey office building on an industrial street just north of the Gardiner Expressway in the western Toronto borough of Etobicoke. Inside, Paul Henderson commandeers the small board-room table and fields questions about the '72 series for easily the five-thousandth time. At fifty-three, he's enviably trim, Hollywood-handsome. His well-articulated features are not particularly marred by his hockey veteran's badge, the nose twisted inevitably sideways. His full head of tightly curled hair is still more brown than grey.

Charisma is an overworked noun, but Henderson possesses it. As the whiplash energy and rapid-fire words come pouring out of him, colours spark from his penetrating hazel eyes, sentences and fragments of sentences tumbling over and into each other. His self-esteem seems to verge on egomania, until a radiant smile breaks out and banishes such impressions. It's a smile that makes you feel good.

You mention what Henderson's best friend Ron Ellis has told you about how different they are.

He grins with pleasure. "Yeah, I'm the eternal optimist. It doesn't matter what it is, I always think I can do it. If I'm playing golf and start out badly, I'll be two-under the rest of the way. I'd be out on the ice with Ronnie and we'd need a goal, and I'd say, 'I've got one. I'll get one for us.' "

In Moscow, Henderson was absolutely convinced the team would win, and his faith paid off in spades. He got hooked, tripped, spun off his feet, yet always came back with as much heedless dash and demonic determination as before. Without detracting from anyone else's contributions, it's arguable (as with Phil Esposito) that without Henderson's opportunism and self-made luck, Canada would have lost. "I just thought, 'How the heck can we live with the Russians beating us?' So you tell yourself, *'We're not gonna lose.'* Ronnie is the direct opposite. Maybe that's why we're so close. He's ten times better than he ever thought he was. And if I was ever *half* as good as I thought, I'd be great."

Henderson pauses to think a moment. "I don't know where I get that from. It's funny, my siblings aren't much like me. My wife says as a joke, 'I think they put you in the wrong family.' I get up in the morning and I'm excited. I just can't wait to get at the day to see what's going to happen."

In summer 1972, when Henderson received his invitation to attend Team Canada's training camp, what was exciting him was an impending holiday on the Rhine River. His wife, Eleanor, a Lucknow girl he'd married at nineteen, was looking forward to the trip too, and Henderson was far from sure he'd take up Harry Sinden's invitation. He changed his mind after his agent, the ubiquitous Alan Eagleson, had a word with him; and after he'd met an Olympic athlete, shooter Susan Nattrass, who told him how great it felt to represent Canada internationally.

Once at camp, Henderson threw himself into the challenge of making the team. Although he'd scored a career-high thirty-eight goals the previous season, putting him among the NHL's top ten goal scorers, he wasn't considered a shoo-in. He was known as a streak scorer; when he was hot, he was hot, but he wasn't always. In '72, nobody dreamed just how hot he'd get, and at just the perfect time.

Henderson is under no illusions about his personal gifts as a hockey player. He knows his limitations, his need for the right kind of linemates to help him shine: "Some luck's involved. The better the players I was paired with, the better I looked. Ronnie and Clarke and I complemented each other. I wasn't the greatest stick-handler—speed was my asset. I had good anticipation, and I could break into the holes. So if I had guys who could get me the puck, I could do the things I was good at."

Reflecting on his achievement in '72, he credits not so much his hockey skills as the attitude he brought to the whole experience. Today, whenever he does motivational speaking as part of his Christian outreach ministry, he cites "some wonderful lessons in life from that series," lessons that he considers crucial to success in any endeavour, from work to relationships: "Basically, I made a commitment to Team Canada. I said, this is what I'm going to do, and whether I play or don't play, I'm going to shut my mouth, I'm not going to cause problems, I'm going to do whatever I have to do as a *team* member. That's really freeing, you know. And of course you become a very positive influence in that type of situation."

At camp, Henderson decided it didn't matter that he, Ellis and Clarke were considered add-ons to the team; he would just "enjoy the process. I went in and decided I was going to enjoy myself. Make a commitment and pay the price. And if I get a chance to play, I'm going to be ready. You can bring that attitude back over into life all the time. It's a matter of taking responsibility."

Today, everyone remembers The Goal in Game 8. Fewer remember Henderson actually scored the winning goal in each of the final three games in Moscow. Fewer still remember that if Team Canada hadn't blown its Game 5 lead to lose 5-4, Henderson's goal—the fourth for Canada—could have been the winner that time, too. Four game-winners would have been incredible; three were simply extraordinary.

To the man himself, the Game 7 masterpiece has always been the best goal of his career. Henderson says he'd never before beaten two defensemen head to head, gone in alone on the goalie and beaten him, too—and the goalie one of the greatest who ever played. And he never did again. Not only that, but Team Canada was dead in the series if it let Game 7 slip away, or even settled for a tie: "No question. If I don't score that sucker—and there are only a couple of minutes left in the game—it's all over, the last game means nothing. I scored seven goals in that series, and the only garbage goal I got was the last one—it drives me *nuts*. Kids nowadays don't see the other goals, they only see that one."

How did he feel towards the Soviet players during the series?

"I was very cognizant of their skill level. I'd find myself watching them and really feel enamoured and even jealous of their abilities. I mean, they were much more skilled than we were—much more. I wasn't proud of a lot of the ways we conducted ourselves. We gave them ten shots for every one they gave us. But that's the Canadian way. And that's the thing the Russians never understand—our intensity. And probably our brutality. They were much better sportsmen than we were."

Some Team Canada members deny knowledge of Clarke's two-hander on Kharlamov, or at least downplay its importance. Not Henderson. "That's Clarke's mentality. It's a mentality that's always been there. But I'd never subscribe to it. If you have to win that way, it's not worthwhile to me—get out of the game. If it's war, that's fine. If it's a life-and-death situation, if somebody's going to rape my children, then that's different. But to me, a sportsman is a person who plays within the rules."

Henderson cites the fierce competitive rivalries among Olympic athletes—swimmers, runners, decathletes—who nevertheless put their arms around each other when the competition is over. That, he says, is what sportsmanship is all about. Could he have extended that spirit to his Soviet rivals in '72?

"No," he admits, "we hated their guts. They were embarrassing us. I hated the suckers. You get caught up in the emotion. Even Whitey Stapleton told me he found himself doing things he'd never have done in the NHL. It's easy to use this as an excuse, but basically we wanted to win so badly, we justified it as their ideology, their whole system, the Russians wanting to take over the world, it's a corrupt society and all that. So it was a winning-at-all-costs attitude."

Henderson became part of the general panic and hysteria: "I mean, I was ready to walk off the ice. You get so sick of it—the manipulation of the referees and that kind of stuff. But why lower yourself to that level? The problem wasn't the Russian players— they were ten times the sportsmen we were—it was the things going on behind the scenes. So you took it out on their players."

Now, it all looks different. "Now we've gotten to know them. Tretiak, Petrov, Mikhailov, they're wonderful people. I was able to meet some of them in '90 when I went over for the ministry. They had a do at the embassy in Moscow. Yakushev was there, Tarasov came, we had a great time. We met some of their wives. They're very nice people trying to raise a family in a not very encouraging situation."

During the "Relive the Dream" series in 1987, when godless Communism still reigned supreme in the USSR, Henderson made a rather unusual overture to his former enemies. He gave each of them a copy of the Bible in Russian. "I told them that in '72 I'd hated them, but that I didn't hate them any more because I understood the love of Christ and how much he loved me. I think that broke down the barriers between us. They were touched by it, and I got some real good feedback from them. Six of them asked for another Bible. They wanted to give it to their mothers, but they didn't want to give away the one I'd given them."

•

Henderson's Christianity is so inseparable from his life now that it's also his work.

Before he became born-again in 1975 under the tutelage of chaplain Mel Stevens, Henderson endured what he has called his "dark days": two years in which he "received enough attention to last me a lifetime," developed an ulcer, and "didn't know who I was or where I was going in my life." After the '72 series, he faltered through two difficult, anticlimactic seasons with the Leafs, then jumped leagues to the Toronto Toros of the WHA, owned by the late Johnny F. Bassett. Henderson felt good about the move: it got him out from under the tyranny of Harold Ballard, and at least somewhat away from the tyranny of being expected to score the winning goal every night he played at home. He felt even better when the Toros moved to Birmingham, Alabama, in 1976 and became the Bulls.

In the Deep South, Paul Henderson wasn't a national hero,wasn't an icon, wasn't an autograph. He was just another guy pushing a supermarket cart with his wife or taking his family to church. Away from the constant media glare of Toronto, he played golf and tennis year-round to his heart's content, and indulged himself on long rides through the countryside on his dirt bike. The WHA wasn't the NHL, and Birmingham wasn't a knowledgeable hockey town, but the fans came to watch, the team paid well, and Henderson was one of the league's top scorers (thirty-seven goals in his best year).

Ironically, in the magnolia-scented Bible Belt, Paul Henderson felt he'd come home. He left behind in Toronto the unbearable burden of a Hockey Messiah, the impossibility of satisfying other people's continuing expectations, the tidal wave of moral and spiritual confusion he'd tried to turn back with alcohol. Christian faith, he decided, did a better job than booze of restoring a sense of purpose to a life knocked off balance. "With hindsight, moving to Birmingham was the best thing I ever did. I needed to get out of here. We needed to slow down as a family. My wife and I were a couple of country kids, and it got us reestablished and back on a solid foundation in our marriage. And the kids [their three daughters, Heather, Jennifer and Jill] loved it."

The Hendersons stayed eight years in Birmingham—four years past his retirement from hockey in 1980, after a final season back in the NHL with the Atlanta Flames. Paul Henderson, private citizen, worked in the brokerage business awhile, then entered a seminary to prepare to "do Christian work" as a layman. When he was repeatedly unable to obtain the necessary documents to work in the U.S., the Hendersons reluctantly recided to return to Toronto in 1984. And yet, Henderson wrote in his 1992 autobiography *Shooting for Glory,* "I realized I had a natural platform that few others have, so why waste it? Canada was the place the Lord could use me the most."

He opened a Toronto branch plant of Campus Crusade for Christ and its offshoot, Athletes in Action, a ministry to pro athletes in football, hockey, baseball and other sports. These days, Henderson devotes the greater part of his energies to another off-shoot of these organizations, Leadership Ministries, which he developed himself: a ministry directed to men in business and the professions, whose aim he describes as "getting them to slow down and examine the spiritual side of life"—essentially what he feels he did to bring his own dark days to an end.

If you're interested, Paul Henderson, softcore evangelist, will come and speak to your group about how Paul Henderson, hockey immortal, learned to take his personal walk with the Lord. It wasn't easy for him. But Henderson feels able to say, "I wouldn't change places with anyone." He can say it today, just as he could have said it on September 28, 1972. Perhaps it's a little easier, knowing things have all been ordained this way.

GAME 8:
SPIRIT TO DRAW ON

"We do not have the spirit to draw on that these Canadians
do. . . . [They have] a light that cannot be put out. You
defeat them sometimes, but you discourage them never."

— ANATOLY TARASOV, quoted in *Country on Ice*
by Doug Beardsley

●

At the news conference after Game
7, Harry Sinden predicts the final game of the series "will be the greatest ever in hockey." Game 8 is that and more. Technically or artisti-
cally, other games may have been as great or greater, but unquestionably this is the *biggest* game in the history of the sport—before or since.

It's extraordinary in several ways. For the intangible yet enormous prize at stake, the unofficial global championship of the real
world of hockey. For the gut-wrenching drama and intolerable suspense. For the superb quality of the hockey itself. For the shocking
extracurricular events that transpire on ice, which threaten to over-
shadow the game. And for the equally bizarre off-ice intrigues that
precede it, which nearly prevent the game from happening at all.

The substance of those intrigues are the continuing machinations
over the refereeing. These now reach their logical yet absurd climax: absurd because all the anguished, tortured twists and turns
(mostly introduced, it must be said, by the Soviets) simply result in a
fairly normal and predictable compromise.

Until Team Canada won Game 6, the Soviets have been, if not

perfect hosts, at least hospitable. Floating on the self-satisfaction generated by their showing in the first five games, the Soviet hockey authorities believed they were on their way to an athletic and propaganda victory, and so could act generously towards their guests. But with the Canadian victory in Game 6, the funny stuff began—the mix-ups over practice times, the military presence in the arena, and the various mind games, especially around the choice of referees.

Nothing else gets Harry Sinden, John Ferguson, Alan Eagleson and their players so upset as the officiating. Do we think the wily Soviets haven't noticed? They're counting on their opponents getting their long johns in a thorough knot. The tempest this matter stirs in the wild Canadian breast may be an even more potent Soviet weapon than any actual bias in the refereeing.

That bias, incidentally, is debatable: it's a bias more towards the international style played by the Soviets, and against the NHL style, than towards the Soviet team itself. But to the Canadian sensibility, it amounts to the same thing. The fact that both sides now get so exercised over the selection of referees is hardly surprising: with the series in a dead heat after seven games, about to be settled by a single match, every advantage counts.

Back when they were still leading by a game, the Soviets agreed to Sinden's demand that the two West Germans would no longer officiate in the series. Sinden explicitly reiterates that agreement during the post–Game 7 news conference, and none of the Soviet officials present contradicts him. But next morning, as Team Canada practises, Gary Smith has the unenviable task of relaying the news to Sinden: the Soviets have gone back on their word. They've told Smith they insist on Baader and Kompalla being used in Game 8.

It seems the Soviets have met privately with all the international referees assembled in Moscow—referees, as noted earlier, angling to work the following year's World's championships—and those impartial gentlemen have collectively declared their wish (without any external pressure, of course) not to see their West German colleagues "discriminated against." It's unclear to Sinden what business the Soviets have meeting unilaterally with the referees anyway. Raging, he returns to the Intourist, where Eagleson is closeted in his room having a word with Alexander Gresko.

Told that his side has a commitment to live up to, Gresko replies with vague excuses about translation problems. Eagleson keeps his poker face: "If either of the Germans works," he says, "we won't play." Gresko phones his superiors to relay the Canadian position, but they won't budge either. At an impasse, the two sides agree to sleep on it and meet the next morning—the day of Game 8.

Meanwhile, the Soviets have another trick up their ample sleeve. Aware there are rival factions within the Canadian delegation, they try to go over Eagleson's and Sinden's heads to find more compliant Canadians—specifically, Hockey Canada and federal government officials.

The senior Canadian government representative at the series is Arthur Laing, a Liberal senator from British Columbia who is a member of the Trudeau cabinet. Laing has been occupying the official box with Brezhnev, Kosygin and Podgorny, but his presence is purely ceremonial. Naively, the Soviets figure that if everything gets decided at the top in their country, why shouldn't this Canadian bigwig be able to bind Team Canada? So they meet with Laing, Ambassador Ford and Hockey Canada officials, unbeknownst to Eagleson or Sinden. Laing, anxious to avoid a political incident, blows Eagleson's negotiating position by reassuring the Soviets that Team Canada will show up to play the final game, no matter what.

That evening, all those Team Canada ballet lovers attend a gala evening at the Bolshoi to watch prima ballerina Maria Plisetskaya dance *Anna Karenina*. Eagleson and his wife, Nancy, are sitting in a stall in the balcony when Gary Smith pokes his head through the curtains and whispers, "Alan, we've got a little problem. Would you come and see Mr. Ford?"

Like any diplomat, Ford wants the conflict settled with the minimum fuss and least disruption to friendly international relations. Finding himself in a thicket of thorny and unfamiliar hockey politics, with the delicate complication of a minister of the Crown thrown in, Ford appeals to Eagleson to be moderate with the Soviets. He's talking to the wrong guy. Informed that his bargaining power has been frittered away, Eagleson retorts, in his own words: "Well, you'd better get back to Senator Laing and tell him to mind his own goddamn business unless he's prepared to go and explain to the players, because I'm not going to. And if he can get them back on the ice, good luck to him."

Eagleson's power lies in his close and privileged relationship with the players as head of their association, and as agent and friend to many. As ever, he doesn't hesitate to use that power.

Senator Laing asks Patrick Reid what he should do now, and Reid wisely replies, "Nothing." Eagleson and Sinden have a meeting with the Soviets scheduled for the next morning: let hockey matters be settled by hockey people. Everyone settles back to enjoy the ballet—more or less. For most of the players, the performance confirms a long-held suspicion that ballet isn't their cup of tea. At the end of each act, Frank Mahovlich asks, "Is that *it*?"

While suffering through the experience, perhaps a few players spare a thought for a fellow Canadian whose fate in the past twenty-four hours has coloured the mood surrounding the series: a drunken Montreal fan whose victory celebration the night before got a little too boisterous. After playing his trumpet in the Intourist bar and inflicting some property damage, the young man's partying was interrupted by two plainclothes policemen who arrested him and dragged him off to jail. There he was given a long cold shower, shorn of his hair, and tattooed on the heels as a prisoner of the state. The bar was closed, and the Canadian patrons were frightened off to their rooms by the sudden, menacing arrival of the militia. Only after the intervention of Smith, Reid and Soviet officials was an agreement reached to let the bar-smasher leave the country quietly instead of spending two years in prison. The Canadian government will pay for the damages. It's the worst incident involving a Canadian visitor; perhaps it precludes others, because there are no more arrests.

•

While Team Canada holds its game-day workout at the arena the next morning, Thursday, September 28, the crucial negotiation takes place upstairs to decide if there will even be a game.

Eagleson, Sinden and Ferguson are present, with Gary Smith as their interpreter; Starovoitov, Romansky and Gresko are there for the Soviets. They review the original, rather loose agreement about the selection of officials for the series, which basically had the two teams picking the referees for alternate games; they discuss the modification to that agreement in Canada, when the Soviets were given their choice in Games 3 *and* 4, as well as Game 1; and the most recent modification after Game 6, dropping Baader and Kompalla. In the Canadians' eyes, the latter agreement was merely reciprocity for their flexibility in the first half of the series. Still the Soviets won't soften their position.

"Listen," Sinden shouts in frustration, "we're going to play this game with the Swede and the Czech or no way at all."

"In Russia," Gresko replies coldly, "we make the decisions, not you."

Finally, Starovoitov announces the whole matter is out of their hands anyway, because it's been decided by the Canadian government. This is too much for John Ferguson. He picks up a water pitcher from the table and smashes it against the wall.

Perhaps Ferguson's little gesture breaks the ice. Gary Smith ventures a solution: both sides could pick one referee each, a concession put forward earlier by Canada, and the formula followed for Game 5. The Soviets go off into a huddle to consider this. When they come back, it's as good as done. There are a few more wrinkles to iron out, but this is the compromise that's finally confirmed later in the day—just a few hours before game time.

When Sinden says Canada will choose the Swedish referee, Uwe Dahlberg, the Soviets report for the first time that Dahlberg is laid up in his hotel with the flu and can't officiate. So the Canadians, suspecting more tampering but sick of the whole rigmarole, and secretly—according to Sinden—prepared to play no matter who referees, make do with their second choice, Rudolph Bata. The Soviets select Joseph Kompalla.

When game time comes, the Canadians will see Dahlberg among the spectators, looking quite chipper.

•

The officiating hassle has kept the Canadian players on edge overnight. Because their coaches have been tied up dealing with it, their usual game-day meeting has to be postponed until arrival at the arena. This—along with rumblings over the missing steaks and beer—could easily have disrupted the equilibrium of players set in their ways, accustomed to observing the same small rituals before each game, acts of sympathetic magic to appease the angry gods of hockey: for instance, Phil Esposito's custom of putting on his equipment in precisely the same sequence every game, his sticks and gloves laid out in front of him and the sticks crossed—in Sinden's memorable phrase, "like a bride preparing for her wedding"; or Gary Bergman's belief that he must be the last man out of the dressing room. But at least the suspense is over now. Everyone knows the game is definitely on, as they suspected it would be.

Ken Dryden will be in goal. Tony Esposito is a little surprised the coaches have passed him up; he feels he's arrived at the top of his form and proved it in Game 7, his best of the series; but he'll dress just in case. Sinden believes Dryden has a big game in him. Even John Ferguson, who has had some doubts about his former teammate's goaltending, especially against the Soviets, agrees. "You're going to start," Sinden has told Dryden at practice. "And finish." Dryden describes the thirty-six hours before the game as "one of the most uncomfortable, tension-filled times of my life. . . . Even when I was doing something totally unrelated to hockey, the feeling was still there—the queasy stomach, rubber legs, fear."

The only other line-up change is Frank Mahovlich for Goldsworthy. Injuries are hurting key Canadian defensemen— Stapleton with a bad ankle, White with a sore heel, Bergman with a tricky back. All three will play over their pain. For the most part, the team is in good shape both physically and psychologically. Yvan Cournoyer remembers that, "In conditioning and mentally, we were getting better and better, while they [the Soviets] were getting tired."

Back home in Canada, so much is riding on this one hockey game that the nation takes the afternoon off to watch it live on television. The broadcast starts at 12:30 p.m. Eastern Time. Employers and school administrators are unusually indulgent about giving their charges time off; after all, *they* want to see it too. In Ontario, the minister of education preempts mass absenteeism by teachers, permitting elementary and high school principals to let their students watch the game because of its national and international significance—thus adding two million young viewers to the audience in that province alone. Those without access to TV at home, work or school resort to bars, the appliance sections of department stores such as Eaton's, Simpson's or Woodward's, and sidewalks outside stores where the game is on view in the window. Across the country that day, scarcely one television set is available for rent.

As we gather in our millions to watch the game, Muscovites are hurrying home from work to catch it on their own TV sets. We know vaguely that a dispute has taken place over the referees, but we don't learn the particulars, and there are many other details we aren't privy to. One scene we miss is a moment in Team Canada's dressing room at the Luzhniki Arena: trainer John "Frosty" Forristal enters and reports excitedly, "I just saw Kharlamov coming into the rink and he's limping like hell!" If Kharlamov plays at all tonight, the team figures, it will have to be on a frozen ankle.

•

The joint CBC-CTV telecast of the final game is introduced as "the series of a lifetime!" Foster Hewitt points out what we all know so well: a Hollywood scriptwriter couldn't have created a more dramatic scenario.

The teams emerge side by side onto the ice to the strains of "Cowards Don't Play Hockey," lining up at their bluelines for the final set of opening ceremonies. The sense of occasion is overwhelming. Through recorded brass-band versions of both national anthems, the players on both sides stand stock-still, their faces rock-solid. The stylized maple leaf on the Canadians' white sweaters is a giant bloodstain splashed across their chests. A sign in the stands held up beside the Canadian flag reads, "Mission Possible."

The Canadian delegation presents a ceremonial totem pole to the president of the Soviet Ice Hockey Federation, a colonel in the Red Army. Laying aside the schisms within Hockey Canada, Alan Eagleson and CAHA president Joe Kryczka lug the man-sized thunderbird figure to centre ice, where it's presented by Hockey Canada president Charles Hay. Notwithstanding the smile on his face, Eagleson's blood pressure has just risen a notch higher:

moments ago, Alexander Gresko told him the television schedule didn't permit time for the Canadians to present their totem pole. But courtesy demands Team Canada reciprocate for the beautiful wooden dolls presented by the Soviets before Game 4 in Vancouver, and Eagleson, who is wearing a badge that reads, "Everything is possible, no problem," was damned if he'd be accused of discourtesy. He told Hay and Kryczka: "Charlie, you stay right close to me and Joe you do the same, we've dragged this goddamn thing with us, and we're going to present it." Eagleson told the red-faced Gresko that Team Canada wouldn't move off the blueline until the totem pole was handed over to the Soviets. Somehow, time was found in the television schedule after all.

Next come the player introductions. Bergman and Clarke both draw loud derisory whistles from the Soviet fans, who have no difficulty identifying them as the Bad Guys of the piece. Phil Esposito gets his share of whistles too, drowned out by the cheers of the Canadian supporters. When the Soviets are announced, the process is reversed for Bad Boris Mikhailov—the loud hometown ovation countered by Canadian boos.

Before the teams head for their benches, the Canadian players skate across to their opponents and hand each of them one more gift, a white Stetson, courtesy of the city of Calgary. Esposito plants his firmly on the head of his opposite number, the captain and veteran defenseman Victor Kuzkin, who grins shyly, looking more pleased than he wants to, before removing it.

Sinden starts Esposito, Cournoyer and Parise against Shadrin, Yakushev and Anisin. Within seconds, Anisin gets in close and drifts a high hard shot right on the net. Dryden bats it away, feeling immediately calmer for having been tested.

At the next faceoff, Sinden changes lines. Bobrov doesn't, then quickly puts out the Maltsev-Kharlamov-Vikulov line on the fly; they get two good scoring chances before Sinden can get the Clarke-Ellis-Henderson line out against them. Kharlamov's lower leg is shot full of painkiller, yet even at half speed he's dangerous.

The game is just two minutes and twenty-five seconds old when Kompalla calls his first penalty against Canada. Alexander Maltsev goes flying over Bill White's stick, good enough for Kompalla but not old Foster, who declares, "That was a dive, a real dive, White hardly touched him!" Off goes White for holding.

Sent out to kill the penalty at centre, Peter Mahovlich does a fine, fired-up job until he collars Yakushev coming out of the Soviet end. Mahovlich gets pushed from behind by a Soviet defenseman, lands on top of Yakushev and is also penalized for holding, a mere thirty-six seconds after White. Suddenly the Canadians are two men short. It's only three minutes into the game. Their worst suspicions of Kompalla are being fulfilled.

Esposito, Park and Bergman set up the triangle and manfully try to keep the puck out of the scoring zone. But with the Soviets, it's only a matter of time. Liapkin blasts a shot from the point which Dryden kicks out with his pad, Maltsev recovers the rebound but hits the post, then Yakushev standing at the crease backhands *that* rebound home with Dryden down—a garbage goal if ever there was one, especially given the two-man advantage. Kompalla 1, Canada 0.

Ten seconds later, a questionable hooking penalty against Petrov appears a feeble attempt to even things up. Petrov shrugs but goes off without further protest, making the teams five a side. A mere twenty-six seconds after that, Kompalla is at it again, calling Jean-Paul Parise when his stick sends Maltsev spinning for a relatively slight tumble. This makes four penalties in just over four minutes —none of them particularly clearcut infractions. It's difficult to avoid the suspicion that Maltsev deserves an Oscar.

A brief calm ensues before the storm. The Canadian players mill about, getting a grip on what's happened. Parise seems to be muttering to himself, and when he learns he's going off for interference, he loses it. He calls the referee a son of a bitch and slams the ice with his stick. This display earns him a ten-minute misconduct. Not content with that, Parise really gets ugly: he hovers menacingly around Kompalla, who is getting an earful from Esposito along the boards, until Guy Lapointe herds Parise into the penalty box beside Peter Mahovlich. But Parise immediately exits the box; he starts for Kompalla, and is only prevented from doing further damage by the watchful Lapointe, who steers him off to centre ice.

Parise roams the rink like some rogue elephant. Swinging his stick in circles about his head, he seems almost demented. He approaches the Canadian bench to seek sympathy. Then, instead of getting himself under control, Parise skates straight back across the ice to where Kompalla is standing and suddenly charges him, pulling his stick back over his shoulder with two hands like a Bobby Clarke out for blood, obviously intending to bring it down on the referee's head. As Kompalla cowers against the boards, raising one leg to ward off the blow, Parise pulls up and veers away at the last second. Naturally he's thrown out of the game.

The ensuing uproar lasts nearly ten minutes. Practically every player in a Canadian uniform disputes the call. Sinden hurls a wooden stool onto the ice, follows it with Ferguson's folding chair, and makes the "choke" sign to the referees. His players throw towels over the boards. The Canadian fans set up the chants, "DA, DA, CANADA, NYET, NYET, SOVIET" and "LET'S GO HOME, LET'S GO HOME!" and some of the players, even Paul Henderson, think they have a point. While bedlam reigns, everyone from Frank Mahovlich to Gilbert to Bergman and even Ellis berates the referees, who are utterly flummoxed by the storm they've unleashed.

"[The referees] were blatantly, openly, and without any hesitation, trying to steal the game from us," Sinden will say in his book. "There was only one thing we could do to make them stop—make them look bad." The Soviet players just look bored and disgusted by it all: to them, it can only appear as childish self-indulgence. The Soviet militia mass behind the Canadian bench—whether to protect Team Canada from the crowd or vice versa is unclear.

Over fifty-five minutes remain in the game. As Brian Conacher remarks drily on television, the referees are going to be in charge all the way, so the Canadians, who are losing and still a man short, better accept it, cool out and play hockey. Still, there is one argument they definitely must win: one of the referees is claiming that, on top of Parise's banishment, Esposito has to serve Parise's ten-minute misconduct. His grounds are that Esposito was on the ice when the infraction took place, and the referee can choose which player serves the time. There is no such rule, international or otherwise, that anyone on Team Canada has heard of. Sinden and Eagleson, who has come down to the bench for the discussion, refuse to accept it. In the end, Dennis Hull serves only the two-minute minor for Parise, which suggests that the referees' grasp of the rules is shaky at best.

At long last, play resumes. After Canada kills off the penalty, Henderson and Tsygankov race each other for the puck into the Soviet end. Tsygankov, who has been burned before by Henderson's speed, interferes with him all the way and gets two minutes. This sets the stage for a long-overdue power-play goal.

Henderson and Ellis are out with Esposito. Henderson does a herculean job outfighting the big defenseman Lutchenko for the puck in the left corner and gets it back to Lapointe, who passes across to Park at the other point. Park one-times the pass right on the net. Tretiak kicks it out, but Esposito stuffs in the rebound, and each side has a goal. Coming at 6:54, the scoring play is critical for Canada: it gets the team back in the game early, settling them down for the tough grind ahead.

With the luxury of two penalty-free shifts, the Canadians show how good they can be offensively. Pressing hard, Esposito and Cournoyer team up and nearly score, as do Ratelle and Gilbert. Before long, however, Ellis goes off for interference, then Petrov. Suddenly the referees, having ignored interference in other games, especially on the Soviets' part, are finding it everywhere. When Cournoyer hooks Vikulov, the Soviet hits the ice face-first and looks back in dramatic appeal to Bata, who gives Cournoyer the gate for interference at 12:51—the fifth interference call of the period.

To the rhythmic chant of "Shai-boo, shai-boo," the Russian for "goal," the serpentine Soviet power play glides into action. Kharlamov is out helping control the play as they move the puck around patiently. Kharlamov fakes a rush, then backhands it to Lutchenko, who blasts a low screened slapshot through a maze of legs to Dryden's stick side, giving the home team a 2-1 lead.

On the whole, the Soviets are playing a more masterful, disciplined game; yet they too make cardinal errors. When Mikhailov and Blinov get a two-on-one against White, Mikhailov sets up Blinov right in front of Dryden, but Blinov inexplicably returns the pass and they lose possession.

Less consistent in their teamwork, the Canadians are nonetheless capable of spontaneously exploding into brilliance at any moment.

On the next shift, Ranger teammates Park and Ratelle work the short give-and-go to perfection. Together they scythe through the Soviet defense, Park to Ratelle and back to Park, who bursts in alone on Tretiak and buries it in the upper corner to tie the game at two. Park's only goal of the series, it comes during his best two-way game by far.

But the team lets down after that goal. Dryden has to be extremely sharp for the rest of the period, especially when Petrov drives a hard one that's labelled. The tie stands up until the intermission. As the players file off to their dressing rooms, Ambassador Ford's wife Maria Thereza is standing with Nancy Eagleson by the ramp. Paul Henderson pauses to say hello to the two women. When Mrs. Ford reaches out to pat him on the back, she is shoved aside by an overzealous militiaman, who apparently considers it his duty to protect Henderson from female advances. When Eagleson hears about this, his blood pressure zooms still higher. It's heading for the roof.

Period two opens with the weirdest goal of the series. Breaking over the Canadian blueline, Yakushev shoots high over top of the net. The puck hits the wire mesh directly behind Dryden and boomerangs past his ear. Disoriented, Dryden takes a swipe at the puck as it flashes past him and lands neatly on Shadrin's stick, about fifteen feet out, and Shadrin has the puck in the net before Dryden can get set. The score is 3-2.

There is neither a goal nor a penalty called for the next ten minutes. The teams play wide-open offensive hockey, and both goaltenders are outstanding. Tretiak robs Cournoyer, who fakes a shot from inside the blueline, then cleverly uses Frank Mahovlich as a screen as he drifts into the high slot and lets go a zinger at the upper-left corner. Somehow Tretiak traps the puck on his stick side between forearm and waist.

Rod Gilbert can't solve Tretiak tonight, no matter how many ways he tries, and he tries several; but in the eleventh minute of the second period, Gilbert truly earns his assist on a marvellous manoeuvre to the left of the Soviet net. Taking the puck from Ratelle off the faceoff, Gilbert dallies along the boards, tracking backwards towards the corner, teasing the Soviet defenders, who watch him carefully but don't move out of position to check him.

Gilbert simply holds onto the puck until the Soviets are mesmerized. Seeing White sneak in unnoticed from the far point, Gilbert fakes a shot, then clotheslines a goal-mouth pass that White tips in over Tretiak. Team Canada has tied the game for the third time. White and Gilbert hug and grin from ear to ear.

Once again, however, the Canadians sag after scoring. The Soviets sense their temporary lapse in energy and turn on the jets, and for several minutes Team Canada needs miracles to keep the Soviets from running up the score beyond reach. The first miracle is Dryden's. On a two-on-one break, Blinov holds the puck on the left wing long enough to draw Stapleton towards him, then slips a pass across to Mikhailov home-free in front of the net—but Dryden, staying in his crease, reads both attackers perfectly and slides across the goal mouth to trap Mikhailov's shot in his pads.

On the following faceoff to the right of the net, however, Shadrin wins the faceoff against Esposito and bounces a pass off Park's skate to Yakushev alone on the doorstep. One little fake, and Yakushev finds the opening between Dryden and the left post to put the Soviets ahead once more, 4-3.

The next miracle is Esposito's. The Canadians are less than crisp in moving the puck out of their own end. Turning to backcheck, Esposito rides Petrov off the puck before he can reach Blinov's centring pass right in front. Then Blinov makes a superb move on Dryden: passing to Petrov, he takes Petrov's return pass to the right of the net, feints Dryden and Stapleton flat onto their backs, and steps nimbly around them to finish off a sure goal. But Esposito, back-stopping Dryden, stretches his stick across the goal mouth to prevent Blinov's shot from crossing the red line, blocks another try by Mikhailov on the rebound, and slides across on nonexistent goalie pads to smother the puck. Dryden, vastly relieved, says later that goaltending must run in the Esposito family. Blinov just hangs his head: he cannot believe it.

But you can go only so far on miracles. When Stapleton takes a penalty at 15:58 for cross-checking Maltsev behind the Canadian net, the Soviet power play once again flexes its muscles. The Soviet players show particular skill in rotating from one position on the ice to another—Kharlamov or Yakushev dropping back to the point when the defensemen Tsygankov or Vasiliev move up. Repeating a manoeuvre that produced goals earlier in the series, Kharlamov stands by the right post and one-times a pass-out straight for the corner, but Dryden anticipates his move and hugs the post in time. Finally, however, the Soviet press is too much. Like Gilbert earlier in the period, Vasiliev holds onto the puck long enough for Shadrin to sneak in and tip Vasiliev's goal-mouth pass into the net. In frustration, White shoots the puck away, almost hitting Kompalla. Afterwards, the normally cool-headed defenseman admits his aim was intentional.

USSR 5, Canada 3. For some reason, the official scorer gives the goal to Vasiliev, not Shadrin. More importantly, it's the first time in the game that either team has been ahead by two goals.

Before the period ends, Dryden makes one more spectacular save on a Petrov-Mikhailov-Blinov rush. But when Kuzkin goes off for elbowing, only the second penalty of the period, the Canadians once again fail to capitalize with a man advantage. The weakness of their power play has begun to appear fatal. Two goals don't exactly represent an overwhelming lead, but the Soviets look steady and confident, their margin formidable, as the teams head for the dressing rooms. And Team Canada seems to be fading fast.

•

For the folks watching at home, trying to stave off mounting despair, there are some encouraging words in an intermission interview with former Toronto Maple Leaf great Syl Apps Sr. "I think everybody in Canada can be really proud of these fellas," Apps tells us from Moscow. "They've worked exceptionally hard, they're trying hard, and the game isn't over yet."

We need to hear that, we really do—because from six thousand miles away, the outlook isn't good. After trailing the Soviets from the very first game of this series, Team Canada has battled back so gamely and come so far, and we with them, that it's bitter to have to face defeat now. And yet with just one period to go, defeat seems to be in the cards.

The Soviets have another possibility on their minds: a tie. Between periods, Alexander Gresko tells Alan Eagleson that if this game does end in a draw, producing a 3-3-2 split in games, the USSR will declare a series victory based on their two-goal advantage in total goals for and against.

This is the first time such an idea has been mentioned. Although it's a commonly used method of settling ties under international rules, it's never done in the good old NHL, and Eagleson is shocked and infuriated by the suggestion. He storms away from Gresko and heads for Team Canada's dressing room. Beside himself, Eagleson charges into the room—the first time he's done so between periods— and for a moment goes "absolutely berserk," in his own words, yelling at all the players that if they get an early goal, the Soviets will fall apart.

In a more nuanced way, that's also what their coach tells them. Sinden says, "We've got to get one back early. But don't gamble to do it." His greatest fear is the Soviets scoring first, putting the game beyond Canada's reach. Keep them from scoring in the first ten minutes, he tells his men, and do all your gambling in the second half of the period.

Apart from Eagleson's eruption, the players remember no hysteria in the dressing room, no panic, no despair: the mood is remarkably calm and collected. Ellis, Henderson and Dryden all recall a collective determination to go out there and do the necessary. They believe they can still win.

As the final period begins, Team Canada bursts out of the starting blocks. Clarke wins the opening faceoff, and from the blueline Ellis powers a drive that Tretiak has to hold onto for dear life, because Henderson and Clarke are immediately on top of him. These guys are primed. But so are the Soviets. Yakushev and Anisin break out on a two-on-one, and Dryden makes a fine save on Anisin's hard shot. The Soviets threaten, creating some tense moments, but shoot wide of the net three times.

Fixation on the net is what makes the difference now. And the fact that Sinden replaces Frank Mahovlich with his younger brother on the line with Esposito and Cournoyer. Peter Mahovlich makes a superb, all-out, end-to-end effort to trigger the game's critical turning point.

From behind his own net, Mahovlich passes up to Montreal

teammate Cournoyer. He takes Cournoyer's return pass and battles all the way up the boards and into the corner to the right of the Soviet net, keeping possession all the way, pursued by three defenders. Finally upended by Kuzkin, Mahovlich still gets off a centring pass to Esposito as he's falling. The puck strikes Gusev's stick in front of the net and flips into the air. Esposito bats it to his feet with his glove, golfs at it, misses on his first try but connects on his second, shooting unerringly between Tretiak's pads.

The Canadian fans erupt in delight. Only 2:27 gone in the third period, and Esposito has made it 5-4! Sinden has his wish for an early goal. Espo and Mahovlich hug but don't smile. There's a ways to go yet.

As Dryden makes a fine save on Tsygankov's dangerous slapshot, a fight breaks out between Gilbert and the Soviets' prime battler, Evgeny Mishakov. Canadian hockey pundits are astonished that Gilbert, hardly known for his fists in the NHL, bloodies Mishakov's nose and emerges unscathed. They christen Gilbert "Mad Dog." Both players get five minutes but, contrary to the usual international ban on fighting, aren't thrown out of the game.

Moments later, a questionable tripping penalty is called against Vasiliev when his hip check sends Clarke flying. Seems not all the bad calls go against the Canadians, who now have a one-man advantage, five men to four, just when they need a goal so badly.

Yet the advantage does Team Canada no good. Although Sinden tries two different power-play combinations—Esposito, Henderson, Park and Lapointe; then Esposito, Cournoyer, Ratelle and Lapointe —they are too unaccustomed to utilizing the big surface against only three defenders and seem to lose their poise, becoming tentative and inept on the attack. When a loose puck comes to Ratelle in front of the net and he has Tretiak at his mercy and the tying goal in his grasp, he shoots a backhander wide.

At the ten-minute mark, the teams change ends with the score still 5-4. But Sinden has noticed something that inspires new hope in him: the Soviets are falling back into a defensive shell, checking very closely and just trying to protect their lead. This surprises the Canadian coach. It's the first time in the entire series the Soviets have changed their strategy and abandoned Tarasov's "attacking style." It may now be their undoing.

The Canadians forecheck fiercely, gunning for the tying goal. Their supporters chant "Go Team Go," the Soviet fans whistle loudly in response. All the offensive momentum is with Team Canada: this is the time they have to go all out.

After a change, Esposito's line takes the faceoff in the Canadian end. Park carries the puck behind his own net, stickhandles away from a persistent Soviet forechecker and moves swiftly up the left boards. He threads a long, rink-wide lead pass through centre to Esposito charging up the right wing. With four Soviets in close pursuit, Esposito carries over their blueline, cuts into the open and lets go a chest-high shot from fifteen feet. Tretiak blocks the shot at the top of the crease but bobbles it. Esposito storms in to stab the puck out of the air, knocking it behind the net, barrelling after it.

His next moment is a marvel of tenacity. Surrounded by three Soviets at the left of the net, Lutchenko, Mishakov and Vikulov, none of whom can knock him off the puck, Esposito refuses to give up until he centres a pass. His first attempt on his forehand is swept back by Tretiak's stick. His second effort on his backhand comes out to Cournoyer a few feet in front. Cournoyer shoots instantly. Making the save, Tretiak drops on his face to smother the puck, but it dribbles away from him, and Esposito and Cournoyer both lunge for it in a mad scramble.

Cournoyer gets there first. Recovering his own rebound, he flicks a backhander over Tretiak and into the net. With four Soviet bodies stacked in the goal mouth, it's amazing Cournoyer can find anywhere to put it, yet he does. The game is tied, 5-5.

Curiously, the red light doesn't flash on. Alan Eagleson finds this not curious but sinister. Even though there's no disputing that Team Canada has scored—the players, the referees, 15,000 fans and about 100 million television viewers around the world are witnesses to the puck going in—Eagleson in his beleaguered and overwrought state sees a ploy to deny Team Canada its tying goal. The little crises of the past forty-eight hours have nearly been too much for him; now this latest one pushes him over the edge.

Clambering over seats and spectators, Eagleson jumps down among the militiamen lining the rink. He starts groping his way towards the official timer's bench to demand the goal be recorded, but never reaches the bench. To the Soviet soldiers, this wild-eyed spectator isn't Alan Eagleson, hockey czar, He Who Must Be Obeyed, but just another of the crazed and probably drunken foreigners they've been warned about. They lay rude hands on him. Preparing to hustle him outside, one soldier twists his arm behind his back, another clamps a headlock on him. Eagleson catches the eye of a Soviet television man nearby, mutely appealing to him for help. The man knows him and could explain his identity and importance to the soldiers; inexplicably, the man looks the other way.

But help is coming from another quarter. Patrick Reid is in the first row behind the very bench Eagleson is trying to reach, seated between his two main contacts from the Soviet foreign ministry. Reid asks the Soviet official on his right to go with him to Eagleson's rescue. The man agrees, and they begin pushing their way through the mob. Reid knows this will be his ultimate, most public challenge but believes he can nip this one too in the bud—if only he and his ally can get through in time.

Meanwhile, big Peter Mahovlich is cruising past the boards. Seeing Eagleson disappear amid a swarm of brown uniforms, Mahovlich converts his hockey stick into the lance of St. George rescuing the maiden: he clobbers two Soviet dragons across the back. Startled, they release Eagleson, and Mahovlich climbs over the boards, yelling to his teammates to join in. As the Canadian players mass along the boards with sticks upraised, like knights in an Uccello painting, Mahovlich takes the dishevelled Eagleson in tow and escorts him through the gate, onto the ice and into the waiting hands of Harry Sinden, who has followed close behind his players. Sinden, Brad Park, Dennis Hull, trainer Joe Sgro and Eagleson employee Mike Cannon conduct him across the ice to a place of supposed diplomatic immunity, the Team Canada bench.

As he crosses centre ice surrounded by his rescuers, Eagleson hears boos. They could easily be Canadian boos protesting his maltreatment, but he must presume they're Soviet boos directed at him (although Soviet crowds whistle instead of booing), because he responds with one last message for the people of this country of which he's a guest: he gives them the finger. Perhaps remembering he's on international television, Eagleson immediately retracts the finger and shakes his fist in defiance, But his original gesture is loyally mimicked by Cannon and Sgro. Worthy ambassadors all.

Trapped in the crowd, Patrick Reid despairs. From his point of view as a diplomat, the incident is "a total and utter disaster." He looks up at the state box to see a row of stony faces: "And there's Ed Ritchie, the Under-Secretary of State for External Affairs and the man who'd put me into this job, sitting beside Kosygin and Brezhnev with his head buried in his hands. I consider that the moment of my abject failure."

But the game must go on—especially if Team Canada is to capitalize on whatever momentum the tying goal has generated.

Seven minutes and four seconds of playing time remain. The Soviets come out of their shell as both sides press the attack, looking for the deciding goal. But the furious, punishing physical pace of the game and the series have taken their toll. Both teams are exhausted, a step or two slower than before. As the forwards wilt, Team Canada actually gets a two-on-one break from its defensemen, Park setting up Bergman for a good scoring attempt that Tretiak kicks out. Moments later, Yakushev carries over the Canadian blueline and tries to split Park and Lapointe, but they pinch in and up-end him high into the air; the Soviets' tumbling regime stands Yakushev in good stead as he somersaults, lands on his shoulder and does a forward roll onto his feet.

Now there is less than a minute to play. The Esposito-Cournoyer-Peter Mahovlich line is nearing the end of its shift. Sinden plans to send out Clarke, Henderson and Ellis for a last stab at a goal, but Henderson, standing impatiently at the bench, can't wait. That inner prompting is working in Henderson again, that conviction he felt in the previous game, *I can score*—but the time is running out.

The way Henderson remembers it, he looks up at the clock and thinks, "This is no good, I gotta get a shot at this, it's now or never." Without waiting for Sinden to dispatch him, he yells "Peter!" three times, and Mahovlich obediently comes off. Henderson vaults over the boards to take his place on left wing.

229

Cournoyer is still out there, beginning to drag. Taking a long clearing pass from Stapleton, he shoots the puck into the Soviets' end from outside their blueline and thinks, "I should go off now." He starts to head for the bench, then tells himself, "No, I'm going to give it one more shot," and stays on.

For his part, Esposito hears his teammates calling him off the ice, "Phil, Phil!" but thinks, "There isn't any way in the world I'm going off. None." He feels a goal coming and he has to be in on it. So all three forwards, all individualists, are out there in a sense without orders.

The puck is behind the Soviet net. Vasiliev takes it from Tretiak and simply clears it around the boards. Perhaps Vasiliev is too tired at the end of his own shift, and perhaps he thinks this is a safe move, since the Canadians are changing, but Cournoyer has gone back to his post on right wing, and is surprised to find the puck coming out to him just inside the Soviet blueline. Nobody is checking him.

Cournoyer sees Henderson on the far wing streaking for the net. He sends Henderson a long, hard diagonal pass that's just half a stride behind him. Overskating the puck, Henderson is hooked by Vasiliev and spun around beside Tretiak. His stick held high, Henderson falls to his knees and slides backwards into the boards behind the net.

The puck ricochets off the boards in the left corner. No fewer than three Soviets are near it as it comes bouncing out to them. Yet unaccountably, they all hesitate, as if thinking to leave the puck for the other guy. None of them takes charge, none of them takes possession. Both Vasiliev and Liapkin touch the puck briefly but mishandle it. Trailing on the play, Esposito is the first to reach the loose puck. Unhesitatingly, he shoots at Tretiak from twelve feet out.

Tretiak blocks the shot easily with his stick. But he allows a rebound, and suddenly Henderson, who has scrambled to his feet behind the net, thinking the Soviets will clear the zone now and he'll have to skate all the way back to his own end before getting one last chance to score, is all alone with the puck in front of Tretiak. Henderson *shoots*—Tretiak makes a pad save and sprawls on his back, and again the puck comes out to Henderson. Henderson *shoots again*—a low slider aimed straight at the narrow space between

Tretiak's body and the right post—and incredibly, the puck is in the net!

It's all over in a second.

Tretiak is still lying flat on his back. Henderson turns like a man entering the sunlight for the first time and laughs for pure joy, raising both arms and his stick into the air, and leaps straight into Cournoyer's arms.

•

The Canadian bench empties. Even Dryden goes lumbering all the way down the rink to join the ecstatic mob of white sweaters hugging, patting, squeezing and slapping Henderson.

The Soviets skate sluggishly about, stunned, their faces drained of hope, their cause apparently lost. Yet thirty-four seconds remain to play, and the Soviets are gifted with the power to score a sudden goal. It's easy to imagine them tying this one up in thirty-four seconds, thus tying the series, and going on to claim victory on goal-differential.

Sinden stays with Stapleton, who was on the ice for the goal along with Savard. He sends out White and his two steadiest defensive forwards, Ellis and Peter Mahovlich, to join the indefatigable Esposito. The five don't let the Soviets anywhere near Dryden. Even the Soviets themselves go halfheartedly through the motions, as if they don't really expect to score. As if it were somehow ordained the Canadians would win.

With Gusev the last Soviet player to touch the puck, with the Canadian fans absolutely roaring out the countdown of the final seconds, Dryden hands off to Stapleton. Carefully, Stapleton carries the puck behind his net and passes up the boards to Mahovlich as the final horn sounds. Mahovlich lets the puck go by, Stapleton races after it, and the fans, as Foster Hewitt says, go wild.

TWENTY

WHERE WERE YOU?

"Cournoyer has it on that wing. Here's a shot—Henderson made a wild stab for it and fell. Here's another shot! *Right in front—THEY SCORE!!! Henderson has scored for Canada!*"

—FOSTER HEWITT, September 28, 1972

●

With the completion of Game 8, the war ends. As they line up at centre ice for the last time, the members of these two magnificent, unparallelled hockey teams emerge from their month-long spell of bitter antagonism and ruthless combat to recognize each other as human beings. Each of them works his way along the line, shaking hands player by player, mumbling incomprehensible words to each other in a foreign language. Their meaning is clear enough. A spirit of mutual admiration and respect and sportsmanship has arrived to dispel the hatred and finally, briefly, reigns. It comes just in time; but probably it could have come no sooner.

Selected by Soviet hockey officials as Canadian players of the game, Paul Henderson and Brad Park pry themelves loose from their jubilant teammates and fans to receive their awards. Afterwards, they're both grabbed for television interviews. A touch comical without his teeth, clearly moved and delighted, yet somehow humbled by the whole ordeal, Park thanks his countrymen thousands of miles away for all the telegrams and letters, and tells us, "I can't express how greatly I feel about being a Canadian." He's speaking for himself, but says he wants to add something on behalf of all his teammates: "We think that Canada's the greatest country in the world."

Henderson is in even bigger demand for interviews. When he finally makes it to the dressing room, the players, team officials, wives and girlfriends have already sung "O Canada," and now they give him a deafening cheer. Completely spent, Henderson collapses on a bench. Somebody hands him a beer. He sits slumped there, beer in hand, soaking up the praise and the precious moments of satisfaction for forty-five minutes before he even begins removing his equipment.

Every player finds his own way of relishing the moment. Ken Dryden sits quietly in reflection and finds "a corner deep inside myself, grinning, burning with twenty-seven days of pleasure, disaster, and relief...."

Dennis Hull has never experienced such feelings as he's having now. He tells Cournoyer he's never won a Stanley Cup: "Is this what it's like?"

Cournoyer replies, "This is better. We've accomplished something nobody's ever done before."

Phil Esposito whoops it up with his brother and the other guys. They reminisce, kibitz, laugh, talk a mile a minute, until Esposito is momentarily struck speechless by the last thing he expects to see, a player from the Soviet team. Young Vyacheslav Anisin enters the room and shoulders his way through the celebrating Canadians straight towards Esposito. With a few words of Russian, Anisin presents him with a somewhat battered and dishevelled package, gift-wrapped.

Inside, Esposito is astonished to find a silver Russian samovar. In spite of, or perhaps because of, his vividly expressed belligerence towards them, the Soviets are acknowledging his role as the Canadians' team leader—not only their leading scorer but the keeper of that "spirit to draw on" that Tarasov spoke about. Wanting to give Anisin something in return, but with nothing prepared, Espo looks around him and grabs a simple but significant object—his hockey stick—and hands it to the Soviet player as a souvenir.

Esposito's was undoubtedly the stick that did the Soviets more damage than any other. Although he didn't score the series-winning goal, although he wasn't selected as the Game 8 star or the series' best forward, Esposito was nonetheless the dominant player on either team throughout—even more than Yakushev, even more than Henderson. In the last analysis, he was the one who made the most difference overall. Leading all players in scoring was only the start of it. Esposito forechecked and back-checked and killed penalties and was frequently double-shifted, logging more ice time than anyone; and more than once he single-handedly lifted his teammates' sagging spirits, both publicly and privately. His contribution in Game 8 alone was enormous: he was involved in four of Canada's six goals, scoring two and assisting on two, including all three goals in the final period. As Brian Conacher said in tribute at the end of the game, "Esposito has to have played one of his greatest games ever, even if he plays hockey until he's a hundred." And as Vladislav Tretiak will tell Dryden in *Home Game*, "Esposito caused the most trouble for me and the team. . . . He played as if he sang. He had this excitation about him and he was charging up his whole team with his enthusiasm." Not bad for a guy who claims he didn't even want to be there.

Finally showered and dressed, Team Canada leaves the Luzhniki Arena for a reception at the Metropole Hotel downtown. Planned by the Soviets as their victory party, it has become their wake. Only a small handful of Soviet players attend—they, too, can feel and act bitter in defeat. The event doesn't last long, just long enough for a couple of sour notes to be struck.

Two of the Soviet players present are Yakushev, who receives the award as best forward in the series—Park is named best defenseman—and Tretiak. Henderson has developed such admiration for Tretiak that he tells him through an interpreter how impressed he was by his play. Tretiak replies, "You know, you were lucky to score that last goal." Stung, Henderson hits back verbally. Today he says, "I took it the wrong way. I *was* lucky. But I told him to take a flying . . . I think he was young, and he was making a comment, but at the time I didn't want to hear it."

Then Alan Eagleson stands up and says a few choice words about how he hopes the series has been a friendly one, in spite of difficult moments in the heat of battle. Alexander Gresko replies that he thought he'd made a friend of Eagleson two months earlier, and that friendship has lasted until the last two days, but now he feels very sorry for him. Eagleson isn't sure what Gresko means and chases him for an explanation, but doesn't get one. At that point, the party is over.

The Canadians return to the Intourist to hold their own victory party. It continues raucously all night until just before dawn, when they have to leave for the airport, bleary-eyed and hungover and without their wives and girlfriends but still elated, to catch a plane for Prague. There they have one more hockey game to play—a superfluous, long-planned exhibition match against the Czecho-slovakian national team—before going home.

•

On the home front, we party too. The team's triumph is ours, just as its defeat would have been ours. If you ask people today how or where or with whom they celebrated on that evening of September 28, 1972, they may be unable to recall. But what most *can* tell you is where they were that afternoon when Henderson scored his goal with thirty-four seconds left to play. For Canadians, the hoary cliché goes, this is our national equivalent of Americans' memories of where they were when John F. Kennedy was shot—except, of course, being Canadian, we get to remember that one, too.

Verne Clemence, for example, then sports editor of the *Enterprise* in the small Saskatchewan city of Yorkton, was in the process of writing his column for the next day's paper. "When Team Canada went into the third period two goals down, I'd given them up," Clemence remembers. He'd been powerfully impressed by the Soviet team throughout the series, and his column contained some comforting philosophical observations about how superbly the Soviets played, and how it's only a game, so let's not get too excited about losing. "But we were having a hell of a time getting the paper out, because there was an Eaton's store two doors down, and they had TVs going in the window and inside the store. All the guys from the composing room kept slipping out to watch the hockey game, so we were getting further and further behind. Finally the publisher said, 'What the hell, let's go,' and we went too and watched the last few minutes of the game at Eaton's. Everyone was getting pretty tense, but when Henderson scored, a great cheer went up. I went back and rewrote my column. I was pretty excited about being on the winning side after all."

For aspiring young novelist Guy Vanderhaeghe, living not far from Clemence in that hockey-mad province, the series began and ended with weddings. The first was his own, which took place September 2, 1972, the day of Game 1. During the reception in Esterhazy, Saskatchewan, Vanderhaeghe learned that Team Canada had scored two early goals, and all was right with the world. He and his bride, Margaret, drove off in a radioless car for their honeymoon in Kindersley. By the time they arrived, the game was over, and Guy was absolutely shocked to be told Canada had lost 7-3; his world had changed, in more ways than one. On the day of Game 8, Vanderhaeghe's former roommate got married in Arborfield. After the bride and groom departed, Vanderhaeghe recalls, "ten of us men, mostly total strangers, huddled on sofas and chairs to see how the series would end. My roommate's father, who'd always hated the Montreal Canadiens, suddenly found himself ecstatically cheering 'Cornbinder' for tying the game 5-5. By the time Henderson scored, it was as if we'd all known each other forever."

In Newfoundland, people living in outports in the northern part of the peninsula couldn't watch the games on television because they lacked electric power. Yet as the series progressed, they too became wrapped up in it. When Pat Stapleton travelled in Atlantic Canada to conduct minor hockey clinics in the 1980s, Newfound-landers told him how they'd followed the games any way they could. Fishermen would sail over to larger, radio-equipped boats to learn the score. "I met an elderly man named Emmanuel," Stapleton recalls, "who told me he used to listen to Foster Hewitt's play-by-play on his transistor radio when he was out fishing. The day of Game 8, he was at the wheel of his boat when Henderson scored, and he got so excited he jumped for joy and punched his fist through the wheelhouse roof."

In the interior of British Columbia, a young publicist for the Red Cross named Joanne Leslie was making one of her road trips on the Trans-Canada Highway between Kamloops and Revelstoke, listen-ing to the game on her car radio. Even the truck drivers must have knocked off early to watch the game, because the highway was absolutely deserted for miles. Henderson scored, and Leslie, with the road all to herself, felt such a rush that she pushed her hand down on her horn and just kept it there for a long, long time.

Driving the same highway that day in the opposite direction was Winnipeg sportswriter Hal Sigurdson, then with the Vancouver *Sun*. Sigurdson had flipped a coin with colleague Jim Kearney to see who would travel to Moscow to cover Team Canada and who would stay home to cover the Vancouver Canucks' training camp. Sigurdson had lost. Driving back over the Rockies after a Canucks exhibition game in Calgary, he tried to listen to Game 8 on the radio, but became desperate whenever the station faded out and he lost the play-by-play. Searching the dial to find Foster Hewitt's voice on some other station, Sigurdson finally picked up a clear steady signal as he came down through Hope, B.C., and got to hear the game's fabulous climax. He too celebrated Henderson's goal with a good blast of his horn.

In Ottawa, Carleton University student Margaret Reynolds was putting herself through school with a temporary job at the Ottawa Credit Bureau. Normally the telephones rang all day long with inquiries from businesses, which Reynolds and her coworkers answered with information from a battery of filing cabinets. But on the afternoon of September 28, 1972, from the moment the puck was dropped in Moscow, they had nothing whatsoever to do: the phones fell eerily silent, only to begin erupting again shortly after the final horn. Meanwhile, Dermot Nolan, watching the game with fellow students and several cases of beer at a University of Ottawa residence, led a riotous victory march onto Parliament Hill and then through the streets to the Soviet embassy, where the surprised students were graciously congratulated by Soviet diplomats.

In Calgary, publisher's sales rep Rob Sanders was selling, among other books, a translation of a work on hockey techniques by Anatoly Tarasov. On board a plane, Sanders had bumped into the owner of an Edmonton Ford dealership by the name of Peter Pocklington, who bought a hundred copies as giveaways for his customers. On the afternoon of September 28, Sanders was staying at the International Hotel and, like most other guests, settled in his room to watch Game 8. The hotel corridor was deathly quiet until

Henderson scored, and suddenly doors flew open up and down the corridor as complete strangers hugged and told each other with grins a mile wide how fantastic it all was.

The image of doors flying open recurs in these tales. Dave King was teaching high-school biology and physical education in Saskatoon back then, as well as coaching Junior B hockey. The classrooms at his school all had TV sets going that day, all showing the same thing. "The teachers felt it was important for the kids to see that last game. Our hockey heritage was on the line, so it was a major Canadian event. Even the girls and the non–hockey fans got caught up in it. After Henderson scored, all the classroom doors opened out onto the corridor, and the kids just came pouring out—it was incredible." In the next decade, King himself went on to make his mark in international hockey—coaching the Canadian national junior team to a gold medal in 1982, and becoming coach of the national team program in 1984 after Father Bauer's concept was revived.

Most Canadians who were in elementary or high school in '72 share variations on the TV-in-the-classroom memory, no matter which province they lived in or what kind of school they attended. It's one of the earliest memories of Toronto journalist Scott Anderson, who was five years old and in kindergarten at Norman Ingram Memorial Public School in Don Mills, Ontario. Anderson's description of the afternoon suggests an innocent kids' version of Mardi Gras, when people throw off society's usual rules and restraints: "We were too young to follow the action, except that when Henderson scored we knew Canada had won and that it was a great moment. All the kids and teachers spilled out into the schoolyard. Everybody was running around and yelling and going crazy. You got the feeling anything could happen—the teachers didn't even care about keeping order."

Ken Juba recalls a similar scene when he was nine in grade five at St. Charles Elementary School in Saskatoon, watching Henderson's goal on a black-and-white TV set in the gymnasium and "everybody running outside and hollering." His memories are close to those of Alain Simard at a similar age, attending St.-Redempteur Roman Catholic school in Hull, Quebec, and Sally Hawks at

Havergal College, an exclusive private school for girls in downtown Toronto: "There must have been six hundred of us girls in the gym," says Hawks, "all in our little green tunics and yellow blouses, all tremendously excited and screaming for Team Canada, even if we weren't all hockey fans. I was—I fell in love with Bobby Clarke."

One eleven-year-old didn't see Henderson's goal at school but at home—not because he was sick, but because his father, Walter Gretzky, overcame the objections of his mother, Phyllis Gretzky, to letting him skip school. Young Wayne watched Game 8 in the living room.

In Luzhniki Arena itself, not all the working stiffs were playing hockey. Brian Pickell, a young photographer from Paris, Ontario, was on assignment shooting the series for the Hockey Canada commemorative book *Twenty-Seven Days in September*. Pickell would use up ten to twelve rolls of film each game, three different cameras slung around his neck. His cameras had no motor drives and had to be rewound by hand. In the late moments of Game 8, he'd been clicking so fast and furiously, anxious not to miss a defining moment, that all three cameras ran out of film. He had to pause and change a roll in one of the cameras, and that's what he was doing—his head down behind the boards—at the magic moment. It was left to Frank Lennon, a veteran staff photographer with the *Toronto Star*, to capture the unforgettable image of Henderson celebrating his series-winning goal. Pickell rues his wretched timing. "Just as I'd changed the film," he remembers, "the crowd erupted. I looked over at the Canadian bench, and Harry Sinden had this *look*—all the muscles in his face were working at cross-purposes, his face was just squirming, as if he didn't know which of his emotions to feel. I wouldn't have been surprised if his eyes had popped out onto his cheeks or the top of his head had blown off. He was *exploding*."

Up in the stands, grizzled media veterans reacted to Henderson's goal in ways that surprised even them. CBC hockey analyst Howie Meeker, a former NHL player and coach with Toronto, "went snakey . . . I waltzed with the guy beside me." Jim Coleman, then with the *Toronto Sun* and already one of the deans of Canadian sportswriters, describes his own reaction as "demented": "There I was, a sixty-two-year-old man, clad in my sincere-blue three-piece suit, my old school tie and my pin-collar shirt. . . . There I was, turning around to face Leonid Brezhnev and the other Soviet Politburo members in their back-row seats, and jamming my clenched right fist and arm upwards in repeated gestures. . . . My parents, who brought me up properly, would have been ashamed of me. But I felt no shame—only exultation! I was gloating in the realization that I was present for the most significant victory in the history of Canadian sports."

Boris Mikhailov, meanwhile, who battled so fiercely and courageously, has said: "Losing that game was the worst moment of my career. I had a sick feeling for a long time."

The two Canadians nearest Henderson when he scored were Cournoyer and Phil Esposito. Esposito remembers the power of his emotions at the moment of the goal. In a reunion with Henderson, Savard, White and Dryden in 1989, taped for Dryden's *Home Game*, Esposito said, "And when he scored it, I mean, that's the closest I ever came to loving another guy." To the laughter of his old teammates, he continued, "I mean, I really loved him. I think if I'd had a million dollars, I'd have given it to him right there."

"Well, you've got it today," Henderson said at the reunion, laughing. "You didn't have it then."

"I don't love you that much any more," Esposito replied.

We don't have to ask where Henderson himself was that day, but we couldn't have guessed what went flashing through his mind at the moment he scored, and the fans went wild in a way they never would again: he thought of his father. Garnet Henderson, that imposing, demanding yet loving man, had died four years earlier. "I remember thinking," Paul Henderson told Roy MacGregor in *The Home Team: Fathers, Sons and Hockey*, " 'Geez, if anybody would've loved to see that goal, it would have been him.' "

One more story. The youngest person to answer the "Where were you?" question for this book is Michel Dubeau, a student at Concordia University in Montreal and a highly knowledgeable hockey fanatic. Dubeau's passion for the game is such that he chose an apartment to live in because it was right across the street from the Forum. When that venerable shrine was shut down in March

1996, Dubeau was there for the old-timers' game and numerous other closing celebrations, rubbing shoulders with his hero, Guy Lafleur, and older saints of Canadiens hockey such as Maurice Richard and Jean Béliveau. Dubeau was just one year old when Henderson scored, so he doesn't remember where he was, exactly: "Probably at home, sleeping or eating." But he *feels* as if he followed the whole saga game by game, just as he would if it were played today. "I've heard so much about the '72 series from my dad and others who were older," he says, "and I've read so much about it and seen all the highlights, especially Henderson's goal, that it's all very real to me—like I was there, and it was only yesterday."

TWENTY-ONE

WHERE HOCKEY HAS GONE

"Nothing ever brought me so low; nothing ever
took me so high. Nothing meant so much."

— KEN DRYDEN, *Home Game*

●

Autumn 1972 was a great time to be a hockey fan—of any nationality.

If you loved hockey for itself, you felt blessed to have watched the two best teams in the world play the game more brilliantly, with more elan and heart and inspiration, than it had ever been played before. If you could leave aside the fatuous posturings of individuals, the preposterous shenanigans induced by small, Cold War minds, you recognized the Canadian and Soviet hockey teams had competed at a higher, more creative, more courageous, more thrilling level than previously known. No Stanley Cup final, no World's championship tournament, could rival the '72 series as athletic *and* dramatic spectacle: as ultimate expression of hockey's artistic potential and battered soul.

To paraphrase Ken Dryden, hockey had never brought you so low or so high; being a hockey fan had never meant so much. Even while participating as one of the principals in the drama, Dryden was able to imagine what an extraordinary spectator experience the series must have been: a part of him wished he'd been back home following its unfolding, just like any other fan. Playing in the series and watching it, Dryden says today, "were two experiences of equivalent value. I got one but missed the other. And they got one but missed the other. I'd have loved to watch the series because it's a great experience that Canadians share."

Team Canada members didn't realize how huge their victory was at home until returning from Europe three days later. But first, they had to stop over in Prague to play an anticlimactic exhibition game, just forty-eight hours after Game 8. The match against the Czechoslovak nationals was memorable chiefly for the triumphant homecoming it provided for Stan Mikita, who had left his homeland at the age of eight to live with an aunt and uncle in Canada, and whose mother, brothers and sisters still lived in Czechoslovakia. Mikita received a standing ovation from the crowd, and an underperforming Team Canada went on to pull off another little miracle —a 3-3 tie on a goal by Serge Savard, his second of the game, with only four seconds remaining.

The team flew home the next day, Sunday, October 1, via London. Their DC-8 landed first in Montreal. A crowd of 20,000 well-wishers, including Prime Minister Trudeau and Mayor Jean Drapeau, plus a national television audience, awaited the plane's arrival at Dorval. When the cameras zoomed in on the aircraft to catch the first conquering hero to emerge, the door swung open and out popped a rumpled, hippie-ish young man with three cameras dangling from his neck. Suddenly the happiest member of the viewing audience was Mrs. Pickell of Paris, Ontario. Her son Brian dashed down the stairs, at the bottom of which he encountered P. E. Trudeau wearing an expectant smile: the election campaign was still in full swing. Trudeau turned the smile up a few watts and beamed it inquiringly at Pickell, who brushed past him to get on with his job—setting up to capture the players as they descended. When Phil Esposito reached the bottom step, he bent over and kissed his native soil: in Quebec, note.

Once all the players were on the ground, they boarded fire trucks and were paraded around the tarmac. Trudeau was there with them, having been hoisted up like a feather by big Savard. In an address to the crowd, Savard got so carried away with emotion that he made Trudeau a gift of a hockey stick autographed by every player on Team Canada; the only problem was that it belonged to John Ferguson, who was a bit surprised by his buddy's generosity.

After the speeches and presentations, the Montreal-based players went home while the rest of Team Canada flew on to Toronto. By the time they arrived, it was dark and raining heavily. A motorcade carried them downtown to Nathan Phillips Square, packed with 50,000 soaked but happy supporters ready to greet and lionize them—this in the city whose new tabloid, the *Sun*, had changed the newspaper's logo the day after Game 8 to the *Hender-Sun*, and had run a headline echoing Harry Sinden's tongue-in-cheek, post-victory remark: "NEVER IN DOUBT!"

In Toronto, a few more players went on home after the speeches—Henderson to discover his neighbours had erected a big illuminated sign, "Home of Paul Henderson," on his front lawn. The rest bedded down at Sutton Place. In the hotel lobby, Bobby Clarke stayed standing on exhausted legs, patiently signing autographs and chatting with fans as long as they wanted him to. Asked earlier by columnist Dick Beddoes about the "wicked two-hander" he'd applied to Kharlamov, Clarke had replied, "Mr. Beddoes, if I hadn't learned to lay on what you call a wicked two-hander, I would never have left Flin Flon, Manitoba." Now the series villain—from the Soviet perspective—resembled a golden-haired, curly-headed cherub, all teeth intact, modestly performing a hockey hero's duty to his people.

●

On Team Canada's triumphant return, there wasn't yet time to understand the full meaning of the '72 series. At that point, we knew only the happy impact on our psyches. But ultimately, the series would have more far-reaching long-term significance than simply providing an emotional catharsis for Canadians: it would transform hockey itself.

Of course, there were still those who saw the series' result as a complete vindication of our game, way of life, socioeconomic system, democratic principles, faith in God and moral superiority. But when people looked more thoughtfully at the outcome, two conclusions became preeminently clear: one, we had every reason to be proud of a team that had shown such heart, battling back from a losing position to win so magnificently by taking the final three games on enemy ice; and two, Team Canada's margin of victory was so narrow, so fragile, so much a product of chance, that the Soviets could just as easily have won by a goal, and consequently Soviet hockey now clearly rivalled our own—stronger in some respects, weaker in others, but on balance equal to ours.

Perhaps the vital difference between the teams had simply been the intangibles of individual human desire, a characteristic that Tretiak has said makes Canadians "stand out from all the rest of the players of the world . . . they always played till the very last second in spite of the score." But at the time, admitting the Soviets as hockey equals represented an attitudinal breakthrough for us, so fixed had been our unquestioned faith in the NHL's, and therefore our own, superiority. The corollary to the breakthrough was to admit we had a lot to learn from the Soviets, and from other Europeans, about teaching and playing our game.

Immediately after the series, one of the most unlikely places this change surfaced was in the sports pages of the plucky but normally not-very-progressive *Toronto Sun*. Sports editor George Gross, himself a European, wrote that while the Soviets, Czechoslovakians, Swedes and Finns had advanced rapidly in hockey by applying scientific methods and the results of medical research, Canadians had stood still, coaching and playing the game in the same old ways for decades. Gross compared our complacency to English soccer in the 1950s; when Hungary defeated England twice in 1953, the myth of English soccer supremacy was destroyed, and the English had to admit their game needed rejuvenating.

Gross introduced into his paper a column by Lloyd Percival— Anatoly Tarasov's inspiration and a long-time critic of NHL training methods. In one column, Percival spoke the heresy that "The Soviets, and European hockey generally, [have] caught up to us, in some ways surpassed us. . . ." They had done so, he argued, by consciously developing better, more skilled players through new coaching and training methods (some of them his own), scientific testing and evaluation, and pragmatic problem-solving. To keep up, Canadian minor hockey would have to train coaches to apply these new methods, devoting more ice time to conditioning and skills development, and less to just playing the game.

Over the next two decades, this was essentially the direction that minor hockey took in North America. During the series in

Moscow, we'd received some glimpses into the Soviets' training methods; those glimpses opened our minds to knowing more about how their players had become so skilled. During an intermission in Game 8, for instance, CBC-CTV showed Howie Meeker visiting the Central Army sports club to watch fifteen- and sixteen-year-olds, the USSR's stars of the future, practising the same drills as the top Soviet teams: intricate passing drills to teach them to keep their heads up, and the rubber-belt-around-the-waist drill to develop skating power. "I think they get more benefit out of an hour here," wise old Howie told Canada, "than the kids at home get out of three hours."

Similarly, Ken Dryden and author Jack Ludwig visited the Central Army club and reported in their respective books what they saw: drills to improve skating agility, balance and strength, and a full conditioning program emphasizing other sports such as weight-lifting, soccer, basketball and gymnastics to produce a complete all-round athlete. "A sound premise, I'd say," commented Dryden.

It wasn't long before minor hockey officials were advocating and introducing these "new" methods here. Belatedly, Lloyd Percival was a prophet with honour in his own country.

Dave King, later coach of Canada's junior and national teams and the NHL Calgary Flames, believes the '72 series was a triumph of Canadian spirit—"The team played on heart and soul." But that fact also posed a warning for the future: "At the hockey administrative level, from university coaches to the CAHA, there was a real concern we'd won only on emotion, and by intimidating the referees to some extent. We realized we'd better work on our game or we'd fall behind. And the best way to improve the quality of our game was to improve the quality of coaching."

Accordingly, the CAHA (now the Canadian Hockey Association, after a long-overdue merger with Hockey Canada in 1994), set to work reeducating coaches. That thrust eventually led to adoption of a national coaching certification program, designed to train qualified coaches at various levels, and a system of developing the most promising young players through participation in Under-18 and Under-17 programs. These and other developmental programs, such as the International Hockey Centre of Excellence in

Calgary, have contributed to keeping Canada highly competitive as a world hockey power.

But when the coaching certification program was introduced, not everybody was on side. Older and more traditional coaches resented the seminars held to teach the new methods, often featuring European coaches. Their attitude, King says, was that "the Europeans can't teach us anything, we have our own game." Consequently, the CAHA had to endure years of criticism and resistance in persevering with its drive to revitalize Canadian hockey at the grassroots.

Player agent and former national team member Herb Pinder recalls the pre-'72 days in minor hockey: "Then there was one coach to a team, and maybe he'd been a player but often knew little about the game. His idea of strategy was to draw imaginary lines down the ice and tell the wingers, 'Now don't you cross that line.' But after learning from the Soviets, we have forwards criss-crossing and doubling back, and teams attacking as a five-man unit. We have better conditioning and nutrition. Now we've got three coaches to a team, extensive videos and advance scouting. We've got players staying in shape, we've got power-play set-ups that only the Soviets used to have. Now we're just as advanced as they are, or more."

The truth was, we Canadians had been an insular, isolationist, self-protective, ignorant lot when it came to "our" game. We needed the shock and comeuppance the series provided, if only to open our eyes to the transforming world around us.

"The Europeans took our game and evolved it, while we stood still or even went backwards," Pinder says. "The Russians had a style, and the Czechs' style was different from that. And the Swedes were a bit timid but had these little guys who could skate and go wide on you like crazy. And the Finns were more hardy and liked to hit. So there was this hockey world evolving through international competition, and we're back here, *stuck*, just playing ourselves. It was a business monopoly. And like any monopoly, the NHL got stagnant—disdainful of the customers, abusive of the employees. The NHL began drinking its own bathwater and believing its own press clippings. Overlay on all of that the element of celebrity, and hockey's importance to Canada, and you can see how we got blind."

The revolutionary impact of the '72 series was reinforced by the advent of the World Hockey Association. Most people remember the WHA's main influence as driving up player salaries, but the league was also important for taking the lead in importing European players, with their own distinctive gifts and style of play. Among the first and finest were the Swedes Ulf Nilsson, Anders Hedberg and Lars-Erik Sjoberg, brought over to play with Bobby Hull and the Winnipeg Jets. The WHA signed many other Europeans, some of the best of them integrated into the NHL after the WHA folded in 1979.

The '72 series triggered another major phenomenon with a chain-reaction effect on hockey: the continuing, though sporadic meetings between European national teams and the NHL, as represented by Team Canada and to some extent Team USA. These included the various Canada Cup tournaments in 1976, 1981, 1984, 1987 and 1991—all but the 1981 edition won by Team Canada; the 1979 Challenge series in New York City, in which the Soviets decisively defeated the NHL All-Stars in mid-season two games to one; and the 1987 Rendez-Vous series in Quebec City, evenly split one win apiece between the Soviets and the NHL. In the seventies and early eighties, there were also exhibition tours involving Soviet and NHL club teams, many of them wonderfully exciting and entertaining match-ups, a few of them violent and bloody—especially if the Philadelphia Flyers were involved. The great majority of these games were won by the Soviet clubs, such as Central Army, Soviet Wings and Spartak. And there was the eight-game WHA-Soviet series in 1974, in which Gordie Howe, Bobby Hull and Paul Henderson played in a losing cause for a Canadian side that sorely missed NHL players and didn't have the depth or character of the '72 team.

All these interactions between North American and European hockey promoted and intensified a cross-pollination of playing styles, producing the hybrid style we see in the NHL today. As the Soviets reinforced their reputation with clearcut victories over the NHL, culminating in their 8-1 trouncing of Team Canada in the 1981 Canada Cup, Canadian coaches borrowed more and more from the Soviets' playing style and training methods. It was no coincidence that the dominant NHL team of the mid-1980s was the explosive Edmonton Oilers of Gretzky, Mark Messier and company, who excelled at a Soviet-style offensive game utilizing the whole ice surface with speed, polished passing and teamwork. As Winnipeg Jets GM Mike Smith has remarked, "It's safe to say that over the long haul we got more from the Russians than they got from us."

Although we're still some distance from embracing Tarasov's prescription of brains over brawn, brains receive a lot more credit today. In Vladislav Tretiak's view, Canadian teams gave up trying to defeat the Soviets through intimidation in the 1980s, after recognizing "we are on the same professional level as you. You started to respect us and to understand that you couldn't beat us in that way, that we could tolerate all that [violence]." No doubt this change is due to North American acceptance of the high quality of Russian hockey—but also to a decline in Cold War animosity. Tretiak observes that some of his countrymen believed the NHLers' propensity for fighting was just for show, but "I didn't think so in 1972 . . . it was all real, although you hated us more than we hated you."

Dave King believes the current hybrid style merges the best of the physical, driving-straight-for-the-net Canadian game with some of the best features of the Soviet game: its greater mobility, for example, where supporting the puck overrides positional play, and the players interchange positions, constantly moving into the open lane; or its expanded conception of the defenseman's role as an important element of the attack, adding a fourth or fifth man in. The result is a faster and more fluid and, at its best, more exciting sport.

Whether you prefer the frenetic, hyperactive style of today's NHL game, which often seems to have only one speed, or the more modulated tempos and more elegant, individualized styles of play by either side in '72 is a matter of taste. However that may be, Canada's performance in international competition at all levels has unquestionably developed and matured well beyond the '72 series.

First of all, there is no longer the fundamental problem of our players being out of condition. Because they train eleven months of the year instead of eight, pro and would-be pro hockey players now stay in shape year-round, take better care of themselves (pasta instead of steak; far less smoking), and don't have to spend the first two or three months of the season playing themelves into condition. Second, when a Canadian team enters an international tournament, the players start with a respect for their opponents and an understanding of their tactics and strengths. Third, and perhaps the biggest factor of all, Canadians know they have to exercise self-discipline in order to perform at their best and maximize their chances of winning. While sticking with their tough physical style, Canadian teams try not to take penalties that can cost a game, no matter how frustrated they become with the officiating or the other team's sneak tactics.

Consequently, the Canadian record in international play continues strong and is getting stronger. In World's junior competition, Canada has dominated ever since winning the gold in 1982; the 1996 junior gold medal was Canada's fourth in a row. In the emergent sport of women's hockey, Canada has been the perennial World's champion. And even in the annual men's World's tournament, where Canada (like other nations) must still play without NHL players who are competing for the Stanley Cup, the Canadian performance has improved substantially in recent years. In 1994, the reconstituted national team, reinforced by NHL stars such as Joe Sakic, Luc Robitaille and Bill Ranford whose teams were out of the playoffs, ended a thirty-two-year drought by capturing Canada's first World's title since the Trail Smoke Eaters won in 1961.

That 1994 victory was the crowning glory of a year in which Canada won five major international championships, including the Under-17 and Under-18 tournaments; and the same year in which the national team, without benefit of NHLers, came within a shootout of winning Olympic gold against Sweden at Lilliehammer. Even in 1996, a no-name Canadian team given little chance of winning the World's title was the surprise of the championships in Vienna, defeating Russia in the semifinal and narrowly losing the gold to the Czech Republic.

It's instructive to hear the coaches of Team Canada 1972 comment on how our game has evolved since the original series was played. Over a long management career with several NHL teams, John Ferguson, that supreme antagonist and partisan, has developed a keen appreciation of European hockey skills. As former director of player personnel for the Ottawa Senators, Ferguson made nine scouting trips to Europe in two years. He estimates that of all the young talent he recruited for the Senators, 80 per cent were Europeans, including several fast-rising stars: Russian Alexei Yashin, Swede Daniel Alfredsson, and Czechs Stan Neckar and Radek Bonk. Ferguson believes Europe contains "a talent pool that the NHL still hasn't tapped thoroughly"—even though some 40 per cent of the league's players are now non-Canadian.

Harry Sinden has a somewhat different take on things. Although he started off admiring Soviet hockey far more than most North Americans, Sinden now feels the pendulum has swung too far the other way: in trying to capture the mystique of the Soviet playing style, North American coaches have adopted coaching techniques they *think* the Soviets used, but didn't. As a result, says Sinden, our young hockey players are overprogrammed and underskilled at playing the game itself. "With coaches today, it's a contest to see who has the best drills. They've got three-ring binders full of them. By putting our young players through all these drills, we've produced big skaters and big shooters who don't know how to play hockey. We've lost a lot of our creativity."

Sinden believes there is an instinctual side to playing any sport. In swimming, coaching helps, but your body will figure out the best way to get through the water on its own; and similarly in hockey, youngsters will find out what works for them by playing the game. "It's not fun for kids to go to hockey practice any more. They lose interest. They want to play, and they'll become much better by playing than being dominated by coaches."

In Russia, hockey isn't what it was, given the dismantling of the Soviet system and the drain of their best players to the NHL, but Sinden points out the Russian players are still highly skilled—more so than ours. Why? Because when they practise over there, they *play* against each other.

North American fans now enjoy watching many of the most gifted Russian players every week of the season. In 1995-96, fifty-five Russians played in the NHL, including Vancouver superstars Alexander Mogilny and Pavel Bure, and the Detroit Red Wings' famous five led by Igor Larionov and Sergei Fedorov. The oldest player in the whole league plays godfather to these Russian emigres: thirty-eight-year-old Vyachislav Fetisov of the Red Wings, who led the exodus of Soviet players into the NHL when he joined the New Jersey Devils in 1989, after glasnost and perestroika had opened the gates.

Such a situation was inconceivable in 1972. But it symbolizes better than anything else the new era of the globalization of hockey.

Another symbol is an event that will have taken place after this book goes to press: the 1996 World Cup of Hockey, formerly known as the Canada Cup. Canada is no longer permitted to pretend it owns hockey. The world owns hockey now, so the rhetoric goes—although in reality money does, and hence the NHL does. The league has agreed to release its players to their various national teams for the World Cup, just as it had the power to agree (or not) to let them play for Team Canada in 1972.

Beyond that, a new professional circuit known as the European Hockey League is struggling to launch its inaugural season in 1996-97, hoping to boast as many as twenty elite teams from twelve countries, and dreaming of a World's Series playoff against the NHL. And still beyond that, another once-unthinkable event: in the 1998 Winter Olympic Games in Nagano, Japan, for the first time, NHL and other professional players will be allowed to represent their country on "dream teams" for the Olympic gold medal in hockey.

These developments signify not only the globalization but the professionalization of hockey. That process, too, was ushered in by the 1972 Canada-Soviet series—the turning point in breaking down hockey barriers not just between East and West, but between amateur and professional. With pros playing in the Olympics, that old and once-honourable distinction has vanished.

Not all of these transformations were directly caused by the '72 series, but it is difficult to imagine them happening without it. For hockey's Cold War to end, the enemies had to take the first step towards each other, creating common ground to meet on. Once they did so, further steps became possible.

The two sides took that crucial step in September 1972. The Soviet Union didn't lose, except technically, on points. And Canada didn't lose either, except for a little face. The Cold War lost.

SUMMARIES AND STATISTICS OF 1972 CANADA-SOVIET SERIES

•

GAME I, SEPTEMBER 2, AT MONTREAL
SOVIET UNION 7, TEAM CANADA 3

GOALTENDERS

Soviet Union: Tretiak, 60 minutes, 3 goals against
Team Canada: Dryden, 60 minutes, 7 goals against

SUMMARY

First Period
1. Team Canada: P. Esposito (F. Mahovlich, Bergman) 0.30
2. Team Canada: Henderson (Clarke) 6:32
3. Soviet Union: Zimin (Yakushev, Shadrin) 11:40
4. Soviet Union: Petrov (Mikhailov) 17:28. Short-handed goal
PENALTIES: Henderson 1:03, Yakushev 7:04, Mikhailov 15:11, Ragulin
17:19

Second Period
5. Soviet Union: Kharlamov (Maltsev) 2:40
6. Soviet Union: Kharlamov (Maltsev) 10:18. Game-winning goal
PENALTIES: Clarke 5:16, Lapointe 12:53

Third Period
7. Team Canada: Clarke (Ellis, Henderson) 8:22
8. Soviet Union: Mikhailov (Blinov) 13:32
9. Soviet Union: Zimin 14:29
10. Soviet Union: Yakushev (Shadrin) 18:37
PENALTIES: Kharlamov 14:45, Lapointe 19:41

SHOTS ON GOAL BY

Soviet Union	10	10	10 —— 30
Team Canada	10	10	12 —— 32

GAME 2, SEPTEMBER 4, AT TORONTO
TEAM CANADA 4, SOVIET UNION 1

GOALTENDERS

Soviet Union: Tretiak, 60 minutes, 4 goals against
Team Canada: T. Esposito, 60 minutes, 1 goal against

SUMMARY

First Period
No Scoring
PENALTIES: Park 10:08, Henderson 15:19

Second Period
1. Team Canada: P. Esposito (Park, Cashman) 7:14
PENALTIES: Gusev 2:07, Soviet Union bench minor (served by Zimin) 4:13, Bergman 15:16, Tsygankov 19:54, Kharlamov (misconduct) 19:54

Third Period
2. Team Canada: Cournoyer (Park) 1:19. Power-play goal; game-winning goal
3. Soviet Union: Yakushev (Liapkin, Zimin) 5:53. Power-play goal
4. Team Canada: P. Mahovlich (P. Esposito) 6:47. Short-handed goal
5. Team Canada: F. Mahovlich (Mikita, Cournoyer) 8:59
PENALTIES: Clarke 5:13, Stapleton 6:14

SHOTS ON GOAL BY

Soviet Union	7	5	9 —— 21
Team Canada	10	16	10 —— 36

GAME 3, SEPTEMBER 6, AT WINNIPEG
SOVIET UNION 4, TEAM CANADA 4

GOALTENDERS

Soviet Union: Tretiak, 60 minutes, 4 goals against
Team Canada: T. Esposito, 60 minutes, 4 goals against

SUMMARY

First Period
  1. Team Canada: Parise (White, P. Esposito) 1:54
  2. Soviet Union: Petrov 3:15. Short-handed goal
  3. Team Canada: Ratelle (Cournoyer, Bergman) 18:25
PENALTIES: Vasiliev 3:02, Cashman 8:01, Parise 15:47

Second Period
  4. Team Canada: P. Esposito (Cashman, Parise) 4:19
  5. Soviet Union: Kharlamov (Tsygankov) 12:56. Short-handed goal
  6. Team Canada: Henderson (Clarke, Ellis) 13:47
  7. Soviet Union: Lebedev (Vasiliev, Anisin) 14:59
  8. Soviet Union: Bodunov (Anisin) 18:28
PENALTIES: Petrov 4:46, Lebedev 11:00

Third Period
No Scoring
PENALTIES: White 1:33, Mishakov 1:33, Cashman (misconduct) 10:44

SHOTS ON GOAL BY

Soviet Union	9	8	8 ——	25
Team Canada	15	17	6 ——	38

GAME 4, SEPTEMBER 8, AT VANCOUVER
SOVIET UNION 5, TEAM CANADA 3

GOALTENDERS

Soviet Union: Tretiak, 60 minutes, 3 goals against
Team Canada: Dryden, 60 minutes, 5 goals against

SUMMARY

First Period
  1. Soviet Union: Mikhailov (Lutchenko, Petrov) 2:01. Power-play goal
  2. Soviet Union: Mikhailov (Lutchenko, Petrov) 7:29. Power-play goal
PENALTIES: Goldsworthy 1:24, Goldsworthy 5:58, P. Esposito 19:29

Second Period
  3. Team Canada: Perreault 5:37
  4. Soviet Union: Blinov (Petrov, Mikhailov) 6:34
  5. Soviet Union: Vikulov (Kharlamov, Maltsev) 13:52. Game-winning
     goal
PENALTIES: Kuzkin 8:39

Third Period
  6. Team Canada: Goldsworthy (P. Esposito, Bergman) 6:54
  7. Soviet Union: Shadrin (Yakushev, Vasiliev) 11:05
  8. Team Canada: D. Hull (P. Esposito, Goldsworthy) 19:38
PENALTIES: Petrov 2:01

SHOTS ON GOAL BY

Soviet Union	11	14	6 ——	31
Team Canada	10	8	23 ——	41

257

GAME 5, SEPTEMBER 22, AT MOSCOW
SOVIET UNION 5, TEAM CANADA 4

GOALTENDERS

Team Canada: T. Esposito, 60 minutes, 5 goals against
Soviet Union: Tretiak, 60 minutes, 4 goals against

SUMMARY

First Period
 1. Team Canada: Parise (Perreault, Gilbert) 15:30
PENALTIES: Ellis 3:49, Kharlamov 12:25

Second Period
 2. Team Canada: Clarke (Henderson) 2:36
 3. Team Canada: Henderson (Lapointe, Clarke) 11:58
PENALTIES: Ellis 5:38, Kharlamov 5:38, Bergman 8:13, White 20:00, Blinov 20:00

Third Period
 4. Soviet Union: Blinov (Petrov, Kuzkin) 3:34
 5. Team Canada: Henderson (Clarke) 4:56
 6. Soviet Union: Anisin (Liapkin, Yakushev) 9:05
 7. Soviet Union: Shadrin (Anisin) 9:13
 8. Soviet Union: Gusev (Ragulin, Kharlamov) 11:41
 9. Soviet Union: Vikulov (Kharlamov) 14:46. Game-winning goal
PENALTIES: Clarke 10:25, Tsygankov 10:25, Yakushev 15:48

SHOTS ON GOAL BY

Team Canada	12	13	12 ——	37
Soviet Union	9	13	11 ——	33

GAME 6, SEPTEMBER 24, AT MOSCOW
TEAM CANADA 3, SOVIET UNION 2

GOALTENDERS

Team Canada: Dryden, 60 minutes, 2 goals against
Soviet Union: Tretiak, 60 minutes, 3 goals against

SUMMARY

First Period
No Scoring
PENALTIES: Bergman 10:21, P. Esposito (double minor) 13:11

Second Period
1. Soviet Union: Liapkin (Yakushev, Shadrin) 1:12
2. Team Canada: D. Hull (Gilbert) 5:13
3. Team Canada: Cournoyer (Berenson) 6:21
4. Team Canada: Henderson 6:36. Game-winning goal
5. Soviet Union: Yakushev (Shadrin, Liapkin) 17:11. Power-play goal
PENALTIES: Ragulin 2:09, Lapointe 8:29, Vasiliev 8:29, Clarke 10:12,
D. Hull 17:02, P. Esposito (major) 17:46, Team Canada bench minor
(served by Cournoyer) 17:46

Third Period
No Scoring
PENALTIES: Ellis 17:39

SHOTS ON GOAL BY

Team Canada	7	8	7 —— 22
Soviet Union	12	8	9 —— 29

GAME 7, SEPTEMBER 26, AT MOSCOW
TEAM CANADA 4, SOVIET UNION 3

GOALTENDERS

Team Canada: T. Esposito, 60 minutes, 3 goals against
Soviet Union: Tretiak, 60 minutes, 4 goals against

SUMMARY

First Period
  1. Team Canada: P. Esposito (Ellis, Henderson) 4:09
  2. Soviet Union: Yakushev (Shadrin, Liapkin) 10:17
  3. Soviet Union: Petrov (Vikulov, Tsygankov) 16:27. Power-play goal
  4. Team Canada: P. Esposito (Savard, Parise) 17:34
PENALTIES: Mikhailov 2:00, P. Mahovlich 5:16, Mishakov 5:16, Mishakov 11:09, P. Esposito 12:39, White 15:45

Second Period
No Scoring
PENALTIES: Gilbert 0:59, Parise 6:04, Anisin 6:11, P. Esposito 12:44, Kuzkin 12:44, Parise 15:14, Kuzkin 15:14, Stapleton 15:24

Third Period
  5. Team Canada: Gilbert (Ratelle, D. Hull) 2:13
  6. Soviet Union: Yakushev (Maltsev, Lutchenko) 5:15. Power-play goal
  7. Team Canada: Henderson (Savard) 17:54. Game-winning goal
PENALTIES: Bergman 3:26, Gilbert 7:25, Bergman (major) 16:26, Mikhailov (major) 16:26

SHOTS ON GOAL BY

Team Canada	9	7	9 —— 25
Soviet Union	6	13	12 —— 31

GAME 8, SEPTEMBER 28, AT MOSCOW
TEAM CANADA 6, SOVIET UNION 5

GOALTENDERS

Team Canada: Dryden, 60 minutes, 5 goals against
Soviet Union: Tretiak, 60 minutes, 6 goals against

SUMMARY

First Period

1. Soviet Union: Yakushev (Maltsev, Liapkin) 3:34. Power-play goal
2. Team Canada: P. Esposito (Park) 6:45. Power-play goal
3. Soviet Union: Lutchenko (Kharlamov) 13:10. Power-play goal
4. Team Canada: Park (Ratelle, D. Hull) 16:59

PENALTIES: White 2:25, P. Mahovlich 3:01, Petrov (minor, misconduct and game misconduct) 3:44, Parise 4:10, Tsygankov 6:28, Ellis 9:27, Petrov 9:46, Cournoyer 12:51

Second Period

5. Soviet Union: Shadrin 0:21
6. Team Canada: White (Gilbert, Ratelle) 10:32
7. Soviet Union: Yakushev 11:43
8. Soviet Union: Vasiliev 16:44. Power-play goal

PENALTIES: Stapleton 14:58, Kuzkin 18:06

Third Period

9. Team Canada: P. Esposito (P. Mahovlich) 2:27
10. Team Canada: Cournoyer (P. Esposito, Park) 12:56
11. Team Canada: Henderson (P. Esposito) 19:26. Game-winning goal

PENALTIES: Gilbert (major) 3:41, Mishakov (major) 3:41, Vasiliev 4:27, D. Hull 15:24, Petrov 15:24

SHOTS ON GOAL BY

Team Canada	14	8	14 —— 36
Soviet Union	12	10	5 —— 27

TEAM STATISTICS

GOALS BY	1st Period	2nd Period	3rd Period	Total
Soviet Union	9	12	11	32
Team Canada	9	10	12	31

TOTAL ADVANTAGES:	Soviet Union	38	Team Canada	23
POWER-PLAY GOALS:	Soviet Union	9	Team Canada	2
SHORT-HANDED GOALS:	Soviet Union	3	Team Canada	1
PENALTY MINUTES:	Soviet Union	84	Team Canada	147

GOALTENDING RECORDS

Player	Games	Goals Against	Average
Esposito, Team Canada	4	13	3.25
Dryden, Team Canada	4	19	4.75
Tretiak, Soviet Union	8	31	3.87

INDIVIDUAL STATISTICS: SOVIET UNION

Player	Games Played	Goals	Assists	Points	Penalty Minutes
Yakushev	8	7	4	11	4
Shadrin	8	3	5	8	0
Kharlamov	7	3	4	7	16
Petrov	8	3	4	7	10
Liapkin	6	1	5	6	0
Mikhailov	8	3	2	5	9
Maltsev	8	0	5	5	0
Anisin	7	1	3	4	2
Lutchenko	8	1	3	4	0
Zimin	2	2	1	3	0
Blinov	5	2	1	3	2
Vikulov	6	2	1	3	0
Vasiliev	6	1	2	3	6
Tsygankov	8	0	2	2	6
Lebedev	3	1	0	1	2
Bodunov	3	1	0	1	0
Gusev	6	1	0	1	2
Ragulin	6	0	1	1	4
Kuzkin	7	0	1	1	8
Martyniuk	1	0	0	0	0
Solodukhin	1	0	0	0	0
Starshinov	1	0	0	0	0
Shatalov	2	0	0	0	0
Volchkov	3	0	0	0	0
Paladiev	3	0	0	0	0
Mishakov	6	0	0	0	11
TOTALS	8	32	44	76	84[†]

[†] Includes one bench minor to each team

INDIVIDUAL STATISTICS: TEAM CANADA

Player	Games Played	Goals	Assists	Points	Penalty Minutes
P. Esposito	8	7	6	13	15
Henderson	8	7	3	10	4
Clarke	8	2	4	6	18
Cournoyer	8	3	2	5	2
Park	8	1	4	5	2
D. Hull	4	2	2	4	4
Parise	6	2	2	4	28
Gilbert	6	1	3	4	9
Ratelle	6	1	3	4	0
Bergman	8	0	3	3	13
Ellis	8	0	3	3	8
Perreault	2	1	1	2	0
Goldsworthy	3	1	1	2	4
F. Mahovlich	6	1	1	2	0
P. Mahovlich	7	1	1	2	4
White	7	1	1	2	8
Cashman	2	0	2	2	14
Savard	5	0	2	2	0
Mikita	2	0	1	1	0
Berenson	2	0	1	1	0
Lapointe	7	0	1	1	6
Redmond	1	0	0	0	0
Awrey	2	0	0	0	0
Hadfield	2	0	0	0	0
Seiling	3	0	0	0	0
Stapleton	7	0	0	0	6
TOTALS	8	31	46	77	147 [†]

[†] Includes one bench minor to each team

SOURCES AND ACKNOWLEDGEMENTS

●

This work of hockey history is also a memoir: not a personal one—although the feelings I experienced while following the '72 series are still powerful, and a major reason for writing the book—but a collective memoir. To this day, millions of Canadians and more than a few Americans hold the series' high drama and emotional catharsis in common. Whatever else may divide us, that memory is a shared treasure, a communal bond, with very few parallels in our society.

So naturally my most important sources for this book were people. I thank all those, hockey professionals and just plain hockey lovers, who reached into their memories to tell me what the series meant and still means to them, how it felt to be caught up in the extraordinariness of it all. Some of their stories are found in Chapter 20. Many individuals have contributed to this book, although I take sole responsibility for its deficiencies.

In the course of my travels around hockey country by car, plane, train and telephone, I was kindly helped by (from east to west) Harry Sinden, Gary Smith, Yvan Cournoyer, Serge Savard, Paul Henderson, Ron Ellis, Pat Stapleton, John Ferguson, Igor Kuperman, Scott Taylor, Morris Mott, Herb Pinder, Dave King, Verne Clemence, Ken Juba, Ned Powers and Patrick Reid. I appreciate the time they took. Special thanks to Mike Harling of Sports Book Plus in Vancouver for pointing me in the right direction, and to Margaret and Steve Yaholnitsky of Yorkton for sharing their memories, library and hospitality.

The starting point for my archival research was the Hockey Hall of Fame in Toronto. Phil Pritchard, manager of the Hall's resource centre, and archivist Craig Campbell provided access to contemporary newspaper accounts, books and photographs.

Ken Dryden and Roy MacGregor generously made available transcriptions of interviews conducted for the CBC-TV documentary series *Home Game*, material that also formed the basis for a chapter in their superb

book of that name. Ken and Roy contributed other thoughtful sugges-
tions, as did Murray Costello, president of the Canadian Hockey Association, and his colleague Phil Legault.

Books that proved valuable include *Road to Olympus* by Anatoly
Tarasov (Griffin House, 1969); *Hockey Showdown* by Harry Sinden
(Doubleday Canada, 1972); *The Death of Hockey* by Bruce Kidd and John
Macfarlane (New Press, 1972); *Hockey Night in Moscow* by Jack Ludwig
(McClelland & Stewart, 1972); *Face-Off at the Summit* by Ken Dryden with
Mark Mulvoy (Little, Brown, 1973); *War on Ice: Canada in International
Hockey* by Scott Young (McClelland & Stewart, 1976); *The Hockey I Love*
by Vladislav Tretiak (Fitzhenry & Whiteside, 1977); *Hockey Is Our Game*
by Jim Coleman (Key Porter, 1987); *Country on Ice* by Doug Beardsley
(Polestar Press, 1987); *The Days Canada Stood Still* by Scott Morrison
(McGraw Hill Ryerson, 1989); *The Red Machine: The Soviet Quest to
Dominate Canada's Game* by Lawrence Martin (Doubleday Canada, 1990);
Shooting for Glory by Paul Henderson (Stoddart, 1992); and *Hockey Night
in Canada: Sport, Identities and Cultural Politics* by Richard Gruneau and
David Whitson (Garamond Press, 1993). Two articles from the *Journal
of Canadian Studies* provided fresh angles: "Hockey Diplomacy and Canadian Foreign Policy" by Donald Macintosh and Donna Greenhorn (vol.
28, no. 2) and "Hockey as Canadian Popular Culture" by Neil Earle (vol.
30, no. 2).

From the Canadian Broadcasting Corporation I purchased videotape
copies of the games themselves, made from broadcast tapes in the CBC-
TV Sports Video Library. And I benefited greatly from viewing two video
documentaries: *The Canada/Russia Games 1972*, produced by TV Labatt
(1987), and especially *Summit on Ice*, the best visual record of the series to
date, produced by Ralph Mellanby for the series' twentieth anniversary in
1992.

For assistance with research, I am grateful to Andrew MacSkimming;
for assistance with fact-checking, to Ron Wight. Sean Rossiter read the
manuscript in draft form and contributed many extremely useful sug-
gestions. Barbara Pulling's incisive editorial work made the final product
more readable and enjoyable.

My thanks to Frank Lennon and Brian Pickell, both of whom went to
extra efforts for this book, and to other rights holders for permission to

reproduce photographs. And thanks to my publisher and friend, Rob Sanders of Greystone Books, for launching and enabling the whole project.

R. M.
Ottawa
August 1996

INDEX

●

Adams, Jack, 101
Ahearne, J. F. "Bunny," 58–59
Alfredsson, Daniel, 251
Allan Cup, 10, 181
Almetov, Alexander, 101
Anderson, Scott, 238
Anisin, Vyacheslav, 87, 90–91, 153, 195,
   218, 225, 233
Apps, Syl, Sr., 224
Atlanta Flames, 209
Awrey, Don, 21, 43, 51–52, 69, 74, 111,
   114, 135, 160

Baader, Franz, 133–34, 171, 175, 177–78,
   194, 196, 212, 215
Ballard, Harold, 18, 22, 58, 120, 209
Bassett, John, 46
Bassett, Johnny F., 209
Bata, Rudolph, 150, 195, 196, 215, 221
Bathgate, Bernie, 13
Bauer, Father David, 7, 25, 61, 82, 132
Beardsley, Doug, 1
Beddoes, Dick, 51, 57–58, 244
Béliveau, Jean, 156, 183, 184, 241
Bell, Max, 8
Belleville McFarlands, 21
Berenova, Olga, 149
Berenson, Red, 21, 28, 44, 55, 110, 169–70,
   174, 176, 195
Bergman, Gary, 21, 43, 47, 53, 69, 88, 111,
   116, 151, 171, 172, 175–76, 194, 196,
   198, 199, 216, 218, 219, 220
Berton, Pierre, 131, 185
Birmingham Bulls, 209
Blackman, Ted, 57, 129
Blake, Toe, 156
Blinov, Yuri, 53, 112, 114, 153, 195, 221,
   223, 224

Bobrov, Vsevolod, 12, 26, 43–47, 72, 77,
   82, 85, 87, 95, 104–8, 116, 146, 147,
   170, 175, 193–94, 195, 196, 218
Bodunov, Alexander, 87, 90, 195
Bonk, Radek, 251
Boston Bruins, 11, 19–22, 26, 70, 77, 89,
   94, 137, 157, 170, 182, 188
Boston Globe, 27
Boucher, Gaetan, 162
Bowman, Scotty, 156
Brewer, Carl, 102, 103
Brezhnev, Leonid, 105, 149, 213, 229, 240
Bucyk, Johnny, 170, 182
Buffalo Sabres, 21, 145
Bure, Pavel, 251
Burns, Pat, 180

Calder Cup, 11, 122
Calgary Flames, 246
California Seals, 62
Campbell, Clarence, 16, 46, 68, 69, 76, 87
Canada Cup, 99, 124, 126; **1981**, 248;
   1991, 129, 248
Canada-Soviet hockey series: **Game One**,
   21, 23, 27, 30, 33, 41–55, 56, 58, 59, 60,
   63, 66, 67, 68, 69, 70, 71, 74, 83, 85, 90,
   111, 123, 163, 215, 236; **Game Two**, 33,
   67–77, 78, 86, 87, 88, 95, 110, 122, 144,
   157, 163, 185; **Game Three**, 63, 78,
   85–92, 93, 95, 110, 123, 160, 185, 215;
   Game Four, 86, 90, 107–18, 129, 131,
   215; **Game Five**, 139–55, 157, 158,
   163, 166, 167, 168, 169, 171, 178, 180,
   195, 207, 215; **Game Six**, 123, 157,
   160, 163, 166–78, 185, 186, 189, 211,
   212, 215; **Game Seven**, 157, 185, 186,
   189–201, 207, 211, 212, 216; **Game
   Eight**, 31, 33, 157, 163, 185, 186, 206,

211–231, 232, 233, 234, 236, 237, 239, 243, 244, 246

Canadian Amateur Hockey Association (CAHA), 8–9, 22, 217, 246–47

Canadian national amateur team, 7, 8

Cannon, Mike, 28, 229

Carbonneau, Guy, 158

Cashman, Wayne, 21, 50, 70, 72–73, 88–89, 91, 110, 129, 135–36, 192

Central Army team, 25, 26, 81, 100, 101, 102, 104, 105, 160, 246, 248

Cheevers, Gerry, 19, 22

Chelios, Chris, 158

Chernyshev, Arkady, 26, 44, 105

Chicago Black Hawks, 16, 20–21, 33, 69, 70, 183

Clarke, Bobby, 15, 21, 32, 48, 52, 70, 74, 90–91, 113–14, 122, 124, 126, 150–51, 153–54, 157, 171, 175, 186, 187, 206, 207, 218, 220, 225, 226, 229, 244

Clemence, Verne, 235

Coleman, Jim, 10, 12, 27, 239

Colorado Avalanche, 81, 159

Conacher, Brian, 54, 90, 171, 175–78, 220, 234

Corey, Ronald, 159, 161

Cournoyer, Yvan, 21, 32, 43, 46–47, 50, 53, 62, 70–71, 74–75, 88, 113, 115, 133, 150, 154, 156–58, 161–65, 184, 197, 199, 216, 218, 221, 222, 225, 229, 230–31, 233, 240

Crozier, Roger, 122

Czechoslovak national team, 243

Dahlberg, Uwe, 150, 195, 196, 215

Dallas Stars, 159

Davidov, Vitaly, 45, 103–4, 107

Davidson, Bob, 25, 26

Davis, William, 72

Day, Hap, 76

Demers, Jacques, 162, 180

Detroit Red Wings, 21, 101, 157, 202, 251, 252

Diefenbaker, John, 23

Dimanche-Matin, 57

Dionne, Marcel, 21, 90, 138

Dowling, Steve, 77, 85

Drapeau, Jean, 243

Dryden, Dave, 111

Dryden, Ken, 5, 15, 16, 20, 21, 25, 29, 32, 33, 41, 43, 46, 47, 49, 50, 51, 52, 53, 54, 55, 57, 60, 64, 68, 69, 77, 81, 82, 83, 88, 97, 109, 111, 112, 113, 114, 115, 116, 126, 133, 134, 139, 146, 148, 156, 157, 163, 169, 170, 171, 172, 173, 174, 175, 176, 177, 216, 218, 219, 221, 222, 223, 224, 225, 231, 233, 240, 242–43, 246

Dubeau, Michel, 240–41

Dunnell, Milt, 27, 43, 44, 131

Eagleson, R. Alan, 8, 9, 18, 22, 28, 29, 30, 55, 86, 129, 130, 136, 137, 138, 145, 167, 172, 173, 177, 183–84, 189, 206, 212, 213, 214, 217, 218, 220, 224–25, 227–29, 234–35

East York Lyndhursts, 10, 12, 97

Eastern Professional Hockey Association, 182

Edmonton Mercurys, 7

Edmonton Oilers, 79, 249

Ellis, Ron, 21, 39, 48, 53, 70, 113, 119–27, 131, 136, 145, 150, 151, 169, 171, 178, 186, 195, 196–97, 200, 205, 206, 218, 220, 221, 225, 229, 231

Esaw, Johnny, 27, 56, 117, 118, 173

Eskenazi, Gerald, 27

Esposito, Phil, 20, 21, 23, 24, 32, 41, 43, 46, 47, 49, 50, 51, 52, 54, 60, 68, 70, 73, 75, 76, 77, 83, 87, 89, 90, 94, 107, 110, 112, 113, 114, 115, 116, 117, 118, 124, 126, 129, 133, 135, 136, 137, 138, 139, 148, 149, 151, 154, 160, 167, 169, 170, 172, 173, 174, 175, 182, 183, 186, 190, 191, 192, 195, 196, 197, 198, 199, 205, 216, 218, 219, 220, 221, 223, 225, 226, 229, 230, 231, 233, 234, 240, 243

Esposito, Tony, 21, 22, 23, 32, 68, 73, 74, 76, 87, 88, 89, 90, 91, 111, 148, 150, 153, 154, 155, 170, 195, 196, 197, 198, 200, 216

European Hockey League, 252

Federov, Sergei, 251

Fedosov, Boris ("The Snowman"), 5, 6

Ferguson, John, 16, 19, 20, 25, 26, 33, 34, 46, 69, 70, 76, 86, 89, 93, 95, 96, 111, 135, 137, 144, 155, 157, 160, 163, 164, 168, 169, 176, 179, 180, 184–85, 186, 187, 188, 195, 196, 200, 212, 215, 216, 243, 250–51

Fetisov, Vyacheslav, 252

Firsov, Anatoly, 45, 103, 104, 106, 107

Fisher, Douglas, 9

Fisher, Red, 71, 95

Ford, Robert A. D., 7, 142, 194, 213

Forristal, John "Frosty," 217

Francis, Emile, 183

Gagnon, Len, 85, 86

Gainey, Bob, 158

Gazette (Montreal), 27, 57, 78, 129

Geoffrion, Bernie, 158, 181

Giacomin, Ed, 20

Gilbert, Rod, 21, 48, 49, 52, 71, 86, 110, 113, 114, 151, 174, 186, 190, 198, 220, 221, 222, 223, 224

Glennie, Brian, 21, 64, 145

Globe and Mail, 57, 58, 82

Gobeil, Pierre, 136, 137

Goldsworthy, Bill, 21, 70, 86, 110, 112, 113, 116, 129, 195, 216

Green, Ted, 182

Greenhorn, Donna, 18

Gresko, Alexander, 192, 194, 212–13, 214, 215, 218, 224–25, 234–35

Gretzky, Wayne, 79, 173, 204, 237, 249

Gross, George, 245

Guevremont, Jocelyn, 21, 90, 145, 146

Gusev, Alexander, 33, 154, 170, 195, 198, 226, 231

Hadfield, Vic, 21, 48, 49, 71, 86, 110, 113, 114, 135, 144, 145, 146, 160, 198

Haggert, Bobby, 28

Hammarstrom, Inge, 134

Hancock, Peter, 6

Harris, Billy, 27, 94

Hart Trophy, 124

Hartford Whalers, 79

Harvey, Doug, 172

Hatskin, Ben, 87

Hawks, Sally, 238–39

Hay, Charles, 8, 217, 218

Hedberg, Anders, 134, 248

Henderson, Paul, 20, 21, 23, 31, 32, 35, 40, 44, 47, 48, 49, 53, 70, 73, 88, 90, 91, 92, 94, 114, 115, 119, 120, 121, 122, 124, 126, 128, 133, 150, 151, 152, 153, 154, 161, 162, 169, 173, 174, 186, 188, 190, 197, 200, 202–10, 218, 221, 222, 225, 229, 230–31, 232, 233, 234, 235, 236–37, 238, 239, 240–41, 244, 248

Hewitt, Foster, 2, 12, 54, 56, 57, 74, 83, 140, 171, 172, 177, 178, 198, 217, 219, 231, 232, 237

Hockey Canada, 7, 8, 17, 18, 22, 29, 30, 55, 61, 79, 105, 183, 184, 213, 217, 246

Hockey Hall of Fame, 126, 162

Hodge, Ken, 182

Houle, Réjean, 165

Howe, Gordie, 51, 79, 183, 202–4, 248

Huck, Fran, 62

Hull, Bobby, 15, 16, 17, 18, 19, 44, 45, 62, 78, 79, 83, 87, 123, 147, 184, 248

Hull, Dennis, 21, 110, 117, 145, 170, 171, 174, 175, 189, 198, 204, 221, 228, 233

Imlach, Punch, 6, 95, 121, 122, 125, 167

International Ice Hockey Federation (IIHF), 8, 9, 58, 105

Irvin, Dick, 156

Izvestia, 5, 6

Jagr, Jaromir, 164

Jennings, Bill, 17

Johnston, Eddie, 22, 111, 131, 132, 135, 145, 146

Johnston, Marshall, 62

Juba, Ken, 238

Juckes, Gordon, 8

Kearney, Jim, 237

Kernaghan, Jim, 31, 32, 58, 59

Kharlamov, Valery, 32, 37, 44, 45, 51, 52, 58, 63, 71, 73, 74, 88, 89, 95, 101, 102, 113, 114, 122, 123, 124, 150, 151, 153, 154, 175, 176, 177, 186, 187, 195, 207, 217, 218, 221, 223, 224, 244

Kidd, Bruce, 78, 79
King, Dave, 238, 246–47, 249
Kitchener-Waterloo Dutchmen, 182
Kompalla, Joseph, 133, 134, 171, 177, 178,
    194, 196, 212, 215, 218, 219–20, 224
Kosygin, Alexei, 18, 149, 213, 229
Kryzcka, Joe, 8, 9, 172, 173
Kukulowicz, Aggie, 28
Kulagin, Boris, 26, 76, 87, 105, 108, 116,
    131, 195
Kuperman, Igor, 81, 82, 83, 84, 101, 147
Kuzkin, Victor, 46, 73, 75, 90, 112, 115,
    170, 195, 218, 224, 226

Lafleur, Guy, 156, 241
Laing, Arthur, 213, 214
Laperriere, Jacques, 20
Lapointe, Guy, 21, 43, 46, 49, 52, 53, 54,
    68, 69, 75, 111, 138, 151, 157, 174, 199,
    219, 221, 226, 229
Larionov, Igor, 251
Larochelle, Claude, 27
Larsen, Frank, 77, 85
Lebedev, Yuri, 87, 88, 89, 90, 172, 195
Lee, Gord, 85, 86
Lemieux, Claude, 158
Lemieux, Mario, 164
Lennon, Frank, 162, 239
Leslie, Joanne, 236–37
Lewis, David, 72
Liapkin, Yuri, 49, 74, 87, 153, 171, 173,
    176, 197, 198, 219, 230
Loktev, Konstantin, 101
London Free Press, 32
Los Angeles Kings, 103
Ludwig, Jack, 73, 246
Lutchenko, Vladimir, 74, 112, 113, 151,
    174, 176, 221, 227

McAvoy, George, 13
McClelland, Ivan, 13
Macfarlane, John, 78, 79
MacGregor, Roy, 5, 81, 139, 234, 240, 242
Macintosh, Donald, 18
McIntyre, Jack, 13
McKenzie, Johnny, 182
MacLaren Advertising, 22

McLellan, John, 25, 26
McLeod, Jackie, 61
Mahovlich, Frank, 21, 32, 46, 47, 49, 50,
    51, 52, 70, 71, 75, 76, 88, 89, 112, 113,
    114, 115, 119, 123, 144, 150, 152, 154,
    157, 170, 190, 192, 202, 214, 216, 220,
    222, 225
Mahovlich, Peter, 20, 21, 32, 43, 46, 52,
    55, 70, 75, 76, 78, 138, 144, 157, 175,
    196, 219, 225–26, 227, 229, 231
Maltsev, Alexander, 37, 45, 51, 52, 91, 95,
    114, 116, 150, 151, 152, 171, 172, 197,
    198, 200, 218, 219, 223
Marsden, Pat, 194
Martin, Lawrence, 82, 101, 102
Martin, Richard, 21, 90, 145, 146, 167
Massey, Vincent, 12
Matheson, Jack, 79
Meagher, Margaret, 136
Meeker, Howie, 151, 239, 246
Memorial Cup, 121, 126
Messier, Mark, 249
Mikhailov, Boris, 37, 46, 47, 48, 49, 50, 53,
    54, 63, 73, 89, 107, 112, 113, 114, 117,
    195, 196, 198, 199, 208, 218, 221, 223,
    224, 240
Mikita, Stan, 21, 44, 70, 75, 88, 177, 243
Minnesota Moose, 84
Minnesota North Stars, 21, 70
Mishakov, Evgeny, 45, 195, 196, 226, 227
Mogilny, Alexander, 251
Montreal Canadiens, 11, 19, 20, 21, 22, 43,
    46, 47, 68, 69, 156–65, 182, 183, 236
Montreal Junior Canadiens, 159, 181
Montréal Matin, 137
Montreal Roadrunners, 164
Montreal Star, 27, 58, 71, 95, 107
Moog, Andy, 13, 64
Moog, Don, 13
Moore, Dickie, 187
Morrison, Scott, 131, 191
Moscow Maple Leafs, 6
Moscow Spartak, 100, 104, 196, 248
Mott, Morris, 61, 62, 63, 64, 66, 101, 187
Mulroney, Brian, 46
Mulvoy, Mark, 27
Murray, Jim, 135, 152

Naslund, Mats, 158
National Hockey League (NHL), 1, 7, 9,
    10, 11, 13, 16, 17, 18, 19, 20, 21, 22, 27,
    32, 35, 43, 45, 54, 57, 58, 61, 62, 63,
    65, 71, 73, 78, 79, 81, 82, 91, 95, 96, 98,
    111, 122, 123, 134, 159, 165, 180, 182,
    183, 195, 203, 209, 242, 247, 248, 251,
    252; Canadiens' domination of, 156–65;
    playing style, 20, 42, 70, 111, 123, 131,
    154, 187, 212, 224; and the '72 series,
    16, 17, 18, 19, 22
Nattrass, Susan, 206
Neckar, Stan, 251
New Jersey Devils, 252
New York Rangers, 11, 17, 19, 20, 21, 48,
    49, 65, 135, 157, 159, 183, 188
New York Times, 27
NHL Players Association (NHLPA), 8, 17,
    18, 127, 184
Nieuwendyk, Joe, 64
Nilsson, Ulf, 134, 248
Nolan, Dermot, 237

Okanagan Senior Hockey League, 10
Olympic Games, 6, 8, 10, 23, 24, 26, 27,
    59, 62, 77, 182; **1952**, 7; **1960**, 25;
    1968, 65; **1972**, 85, 105; **1984**, 65;
    1994, 250; **1998**, 252
O'Malley, Terry, 63
Orr, Bobby, 8, 16, 19, 22, 26, 45, 50, 51,
    62, 67, 83, 94, 110, 124, 147, 159, 177,
    182, 183, 184, 194
Ottawa Senators, 188, 251
Ozerov, Nikolai, 83, 140

Paladiev, Evgeny, 49, 74, 75, 87
Parise, Jean-Paul, 21, 72, 87, 88, 89, 129,
    151, 167, 174, 197, 218, 219–20, 221
Park, Brad, 21, 32, 43, 49, 50, 53, 69, 73,
    74, 83, 89, 111, 113, 116, 129, 137, 171,
    175, 191, 196, 198, 219, 221, 222, 223,
    226, 227, 228, 229, 232, 234
Park, Gerry, 173
Patrick, James, 65
Pearson, Lester B., 46
Penticton Herald, 13
Penticton Vees, 10, 11, 12, 13, 24, 106, 172

Percival, Lloyd, 98, 99, 245, 246
Perreault, Gilbert, 21, 90, 110, 113, 115,
    151, 167, 170
Petrov, Vladimir, 37, 46, 49, 50, 54, 63, 73,
    88, 104, 112, 113, 114, 116, 153, 155,
    176, 177, 195, 196–97, 208, 219, 224
Philadelphia Flyers, 21, 161, 248
Phoenix Coyotes, 79–80
Pickell, Brian, 239, 243
Pinder, Herb, Jr., 64, 65, 66, 187, 247
Plante, Jacques, 27, 43, 49, 114, 159
Pocklington, Peter, 237
Podgorny, Nikolai, 213
Pollock, Sam, 156
Pravda, 28, 58
Province (Vancouver), 131

Quebec Nordiques, 79, 81

Ragulin, Alexander, 45, 46, 47, 49, 74, 87,
    154, 173, 176
Ranford, Bill, 250
Ratelle, Jean, 21, 46, 48, 49, 71, 86, 88,
    110, 149, 150, 154, 172, 198, 221,
    222, 226
Ratelle, Nancy, 173
Redmond, Mickey, 21, 49
Reid, Patrick, 190, 191, 192, 201, 214,
    228–29
Reynolds, Margaret, 237
Rheaume, Manon, 120
Richard, Maurice "Rocket," 16, 68, 73,
    156, 158, 241
Richer, Stéphane, 158
Richter, Mike, 64
Ritchie, Ed, 229
Robertson, John, 27, 28, 58, 94, 107
Robinson, Larry, 158
Robitaille, Luc, 250
Roller Hockey International, 164
Romansky, Karel, 194, 214
Rosa, Fran, 27
Roy, Patrick, 158

Sakic, Joe, 250
Salming, Borje, 134
Sanders, Rob, 237

Sanderson, Derek, 19, 182

Savard, Serge, 22, 32, 41, 69, 110, 111, 126, 129, 130, 157–62, 170, 172, 176, 196, 199, 231, 240, 243

Schmidt, Milt, 183

Seiling, Rod, 21, 43, 49, 50, 51, 52, 53, 54, 64, 69, 74, 111, 152, 154, 170

Seiling, Sharon, 173

Selke, Frank, 156

Sgro, Joe, 152, 228–29

Shabaga, Mike, 13

Shadrin, Vladimir, 49, 54, 116, 150, 153, 173, 196, 218, 222, 223, 224

Shatalov, Yuri, 87, 91, 170, 172

Sidelnikov, Alexander, 195

Sigurdson, Hal, 237

Simard, Alain, 238

Sinden, Harry, 15, 16, 19, 20, 21, 23, 24, 26, 28, 33, 34, 42, 43, 45, 46, 49, 50, 51, 52, 54, 55, 56, 60, 67, 68, 69, 70, 71, 72, 76, 85, 86, 87, 89, 90, 91, 93, 94, 95, 110, 111, 112, 113, 114, 116, 117, 130, 131, 133, 134, 135, 136, 137, 138, 142, 144, 145, 148, 151, 152, 153, 155, 163, 164, 166, 167, 168, 169, 174, 176, 177, 178, 179–88, 190, 193–94, 195, 196, 199, 206, 211, 212, 213, 214, 215, 216, 218, 220, 225, 226, 228, 231, 239, 244, 251

Sittler, Darryl, 125

Sjoberg, Lars-Erik, 135, 136, 248

Smith, Bobby, 158

Smith, Dallas, 20

Smith, Floyd, 202

Smith, Gary, 5, 147, 191, 212, 213, 214, 215

Smith, Mike, 82, 125, 249

Le Soleil, 27

Solodukhin, Vyacheslav, 87

Soviet Ice Hockey Federation, 217

Soviet national team, 10, 55, 112, 128, 131, 143, 147, 151, 163, 168, 169, 171, 184, 186, 204, 208, 211–12, 213, 215, 242, 244, 248; Canadian attitudes towards, 11, 13, 14, 18, 27, 28, 29, 37, 47, 60, 63, 91, 93, 117, 131, 132, 140, 160, 161, 207, 245; comparison to

North American teams, 9, 26, 63, 71, 96, 110, 116, 150, 151, 160, 163, 216; playing style, 36, 47, 48, 49, 50, 70, 94, 99, 110, 111, 112, 114, 116, 153, 168, 199, 212, 247

Soviet Wings, 248

Sports Illustrated, 27

St. Catharines Teepees, 34

St. Laurent, Louis, 12

St. Louis Blues, 183

Stanfield, Fred, 182

Stanfield, Robert, 46, 71, 72

Stanislavsky, Konstantin, 102

Stanley Cup, 6, 18, 23, 26, 27, 40, 42, 49, 50, 58, 76, 86, 126, 156, 162, 163, 170, 233, 242, 250; **1967**, 122; **1970**, 183; **1996**, 81

Stapleton, Pat "Whitey," 20, 21, 26, 28, 31–40, 67, 69, 72, 74, 87, 89, 91, 109, 110, 111, 112, 113, 114, 119, 126, 132, 148, 150, 153, 174, 193, 198, 200, 208, 216, 223, 230, 231, 236

Stapleton, Jackie, 193

Starovoitov, Andrei, 6, 77, 85, 190, 192, 214, 215

Starshinov, Vyacheslav, 87, 100, 104, 109, 110

Steen, Thomas, 80

Stemkowski, Pete, 202

Stephenson, Wayne, 62

Sterner, Ulf, 135–36

Stevens, Mel, 120, 209

Storey, Red, 27

Sudbury Wolves, 10

Sunday Express, 57

Swedish national team, 132–34

Tallon, Dale, 21, 90, 136, 145

Tarala, Hal, 12

Tarasov, Anatoly, 11, 16, 26, 93, 95, 96–106, 142, 146, 147, 160, 168, 181, 208, 211, 227, 233, 237, 245, 249

Tass (Soviet news agency), 59

Team Canada, 9, 23, 60, 63, 77, 112, 114, 115, 116, 118, 119, 122, 123, 124, 129, 134, 140, 144–46, 150, 151, 156–65, 167, 169, 171, 172, 173, 175, 176, 178,

197, 200, 206, 207, 211, 212, 214, 218, 220, 223, 224, 226, 229, 234, 236, 237, 242, 243, 248, 252; Canadian attitudes towards, 27, 28, 29, 37, 38, 43, 47, 57, 58, 59, 62, 66, 68, 78, 111, 113, 115, 117, 131, 132, 148, 167, 235, 239, 244; in Sweden, 132, 133–138; player selection, 16, 19, 20, 21, 22, 33, 122, 184; playing style, 36, 48, 72, 73, 88, 112, 114, 123, 130, 151, 153, 161, 168, 185, 187, 250; Soviet attitudes towards, 44, 45, 49, 59, 83, 107, 108, 131, 147; training camp, 15, 19, 20, 21, 25, 26, 44, 160, 205

Team Five, 29
Team USA, 248
Templeton, Charles, 185
Tkaczuk, Walt, 20
Toronto Maple Leafs, 6, 18, 20, 21, 25, 26, 27, 43, 64, 76, 102, 120, 121, 123, 125, 157, 159, 183, 202, 209, 239
Toronto Marlboros, 121, 159
Toronto Star, 27, 43, 57, 58, 72, 78, 131, 239
Toronto Sun, 167, 239–40, 244, 245
Toronto Toros, 209
Trail Smoke Eaters, 7, 250
Tremblay, J. C., 19
Tremblay, Mario, 165
Tretiak, Vladislav, 25, 26, 27, 31, 32, 41, 43, 45, 47, 48, 49, 50, 52, 53, 62, 73, 74, 75, 78, 87, 88, 89, 90, 91, 92, 95, 107, 110, 113, 114, 115, 116, 117, 130, 146, 147, 148, 149, 150, 151, 152, 154, 155, 171, 173, 174, 195, 196, 197, 200, 208, 221, 222, 223, 226, 227, 229, 230–31, 234, 245, 249
Trudeau, Pierre Elliott, 17, 18, 30, 46, 60, 72, 148, 243
Tsygankov, Gennady, 74, 89, 151, 174, 200, 221, 224, 226

Ullman, Norm, 21, 122, 202
Unger, Gary, 202

Vancouver Canucks, 145, 237
Vancouver Sun, 237

Vanderhaeghe, Guy, 236
Vasiliev, Valery, 87, 88, 90, 113, 174, 197, 200, 224, 226, 230
Vikulov, Vladimir, 46, 114, 115, 150, 154, 171, 172, 196, 197, 218, 221, 227
Volchkov, Boris, 170, 173

Walter, Ryan, 64
Warwick, Bill, 11, 13
Warwick, Dick, 11, 13
Warwick, Grant, 11, 13
Weekend Magazine, 18
Whitby Dunlops, 23, 24, 181
White, Bill, 21, 23, 33, 69, 75, 87, 90, 109, 110, 111, 112, 113, 114, 150, 174, 196, 200, 216, 218–19, 221, 223, 224, 231, 240
Whitehead, Eric, 131
Williams, Tiger, 125
Williamson, Murray, 77
Winnipeg Jets, 16, 78, 79, 80, 81, 82, 83, 84, 87, 188, 248
Winnipeg Tribune, 78
World Cup of Hockey, 252
World Hockey Association (WHA), 16, 17, 19, 58, 68, 78, 79, 125, 134, 183, 209, 248
World's hockey championships, 6, 7, 8, 10, 21, 23, 61, 62, 63, 64, 79, 82, 97, 99, 100, 101, 105, 242, 250; **1954**, 10; **1955**, 11; **1958**, 24, 181; **1967**, 102; **1969**, 83; **1994**, 250; **1996**, 250

Yakushev, Alexander, 32, 37, 45, 47, 49, 54, 55, 71, 95, 104, 116, 154, 173, 175, 176, 196–97, 198, 208, 218, 219, 222, 223, 229, 234
Yakushev, Victor, 101
Yashin, Alexei, 188, 251
Yorkton Enterprise, 235
Young, Scott, 167

Zhamnov, Alexei, 82
Zimin, Evgeny, 47, 49, 53, 73, 74, 87, 104
Zinger, Victor, 195